Adventures in Peacemaking

This project was developed by Educators for Social Responsibility and Project Adventure, Inc. in conjunction with Work/Family Directions.

EDUCATORS
for
SOCIAL
RESPONSIBILITY

23 Garden Street
Cambridge, MA 02138
(617) 492-1764
(800) 370-2515

Project Adventure, Inc.
P.O. Box 100, Hamilton, MA 01936
(508)468-7981

The "ABC's of Meditation" is adapted with permission from *Fussbusters* by Paul Godfrey and Barbara Davis. © 1986 The Mediation Center, Asheville, NC. If you would like to learn more about setting up a peer mediation program in your setting we recommend *Fussbusters*, available from The Mediation Center, 189 College St., Asheville, NC 28801, (704) 251-6089.

Adventures in Peacemaking

by William J. Kreidler and Lisa Furlong with Libby Cowles and IlaSahai Prouty

Adventures in Peacemaking

by William J. Kreidler and Lisa Furlong
with Libby Cowles and IlaSahai Prouty

Project funded by the
AT&T
Family Care
Development Fund
a joint project of
AT&T/Lucent Technologies,
the Communications Workers
of America and the
International Brotherhood
of Electrical Workers.

About the Authors

William J. Kreidler is a former teacher with more than twenty years of experience. He works with educators internationally on issues of conflict resolution, violence prevention, and appreciation of diversity. Mr. Kreidler is the author of the highly-praised guides for teachers, *Creative Conflict Resolution*, *Elementary Perspectives: Teaching Concepts of Peace and Conflict*, *Teaching Conflict Resolution Through Children's Literature*, and *Conflict Resolution in the Middle School*. His column, "The Caring Classroom," appears monthly in *Instructor* magazine. He is currently senior conflict resolution specialist at ESR.

Bringing Adventure Home is the motto of Project Adventure, Inc. For the past eight years, **Lisa Furlong** has worked at helping people do just that. As the Editor of *Zip Lines*, a magazine for the Adventure field, she helps practitioners share their programs and expertise with people throughout the US and abroad. As a trainer for Project Adventure, she has traveled the country teaching Adventure techniques to staff in camps, schools and recreational settings. As a mother of two young boys, Lisa continues to promote the development of Adventure programs for children.

Libby Cowles has experience facilitating workshops, designing curriculum, evaluating schools, and developing programs for young people on issues related to gender equity. Ms. Cowles served as program associate at ESR, coordinating conflict resolution and peer mediation programs nationwide. She has worked with middle and high school students in language arts classrooms, after-school programs, wilderness expeditions, and academic study programs for the past ten years.

IlaSahai Prouty has been involved with the Adventure process since middle school both as a participant and a facilitator of groups. She is an artist and has taught secondary school art in Massachusetts. Ila has worked as a writer for Project Adventure for the past two years an is currently involved with various publishing projects in the Portland Office of Project Adventure.

Table of Contents

Part One

Getting Started

Introduction

The goal of this guide is to help staff in school-age child care settings teach children effective, nonviolent ways to resolve conflict. It is clear that there is a growing need for such work in school-age child care. Over the years providers have been ingenious and creative in adapting materials designed for school programs to their own settings. This guide was developed to meet the unique needs of school-age child care providers and provide assistance in the following three areas:

1. implementing instruction in key conflict resolution concepts

2. further developing children's skills using experiential education strategies

3. developing approaches for resolving conflict in child care programs

The Peaceable Program*

This guide is based on an approach to teaching conflict resolution skills called the Peaceable Program model. The Peaceable Program approach looks at the school-age child care setting as a caring, respectful community. To establish this caring community five themes are emphasized:

1. cooperation

2. communication

3. emotional expression

4. appreciation for diversity

5. conflict resolution

You will see these five themes throughout this book. While they are the focus of individual chapters, all of these themes also are infused into every aspect of the guide. Conflict resolution is the main focus of the book, but you will find that most of the activities are cooperatively structured and encourage children to communicate with each other. Similarly, the activities help children to identify and discuss the affective aspects of the activities. Many of the activities address issues of cultural and ethnic diversity, as well as other types of diversity.

The Peaceable Program is an important part of creating a total conflict resolution approach. Conflict resolution is taught most effectively not in isolation, but rather in the context of a caring and respect-filled community. Establishing a Peaceable Program is one of the ways you can prevent conflict by addressing some of its root causes. Being part of a caring program community helps motivate children to resolve conflict nonviolently.

A Three-minute Introduction to Conflict Resolution

All of us can use some improvement in the ways we handle conflict. The following will give you a quick introduction to some of the key concepts about conflict and its resolution that underlie the activities in this book.

Conflicts are a normal and natural part of everyone's life. Conflicts are simply the disputes and disagreements that occur between people. While we tend to think of conflict only in terms of its negative effects, conflict can also be very positive. Without conflict there is no growth or progress. There is stagnation. It is the constructive use of conflict that allows society to move forward.

There is also, of course, destructive conflict. The goal of conflict resolution education is not to eliminate conflict. That is neither possible nor desirable. Instead the aim is to help children learn from conflict, use it constructively and avoid its destructive aspects.

---

* The Peaceable Program model is based on the Peaceable Classroom model which is discussed more thoroughly in William J. Kreidler, *Creative Conflict Resolution: More than 200 Activities for Keeping Peace in the Classroom*, (Glenview, IL: Scott, Foresman and Company, 1984) and William J. Kreidler, *Elementary Perspectives: Teaching Concepts of Peace and Conflict*, (Cambridge, MA: Educators for Social Responsibility, 1991).

Many children – and more than a few adults – look at conflict as if it were a contest in which one person wins and the other must lose. This book promotes Win-Win conflict resolution, where all parties get what they need and feel good about the resolution.

There is no one right way to handle all conflict. Different conflict resolution approaches are appropriate for different situations. Conflict resolution is an umbrella term that covers every approach, from a punch in the nose, to sitting down and talking it out, to running away and hiding. The activities in this book will help children recognize the options they have in conflict situations and encourage them to choose options that are nonviolent, meet the needs of the people involved and improve relationships.

Developmental Considerations in Teaching Conflict Resolution[*]

There are developmental considerations to keep in mind as you work with elementary grade children on conflict resolution skills. Here are some general guidelines:

❖ Think in terms of readiness, as well as mastery. Many conflict resolution skills and concepts (for example, problem solving and point of view) are difficult for young children. This means children may not be at an age where they can master the skill or concept. However, they may be ready to work with it, which will prepare them to master the skill when they are older.

❖ Be as concrete as you can. It's very easy to start talking about conflict in abstract terms, but this goes over the heads of young children. Discuss conflicts first in terms of specific actions and objects, then move to more abstract aspects of conflict, such as motivations or positions and interests.

❖ Help children see cause and effect. Primary grade children need help to understand the relationship between cause and effect, a relationship that is central to learning to resolve conflict. When discussing either actual or hypothetical conflicts with children, help them to see the whole problem and how specific actions and behaviors have contributed to it.

❖ Strive to expand children's choices. Young children tend to have a limited array of conflict resolution approaches, and they will try to apply these to all conflicts, regardless of the potential consequences. Gently help them see that there are other options. For example, during a discussion a child will sometimes insist that violence is the only solution to a conflict ("I'd kick his head."). Rather than arguing with the child, help the child to understand the consequences of that action ("If you kick his head, that will hurt him and you might get into trouble."). Then present some alternatives.

---

[*] For further discussion of the developmental considerations in teaching conflict resolution, see Diane E. Levin, *Teaching Young Children in Violent Times: Building a Peaceable Classroom*, (Cambridge, MA: Educators for Social Responsibility, 1994).

Using an Adventure Based Approach to Teaching Conflict Resolution

Adventure activities are uniquely suited to helping children understand, in concrete ways, the conflict concepts you are trying to teach. Underlying the Adventure approach to teaching is the assumption that we learn best by doing. The activities included in this guide have been framed to fit the themes of the program – cooperation, communication, diversity, conflict resolution and expressing feelings. You will find that your children engage easily in the activities. The important piece for you, as the facilitator, is to help the children see how the activities they are participating in have relevance to the topic of conflict.

How can this be done? By "framing" the activity in a way that makes it relevant and offering a "reflection" time when the group can talk and think about what they have learned. Most of the activities are written with ideas for "Setting the Scene" and "Reflecting." In order to get as much learning out of the activities as possible, we encourage you to use these ideas and spend time reflecting with your group.

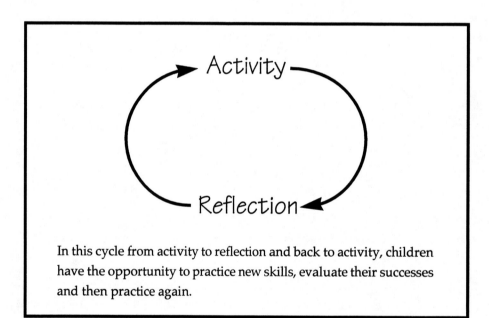

In this cycle from activity to reflection and back to activity, children have the opportunity to practice new skills, evaluate their successes and then practice again.

Let's Get Started!

We have taught conflict resolution for many years in all kinds of settings – urban, suburban and rural – to all kinds of children. We have rarely met a child who is not, in some way, interested in and able to learn to be more effective at handling conflict. Because conflict is an essential part of children's lives, it's one of the most motivating topics you can teach. It's also a lot of fun. Conflict resolution skills, like reading skills, are something that children will use every day of their lives. By starting now, when children are young, we can get a head start on helping children acquire skills that will not only make a difference in children's lives now, but will also lead to a more peaceful world.

Handling Conflict in the Peaceable Program

Around the country, directors of afterschool programs, camps, recreation centers and other programs agree that planning is the key to handling conflict in such settings. But what kind of planning? In this chapter we will discuss the kinds of planning that will help you both reduce conflict in your program and handle the conflict that does occur more effectively.

Get Ready for Conflict

Conflict is a normal, natural part of life and is certainly part of life in afterschool programs for children. Planning and preparation will help you and your children use conflict for its productive potential. Here's an approach that works:

1) Find out how conflicts are handled in your program.

Start by exploring your own conflict resolution styles and the most common approaches used by your staff. One way to do this is to observe their behavior. Try setting aside five, 30-minute blocks of time for a week. These blocks should be at different times of the program day. Have an observer watch with these questions in mind: What kinds of conflict occur in the thirty minutes? How are they handled? What words do the staff members use in resolving conflicts? This observation can be done by a staff member who is released for a half hour to observe.

Another somewhat less effective option is to have staff members observe themselves for half an hour. It's important to stress that the observation is for information-gathering purposes, not evaluation.

Once the observations are completed, analyze the results as a staff. What conflict resolution approaches are you using most often? Are they the ones you want to be using? What could be added to your repertoire?

TIP!

Using a Peace Place

When children have conflicts in your program, first send them to the 'Cool Off' chairs. Once they've calmed down, then send them to the Peace Place to try to work it out. We've found it helps to set a timer for five minutes. When the timer rings, the adult in charge checks in to see how the children are doing. If they need help, the adult is there. If they need more time, the adult sets the timer again. If they've worked everything out, they tell the adult what they've agreed to, then they're on their way!

2) Train the staff in conflict resolution.

Most adults who work with children have incorporated a few standard approaches for dealing with conflict that they use for all situations. Try using the activities in this guide to help them improve and broaden their own skills. Some of the activities that can be used with adults include those dealing with conflict styles ("Conflict Resolution Chart," p. 249), the conflict escalator ("Conflict Escalates," p. 241), appreciating diversity ("Human Bingo," p. 214) and many others.

3) Set up a Peace Place.

A Peace Place is a designated corner or place in the room where children can go when they have a conflict. A problem-solving process is posted there (see "A B C D Conflict Solving," p. 256), and all children are trained in the process. When children have a conflict, they can ask to go to the Peace Place or be sent there to work out the problem.

The Peace Place need not be a corner. An old rug can become the "Conflict Carpet" or a table can be the "Talk It Out Table." The point is to have a place for children to go where an adult can keep an eye on them while they work out their problem by themselves. The adult is nearby, but is not involved in the process unless asked by the children.

Uses:	Encourages independence in conflict solving. Gives children the security of a process and a place to solve conflicts without an adult having to take time to help.
Limitations:	Not all conflicts can be handled without adult help. Students must be thoroughly trained in problem solving and the Peace Place must be monitored.

Naturally, children need to be taught how to use a Peace Place. Activities for helping children learn to effectively use one are found under "Conflict Resolution Skill Building" in Chapter 9 or "Helping Children Learn to Use a Peace Place," (p. 30).

4) Hold group meetings.

Group meetings are especially effective for handling conflicts that affect the whole group. They are really problem-solving meetings, and as such they are also a good way to help children practice the ABCD problem-solving method discussed in Chapter 9.

Conflicts may be brought to the meeting by the children or the staff person. Once the conflict is raised, the meeting should follow a clear conflict-solving procedure, including scheduling a follow-up to see if the solution is working.

Uses:	Group meetings are a way to involve the whole class in solving conflicts and are also great teaching opportunities.
Limitations:	Not all conflicts are appropriate for class meetings. Children should not be embarrassed or humiliated in this public forum. Children may also have trouble implementing solutions.

Conducting group problem-solving meetings involves several steps:

1. Call the group together.

2. Set an agenda.

3. Identify problems that need to be addressed in the meeting.

4. Choose one problem to discuss.

5. Brainstorm possible solutions to the problem.

6. Choose a solution and develop an implementation plan.

7. Discuss when and how the solution will be evaluated.

8. Later, evaluate how the implementation went.

Noise Control with a Talking Teddy Bear*

During group meeting children can get very excited – even heated – as they discuss the problem and potential solutions. If they start interrupting each other it can get hard to hear or get anything done. Try implementing a "talking bear" approach for these situations. When the meeting gets excited bring out the talking bear with the rule that only the person holding the talking bear may speak. If the children are sitting in a circle, have them pass it to the right. The child who receives it may then talk or simply pass the bear along, it's up to her. The bear keeps going around the circle so that everyone gets many chances to speak. (Any object will do – use one the children will enjoy.)

* This is adapted from a tradition shared by many Native American peoples (e.g., the Ojibwa pass an eagle feather in a Talking Circle to give full attention and respect to the person talking.)

5) Establish a peer mediation program.

Mediation takes place when a neutral third party helps disputants resolve their conflict. In a peer mediation program, the mediator is a child who helps other children resolve their disputes. Once mediators have been trained they are available on certain days and times to deal with disputes between children. This relieves the staff from having to settle all the conflicts. It also helps children practice conflict resolution skills.

Uses: Children learn to handle conflicts without adults having to mediate. Adults have another option other than handling the conflict themselves. Mediators receive intensive training in conflict resolution. Children like peer mediation.

Limitations: Some conflicts are not appropriate for mediation. Some conflicts need adult intervention. Only the mediators acquire conflict resolution skills. Mediation does not help the children who have the conflict learn how to solve it themselves. Setting up a mediation program takes a lot of staff time and attention for training, supervising, follow-up, etc.

To establish a peer mediation program you need to:

❖ have realistic expectations for what a mediation program can do and how much work it entails;

❖ explain to the entire group what mediation is and how the mediation program will work;

❖ select children to act as mediators;

❖ train the mediators;

❖ schedule mediators so that someone is always available, but no one mediator is on call all the time;

❖ encourage children to use mediation when they have a conflict;

❖ supervise the mediations;

❖ continue to meet with the mediators and help them improve their skills;

❖ keep mediation within a larger framework of a conflict resolution program.

❖ Training children to mediate disputes is one of the clubs described in Chapter 2 (Peer Mediation, p. 24).

TIP!

Building Relationships

There are probably some children in your afterschool program who have difficulty managing their behavior. With these children there is, by necessity, a lot of limit-setting and imposing consequences. This can add up to a lot of negative interactions, so try to engineer positive interactions as well. For example, you might have staff members relieve each other so that one is free to spend half an hour just with that child. Or perhaps a staff member can have that child participate in a special project with a few other children. The time it takes to do this is worth it, because the next time there is a negative interaction, there will be a history of positive interactions to balance it.

6) Build relationships.

Even though it may not have anything directly to do with resolving conflict, developing positive relationships between adults and children is one of the most important pieces of groundwork to lay. According to research on violence prevention, one of the qualities that distinguishes programs with low levels of conflict and violence is the strong relationship between staff and children. In particular, children who report feeling respected, listened to, liked and treated fairly are likely to have lower levels of violent conflict.

Walking Your Talk:
The Importance of Modeling

Children mirror what the adults around them do. This is one of the primary ways children learn what is appropriate – or what seems to be appropriate – behavior. If we want the children in our program to handle conflict constructively and nonviolently, then we need to look at how *we* handle conflict – both conflict with children and with other staff members. Are we walking our talk?

This does not mean that you need to negotiate every conflict that arises among children and adults in the program. It does mean that you strive for consistency between what you ask children to do and what you do yourselves.

Suggestions for Modeling Conflict Resolution:

❖ As a staff, think about how you handle conflicts among yourselves: what procedures, either formal or informal, are in place for handling staff conflicts? Do they work? What's missing? What skills in handling conflict do you think you need to develop?

❖ When you handle conflicts between children, remember that you are teaching with every action you take, every word you say. Take care to model good listening, mutual respect and the kind of problem solving you want children to do.

❖ When you deal with children, it isn't necessary to always be calm. However, it is important to be aware of what you are modeling. Model nonaggressive behavior at all times, no matter how angry you are. You can say, "I am very angry with you," without being abusive or aggressive in that expression.

❖ Emphasize positive behavior whenever and wherever you can. Develop the philosophy of "catch them being good." Research on behavioral change is clear that children learn more from being told what to do than from being told what *not* to do.

❖ Think in terms of prevention. We call this "constructive negative thinking." It means trying to predict where problems will occur and why, then trying to prevent the problems. For example, if you're doing an art project where everyone needs scissors and you have a group of seven children but only five pair of scissors, there is potential for conflict. Two positive approaches to this problem are: explaining the problem to the children and asking what they think can be done about it, or finding more scissors.

❖ When you use conflict resolution techniques with children, explain what you are doing. For example, you can say, "I am listening to both sides," or "I'm trying to put myself in your shoes to understand how you feel about it."

The PII Approach

PII is a simple and proven approach to thinking about conflict and planning for action. It has been used by both school and nonschool programs. PII stands for *Prevention, Intervention* and *Invention.*

Prevention is anything we do to prevent conflict in our programs or to prepare for it before it happens. Prevention means laying groundwork such as:

❖ establishing procedures and routines for common activities so they happen smoothly and without incident;

❖ creating a feeling of community and caring in the program;

❖ building relationships with children;

❖ building relationships among the staff;

❖ doing some constructive thinking – such as asking where conflicts are likely to occur and what can be done to prevent them;

❖ setting up ways to handle conflicts when they do occur.

Intervention is responding when conflicts do happen. It means dealing with the conflict in ways that:

❖ solve problems;

❖ help children to be more independent in their conflict resolution;

❖ help children learn from the experience;

❖ improve relationships among children as well as between children and staff.

Invention is creating something new and constructive out of the situation. Invention is using the conflict productively to:

❖ help children learn;

❖ build relationships in the program;

❖ identify problems, weaknesses and areas of concern in the program;

❖ identify skills children need to develop in conflict resolution.

Prevention – Laying the Groundwork

We seek to prevent conflict in order to reduce conflict in the program and prepare to use conflicts constructively.

We can achieve these goals by building a feeling of community. Two approaches to prevention can help:

1. Build a Feeling of Community

2. Set Group Standards

Build a Feeling of Community

Community is a feeling of respect and caring in the program. You build community in a program by bringing the group together in a positive way, through games, whole program events, group projects and so on. Many of the projects and activities presented in this guide are designed to contribute to the feeling of community in Peaceable Programs.

Set Group Standards

As you set standards for group behavior, involve children in the process. Set up a procedure by which they can participate in setting standards, rules and procedures for the program. Let children help decide what the consequences should be for not following rules. Children who have a role in establishing rules and procedures will be more invested in and have more ownership of what they create.

Involving children in the process is not giving up your authority. The parameters for rules, procedures and standards will still need to be determined by you. Decide as a staff what's not negotiable – what rules and procedures does the staff want and need to have? Similarly, children's input will need to be tempered by adults.

Generally, there are five possible problems with the rules children set. Without careful guidance from adults, the rules children make are likely to be:

❖ **too general** – Rules like "Be nice to each other" do not specify what "nice" is.

❖ **too harsh** – The consequences feel more like punishments, such as, "Anyone who runs in the art area has to stay in from games for a month!"

❖ **too many** – There are rules to cover every specific situation rather general rules covering categories of problems.

❖ **too negative** – The rules are a series of descriptions of what people shouldn't do ("Don't yell," "Don't call names," "Don't hit") with no guidance on what they should do ("Use inside voices when inside," "Call people what they want to be called," "Keep your hands to yourself").

❖ **ignored** – Time and energy is spent developing standards and rules, then nobody pays any attention to them.

On the following pages are two positive and fun ways to involve children in establishing standards of behavior for the program.

Age: 5–12

Activity Type: Team Challenge

Activity Level: Moderate

Space: Any

Concentration Level: Medium

Time: 20 minutes

Group Size: 5–20

Prerequisite: None

The Peaceable Being *

Children create a Peaceable Being as a way to begin thinking about the kinds of behavior they want in their Peaceable Program.

● ● ● ● ● ● ● ● ● ● ● ● ● ● ● ● ●

Materials

❖ Large paper (7' by 4')

❖ Markers

Suggested Procedure

1. Have a volunteer lay down on the paper and have a few group members trace his or her body. This outline becomes the outline of the "Peaceable Being."

2. Gather everyone around the Being and ask them to think about what behaviors and attitudes would be helpful to the group. After they have had a minute or two to think, have them take markers and write these positive things inside the outline of the Peaceable Being.

3. Next ask the group to think of some actions/behaviors that they do not want as part of the group because of their negative consequences. Have them write these words on the outside of the Peaceable Being.

4. Have each group member say what he or she meant by the words chosen. Even if the words were the same as someone else's, the meaning may be slightly (or greatly) different.

5. Ask children if they think they can agree to use the Peaceable Being as a set of guidelines for their behavior in the program. Once you have this agreement, post the Peaceable Being prominently in the program space. If the group is going to name the Being, this is a good time.

Note: The Peaceable Being can be adapted for younger children. Make two tracings and have the children color and decorate them. For the key words, have the beings wear T-shirts. Designate one being's T-shirt as the positive and the other's as negative. Making it more of an art project makes it more interesting for young children.

Reflection

❖ What do you notice about the words that are inside the Peaceable Being?

* This activity is adapted from Youth Leadership in Action (Hamilton, MA: Project Adventure, 1994)

- ❖ What do you notice about the words that are outside the Peaceable Being?
- ❖ What kinds of rules could we make based on the Peaceable Being?
- ❖ What would be a good name for our Peaceable Being?

The Peaceable Being

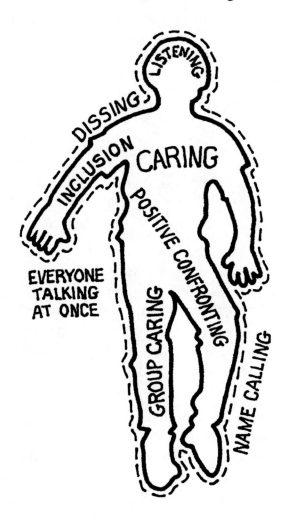

Age: 5–12

Activity Type: Chart

Activity Level: Quiet

Space: Any

Concentration Level: Medium

Time: 20 minutes

Group Size: 5–20

Prerequisite: None

The Peaceable Program Compact

Children establish guidelines for program behavior by creating a simple compact.

Materials
- ❖ Chart paper and markers

Suggested Procedure

1. The Peaceable Program Compact is a set of guidelines for how to behave and treat each other in a caring Peaceable Program. With older students you can explain that this is similar to the Mayflower Compact that the Pilgrims wrote when they first landed in America.

2. With primary grade children, keep it simple. Use three sentence starters:
   - ❖ In this program we treat people with respect. That means. . .
   - ❖ In this program we care about each other. That means. . .
   - ❖ In this program we use conflict resolution. That means. . .

3. Present these to the group and focus the discussion on completing the sentences with three specific behaviors for each. Help children frame the compact in positive language that says what children should do, rather than what they should not do. For example, instead of saying, "Don't call names," try restating it as, "Call people what they want to be called." Write up the results of the discussion on a chart to post in the program.

4. With upper elementary children, the Peaceable Program compact can be more elaborate. But the three sentence starters are still good places to begin the discussion. Keep the compact as concrete as possible. If it becomes too elaborate or abstract, children will have trouble sticking to it. When the class compact is finished, post it in a prominent place. Make an effort to refer to the compact at least once a day.

5. Your compact is different from setting up rules and consequences for the program. The compact is a set of guidelines for how the class members should treat each other. You can use it as a starting point for rule setting by asking the class: "What rules would help us to maintain the class compact?"

Intervening in Conflicts

Why do we intervene in conflicts? The obvious answer is: to stop the fight before someone gets hurt.

But there's more to it. We have at least six possible goals when we intervene in children's conflicts. They are to:

- ❖ create safety,
- ❖ establish order,
- ❖ enhance learning,
- ❖ increase independence,
- ❖ solve a problem,
- ❖ improve relationships.

Any intervention we make should contribute in some way to at least three, and preferably more, of these goals. Keeping that in mind, let's look at the possible ways we can intervene in conflicts.

Five Styles of Handling Children's Conflicts

The five primary styles of intervening in children's conflicts are:

1. direction,
2. mediation,
3. arbitration,
4. judgment and
5. listening sympathetically.

Direction

When you say, in effect, "Do this," you are directing. Direction is a non-negotiating approach. An adult authority decides what needs to be done and gives the direction that it be done. It's important to recognize that directing need not be unkind or authoritarian. Children can be told nicely, but clearly, what they need to do.

Uses: When safety is at stake; when children are out of control and need help getting back into control; when there is no time to discuss or negotiate; when the problem is not important enough to spend much time or energy.

Limitations: Doesn't build children's independence in problem solving; may cause resentment on the part of children; may not really solve problems.

Mediation

A third party – either a staff person or any trained person – sits with children and helps them work out their conflict by creating an environment where problem solving can take place. This is done by strictly enforcing ground rules. The mediator helps the disputants define their problem, develop solutions and choose a workable solution.

Uses: Because the disputants are solving the problem themselves, they are invested in the solution. Also, helps get to the root of some persistent problems.

Limitations: Takes time! The conflict may not be worth the time and effort compared to the learning that comes from it.

Post-problem Mediation

Many conflicts are over by the time an adult learns about them. To bring the conflict to closure, ask children the following questions:

❖ What happened?

❖ How do you feel?

❖ What could you do if this happened again?

❖ What could you do now to make things better?

Uses: Allows children to tell what happened and bring the problem to closure. Helps them learn something from the situation. Doesn't force them to do things like shake hands unless they want to.

Limitations: Students may not practice what they say they would do when the situation is repeated.

Arbitration

Also involves a third party who hears both (or all) sides, then tells the disputants how they should handle the conflict. This may be done with some input from the disputants, or by simply saying, "This is what you're going to do."

Uses: Efficient. Gives the disputants a chance to state their point of view, but doesn't spend a lot of time on problem solving.

Limitations: May not get to the root of the problem. The disputants may not learn anything about solving conflicts.

Judgment

Sometimes the emphasis needs to be not on problem solving, but on determining who was right and who was wrong. Children depend on the adult to act as a judge, to listen and weigh the evidence, and then to pass a fair judgment.

Uses: When there has been clear wrongdoing and the parties involved want justice; when there is a need for consequences to be decided upon for actions.

Limitations: Doesn't build independent problem-solving skills; keeps children dependent upon adults; is by its nature a Win-Lose model.

Listening Sympathetically

Just listening, not asking a lot of questions or giving advice or solutions, is lending a sympathetic ear. Children have a great need to be listened to regarding their conflicts. It is not uncommon for them to be able to figure out their own solutions once they have expressed their feelings and feel they have been heard.

Uses: Respects children and lets them express their feelings and opinions; helps them clarify their positions and feelings; gives them attention and support; can be combined with other methods of resolving conflict.

Limitations: Takes time; may not lead to problem solving; disputants may feel problem is unresolved.

Taking Advantage of Teachable Moments

- ❖ **Remember that there is a difference between teaching and preaching.** Preaching is unlikely to give children new skills or understandings. Use the conflict situation to teach and help children acquire a new skill or reinforce one they have already been taught.

- ❖ **When it's appropriate, give children as much responsibility as you can for solving the problem.** You will often need to supervise this, of course, but try as much as possible to let them solve it. For example, set a timer for five minutes and ask the children to see what solutions they can create in that time. If they can't come up with anything, you will be available to help them. The timer idea works very well with Peace Places.

- ❖ **Help the children invent something new out of the situation.** Ask questions like: "What could you do if this happened again?" or "What could you do now to make this situation better?" Focus children's attention on inventing something new.

Invention

To invent something new out of conflict means to learn from it in a way that leads to preventing the conflict in the future. The key questions of invention are:

- ❖ What did we learn from that conflict?
- ❖ What is this conflict telling us?

For example, is the conflict:

- ❖ a sign something is wrong with program;
- ❖ a sign children need more skills;
- ❖ a sign that the program is not well-planned?

Some related questions may include:

- ❖ Are there new procedures we need to establish in the program?
- ❖ Do we need to revise procedures or schedules?
- ❖ Is our program meeting children's needs?
- ❖ Are we planning in a way that prevents conflict?

Trouble-shooting Guide

Following are some activities and suggestions for dealing with common program conflicts. With problems like these, there are no prescriptions, The sources of and solutions to the problems will vary from program to program. Begin by first looking at what you can do to *prevent*, assessing how to *intervene*, then attempting to *invent* something new.

Teasing and Name-calling

Prevention

❖ Establish standards with "The Peaceable Being" (p. 14) or "The Peaceable Program Compact." (p. 16)

❖ Have children create a rule and consequences for not following the rule.

❖ Discuss the negative effect of teasing/name-calling/put-downs with "Green Poison Darts." (p. 194)

Intervention

❖ Give cool-off time.

❖ Remind children of the standards and/or the rules and consequences, then enforce them.

❖ Refer to "Post-problem Mediation." (p. 18)

Invention

❖ If it's a group problem, use group problem solving.

❖ If it's an individual problem, develop an individual contract.

❖ Determine if children's needs are not being met and develop a plan for meeting them.

Inclusion/Exclusion

Prevention

❖ Establish standards with"The Peaceable Being" (p. 14) or "The Peaceable Program Compact" (p. 16).

❖ Have children create a rule and consequences for not following the rule.

❖ Play "What's Prejudice?" (p. 227) as a way to begin discussing inclusion/exclusion.

Intervention

❖ Help excluded children find alternative activities.

❖ Direct children to include excluded children.

Invention

❖ If it's a group problem, use group problem solving.

❖ If it's an individual problem, try to figure out why the child is being excluded.

❖ Help children who are excluding others to be more inclusive with the "Green Poison Darts" (p. 194) activity.

Fighting

Prevention

❖ Establish standards with "The Peaceable Being" (p. 14) or "The Peaceable Program Compact" (p. 16).

❖ Have children create a rule and consequences for not following the rule.

❖ Establish a Peace Place, peer mediation and/or other ways to handle fights.

Intervention

❖ Give the children who are fighting cool-off time.

❖ Remind children of the standards and/or the rules and consequences, then enforce them.

❖ Use Peace Place, mediation or arbitration to resolve the dispute.

Invention

❖ If it's a group problem, use group problem solving.

❖ If it's an individual problem, develop an individual contract.

❖ Determine which conflict resolution skills children lack and develop a plan for teaching those skills.

❖ Determine if there are needs children have that are not being met and develop a plan for meeting them.

3

Clubs, Clusters, Themes and Projects

Τhis guide will help you effectively plan for and deal with conflict in your program, as well as provide you with plenty of activities to engage the children in your program in acquiring skills in conflict resolution and related themes.

The guide is also intended to be easy to use. This chapter includes "road maps" to guide you in selecting activities that address the needs of your children and your program. These road maps are only a few of the ways you can select and combine activities. They are presented as possibilities, not prescriptions.

There are two parts to this chapter:

1. Clubs: sequences of activities to last several weeks

2. Projects and clusters: activities built around a particular project;

Clubs

Clubs are a popular way of organizing activities in after-school programs. The clubs in this chapter are designed to last from four to six weeks, meeting once a week for 60 to 90 minutes. The clubs presented here were developed as examples of how to use and sequence the material in the guide. You can, of course, feel free to add to, subtract from, or otherwise modify the clubs to meet the needs of your children and your program.

Each club meeting focuses on an active, engaging, meaningful activity, such as a cooking project, a craft project, a play, a story, etc. As children participate in these activities, other activities can be incorporated into the session in order to introduce children to the skills and concepts of conflict resolution.

Below you will find a comprehensive guide to creating a peer mediation club. Included are the plans for six initial sessions as well as recommendations for including peer mediation in your program's structure. This detailed club description gives you an in-depth look at how clubs can be planned. Following the peer mediation club are six other club ideas with suggested activities. Use these club outlines to develop your own customized club.

The clubs included in this section are:

- ❖ Peer Mediation
- ❖ Helping Children Use a Peace Place
- ❖ Getting to Know You
- ❖ Peace Plays: An Improvisational Drama Club
- ❖ Actor's Exercises
- ❖ Peace Puppets Club
- ❖ Community and Trust Building

● Peer Mediation

(see Establish a Peer Mediation Program, p. 10.)

Focus: An on-going group trained to handle conflicts as they arise in the program.

Useful When: You have a high or increasing level of conflict in the program and want to enlist children's help in establishing a procedure for handling conflicts.

Mediation takes place when a neutral third party helps disputants resolve their conflict. In a peer mediation program, the mediator is a child who helps other children resolve their disputes. Once mediators have been trained they are available on certain days and times to deal with disputes between children. This relieves the adults on duty from having to settle all the conflicts. It also helps children practice conflict resolution skills.

To Set Up a Peer Mediation Program You Need To:

1. *Have realistic expectations for what a mediation program can do and how much work it entails.*

   Peer mediation is great for solving some conflicts, but it's not effective with all conflicts. For example, train mediators to give a list of problems that need adult attention and should not be mediated: anything to do with drugs, weapons, or touching on private parts.

   In addition, some conflicts involving breaking rules should not be mediated at first. The consequences for breaking the rules should be automatic. Once regular consequences have been enforced, the conflict can then be mediated so that it can be dealt with differently next time. In other words, mediation should not take the place of your discipline code, it should be an addition to it.

2. *Explain to the entire group what mediation is and how the mediation program will work.*

   The purpose of this introduction is both to interest potential mediators and to introduce mediation as one way for solving conflicts that occur in the program. Some children will be familiar with mediation from school programs, but most will not be very familiar with the process. Doing a mediation demonstration with some other staff members is a great way to introduce mediation and excite interest in it.

3. *Select children to act as mediators.*

   There are several ways to choose children to act as mediators. One is to have the staff suggest the names of children they think would make good mediators. Another is to have the children vote by secret ballot naming who they think would be effective in the role. A third is to have children volunteer to be part of the mediation club. Finally, another method is to combine all three methods and and see which names overlap.

   Whichever method you use, you will need to keep the following criteria in mind when choosing potential mediators:

   ❖ Availability to participate in mediation training;

   ❖ Interest in being a mediator;

   ❖ Evidence of being able to be impartial and fair;

   ❖ Evidence of good verbal skills;

   ❖ Representation of all the groups in your program's population.

   Aside from these, there is no hard and fast rule about choosing mediators. Some mediation experts believe that it's important to include some of the "negative leaders" in your program. Often these children, once given some responsibility, become positive leaders. Expect some children to drop out of the club once the training starts – some lose interest, some can't make the commitment, some aren't good at mediating. If you want to have mediators available for every day of your program, you will need to train three or four mediators for each day.

4. **Train the mediators.**

We recommend that the mediation training club meet six times, preferably twice a week for an hour and a half each session.

Session 1: Basic Conflict Resolution Skills

❖ Warm-up Activity: Humachines (p. 64)

❖ What's Conflict? (p. 239)

❖ Where Does Conflict Occur?

Have the children work in pairs to make maps of the school-age program area. Have them mark the maps where conflicts usually occur. When everyone is finished, have the pairs share their maps and describe the types of conflicts that take place at the marked locations.

❖ Conflict Escalates (p. 241 or p. 245)

If you can, use one of the conflicts described in the previous activity as an example, instead of using the case studies given.

❖ ABCD Problem Solving (p. 254 or p. 258)

Again, if you can, instead of using the case studies given, use as an example the conflicts you used in the escalation activity.

❖ Thumbs Up, Thumbs Down (p. 260)

Finish the session by having children make folders in which to keep their mediation materials.

Session 2: Listening in Mediation

❖ Warm-up Activity: All Knotted Up (p. 63)

❖ Practicing Mediation (p. 294)

❖ Model Mediation

You play the role of mediator with two children acting the roles of disputants using one of the role plays on p. 253. Act out the ABC Mediation process (p. 295), paying particular attention to setting the ground rules. During the discussion afterwards, discuss why the ground rules are so important, what to do if someone won't follow the rules, etc.

❖ Good Listening (p. 102)

❖ Pete and Repeat (p. 104)

❖ Communication Potholes (p. 105)

❖ Listening Role Plays (p. 141)

Set these role plays up as mediation role plays by having two of the children play the disputants and two play the mediators. If you have leftover children they can be observers or, if there are three leftover, you can play one of the roles. When finished, discuss the first part of the mediation; i.e., setting ground rules, listening to both sides, keeping to the ground rules, etc. Emphasize that if one of the disputants says they are not willing to solve the problem, then mediation probably won't work.

Use the following questions to process the role play:

❖ What went well? (Ask this of both mediators and disputants.)

❖ What was difficult? (Ask this of both mediators and disputants.)

❖ Based on this experience, what's one thing you think you could do better next time?

❖ What are some ways you could handle it if someone didn't agree to the ground rules?

Session 3: Practicing Mediation

❖ Warm Up: What Color Is Conflict? (p. 268)

❖ Review the Role of the Mediator and the Mediation Process

❖ Mediation Dos and Don'ts

Make a chart with the children of what they think are good "Dos" and "Don'ts" for mediators. Bring this chart out during the following sessions for the children to add to the lists anything they've learned.

❖ Practicing Mediation

Form groups of four to role play the conflict on p. 296. Set these role plays up with small groups as you did in the previous session. Children who did not get to be mediators previously should get a chance today. Ask the mediators (and observers, if any) to pay close attention to their listening and how it affects the mediation. Depending on the time, have one or two of the groups volunteer to do their mediation before the group. Get feedback from the group by asking the following questions:

❖ Ask the mediators and the disputants to comment on their experience.

❖ What's one thing you saw or heard the mediator do well?

❖ What's one thing you think the mediator could improve?

Session 4: Feelings in Mediation

- ❖ Warm-up: Can You Guess? (p. 133)

- ❖ Creating a Feelings Chart (p. 148)

- ❖ Feeling Pantomime (p. 160)

- ❖ The Anger Thermometer (p. 150)

   Be sure to do the follow-up where children make their own anger thermometers.

- ❖ Ballooning and Draining (p.153)

- ❖ Practicing Mediation (p. 294) or other role plays

   Set these role plays up with small groups as you did in the previous session. If there are children who did not have an opportunity to be mediators previously, they should get a chance today. Ask the mediators (and observers, if any) to pay special attention to the feelings expressed and how they affect the mediation. Emphasize in the discussion that the mediators are in charge of the process, while the disputants are in charge of the solution.

Session 5: Finding Solutions in Conflicts

- ❖ Warm-Up: King Frog (p. 165)

- ❖ Discussion:What's a Good Solution?

   Discuss what makes a "good solution" in a conflict. With the group, develop criteria for good solutions. Refer back to the "Win-Win" charts of session 1.

- ❖ Mediation Practice (p. 296 or 248)

   Set these role plays up with small groups as you did in the previous session. Plan on running two sets of role plays so that everyone practices being the mediator today. The goal is for each group to come up with "good solutions." Focus the discussion on what it's like to help others develop solutions, what's helpful or not helpful when doing this, etc. This is also a good time to discuss how to work in pairs as mediators. What's good about working with another mediator? How can mediators help each other? What problems come up?

Session 6: Preparing to Demonstrate

- ❖ Warm-Up: Human Bridges (p. 74)

- ❖ Discuss the Nuts and Bolts of Scheduling, Supervision, etc.

- ❖ Discuss What to Present to the Group

For the mediation program to work, children in the program need to know what it is and how to use it. Discuss with your club what they think are the important points other children need to know about mediation. Then discuss how to present those to the group during a group meeting.

❖ Brainstorming Conflict Scenarios (p. 281)

Explain to the children that they will do this activity with goal of developing a conflict mediation role play they can show to the group.

❖ Planning a Presentation

Once a role play is developed, choose children who will be the players before the group. Others who are interested in being presenters can come up with ways to present such aspects of the mediation program as: What is mediation? What does a mediator do? What does a mediation not do? How are mediations scheduled? etc.

5. *Designate a Mediation Place and schedule mediators.*

Many programs have a sign posted in a prominent place that lists who is available to mediate that day. You want to have three or four children available each day, but you don't want one or two children to be doing all the mediations. Remember, children will be mediating in pairs. You also need to designate a place where mediations will happen—a table with chairs is all you need.

6. *Encourage children to use mediation when they have a conflict.*

Especially in the early days of your mediation program, the children will need to be reminded that mediation is an option they have whenever they have a conflict.

7. *Supervise the mediations.*

Your mediation place should be located where you – or some other responsible adult – can keep an eye and an ear on things.

8. *Continue to meet with the mediators.*

As children start to mediate they will have a lot of enthusiasm, but they may encounter some difficulties. A meeting every two weeks to help them improve their skills is useful. Make these a combination of skill building, discussing problems, and fun activities.

9. *Keep mediation within the larger framework of a conflict resolution program.*

A mediation program is an excellent addition to conflict resolution work in your school-age program. But it cannot and should not be the entire program. Do some of the other conflict resolution activities in this guide with your entire program, and remember that the more the children in your program know about conflict resolution, the more successful your mediation program will be, and vice versa.

● Helping Children Learn to Use a Peace Place

(see "Set up a Peace Place," p. 8.)

Focus: A method for encouraging children to resolve their disputes.

Useful When: You have a high or increasing level of conflict in the program and want to help children to solve the conflicts independently.

To Introduce the Peace Place you will need to:

1. *Establish a corner or area that is the Peace Place.*

    Post a copy of the Conflict Resolution Chart (p. 252), the ABCD Problem Solving Chart (p. 256), and the Win-Win Grid (p. 263) in the area. It's also helpful to have a kitchen timer.

2. *Introduce the Peace Place during a group meeting.*

    Explain that the Peace Place is a place where children can go and try to solve conflicts. To go there they must first ask permission from an adult, or an adult may suggest that they go to the Peace Place. Explain that there is a timer they can set. If conflict solving in the Peace Place starts to take too long, they can ask an adult for help, but they have to work at it for seven minutes first. Introduce the three charts and discuss how they might be used to solve conflicts. (If you have time to do any of them now, the activities that go with these charts will lead to children being more effective at using the Peace Place. If you don't have time, see step #4.)

3. *Demonstrate how to use the Peace Place.*

    With another staff person, role play two children going to the Peace Place and working out their problem. Set the timer for seven minutes and explain that you will try to solve the problem in that time. Begin the role play by walking through the steps on the ABCD Chart. When it comes time to brainstorm solutions, refer to the Conflict resolution Chart and suggest some solutions based on what's listed there. Try to come up with a solution within the seven minute limit. When the role play is complete, shake hands.

4. Use Activities

In a club format or as part of another group meeting, use any or all of the following activities, which will help children who try to use the Peace Place. The more practice they have with these, the more effective they will be at using the Peace Place and at resolving conflicts generally.

- ❖ What's Conflict? (p. 239)
- ❖ Conflict Escalates (p. 241)
- ❖ Conflict Resolution Chart (p. 249)
- ❖ ABCD Problem Solving (p. 254)
- ❖ Thumbs Up, Thumbs Down (p. 260)

Getting To Know You

Focus: Helping a group get to know each other in positive ways.

Useful When: You have a group of children who don't know each other; e.g., it's the beginning of the year, etc.

Activities:
- ❖ MeYouLisa (p. 52)
- ❖ Don't Forget! (p. 54)
- ❖ Pass the Shoe (p. 56)
- ❖ All Knotted Up (p. 63)
- ❖ The Line Forms Here (p. 65)
- ❖ Warp Speed (p. 70)
- ❖ Find Your Place (p. 205)
- ❖ Orbit (p. 125)
- ❖ Picture Me (p. 204)
- ❖ Pick Your Corner (p. 190)
- ❖ Have You Ever . . . ? (p. 207)
- ❖ Have You Ever . . . ? Yes/No Rope (p. 209)
- ❖ Interviewing (p. 210)
- ❖ Family Bag Projects (p. 212)
- ❖ Tell Me Your Story (p. 213)
- ❖ Silhouette Portraits (p. 218)
- ❖ If (p. 201)

Peace Plays: An Improvisational Drama Club

Focus: An ongoing dramatic group improvisation using conflict themes.

Useful When: You have a group of children interested in developing their own dramatic presentations.

Activities:

Team Building

The activities listed under Actor's Exercises (p. 33) are good warm-ups and team builders for this type of group.

Improvisation and Role Play

- ❖ Humachines (p. 64)
- ❖ Standing in Their Shoes (p. 121)
- ❖ Listening Role Plays (p. 141)
- ❖ Listening for Feelings (p. 143)
- ❖ Feeler Soup (p. 167)
- ❖ How Did It Feel? (p. 173)
- ❖ Mood Glasses Pattern (p. 177)
- ❖ The Anger Suit (p. 184)
- ❖ Hanging Up the Anger Suit (p. 186)
- ❖ Conflict Escalates (p. 241)
- ❖ Conflict Resolution Chart (p. 249)
- ❖ ABCD Problem Solving (p. 254)
- ❖ Thumbs Up, Thumbs Down (p. 260)
- ❖ Brainstorming Conflict Scenarios (p. 281)
- ❖ Craziest Conflict Resolutions (p. 284)
- ❖ Making Peace Punch (p. 309)
- ❖ Peace Punch Role Plays (p. 310)
- ❖ And Now, A Word from Our Sponsors... (p. 313)
- ❖ Filming Peace Ads (p. 315)

● Actor's Exercises

Focus: Conflict-related exercises to help young actors warm up.

Useful When: You have a drama group that is putting on a play and you want to infuse some conflict resolution and related themes into the group.

Activities:
- ❖ Humachines (p. 64)
- ❖ Pete and Repeat (p. 104)
- ❖ Standing in Their Shoes (p. 121)
- ❖ Bumper Cars (p. 124)
- ❖ Slot Machine (p. 129)
- ❖ Feeling Pantomimes (p. 160)
- ❖ Speedy Threesome (p. 161)
- ❖ King Frog (p. 165)
- ❖ Feelings Relay (p. 171)
- ❖ Sculptor, Model, & Clay (p. 181)

● Peace Puppets Club

Focus: An on-going group for younger children based on puppet improvisations.

Useful When: You have a group of children interested in putting on puppet shows.

Sequence:

Team Building

Choose activities from Chapters 5 and 7

Improvisation and Role Play

1. Making Peace Puppets (p. 279)
2. Conflict Escalates – Primary Grade Version (p. 245)
3. Conflict Resolution Chart (p. 249) and Role Plays (p. 253)
4. ABCD Problem Solving – Primary Grade Version (p. 258)
5. Thumbs Up, Thumbs Down (p. 260)
6. Brainstorming Conflict Scenarios (p. 281)
7. Peace Puppet Show (p. 280)

● Community and Trust Building

Focus: Activities that will build community by helping to increase trust and cooperation.

Useful When: You are starting the program year. Also when you see an increase in conflicts related to an inability to work together successfully, miscommunication or negative communication, or lack of appreciation for diversity.

Sequence:

Cooperation Skill Building

1. Toothpicks (p. 47)
2. Cooperative Monster Making (p. 49)

Cooperation

Any Team challenges

Feelings

Choose activities from chapter 7

Diversity

1. Green Poison Darts (p. 194)
2. Interviewing (p. 210)
3. Silhouette Portraits (p. 218)

Peace Projects and Clusters

Focus: Creative and enrichment activities that can be used to introduce basic conflict resolution skills, either formally or informally.

Useful When: You have a group of children who enjoy creative and active projects and you don't want to make the time commitment required for a club.

Sample Projects and Clusters:

Central Project

Tower of Power (p. 331)

Cluster Activities

❖ Conflict Resolution Chart (p. 249)

Making the Activities Adventuresome

Then his book was titled *Adventures in Peacemaking* because we believe learning to work and play together peacefully can be an adventure. Resolving conflicts, learning skills in cooperation and practicing expressing emotions can be challenging, risky and fun. It is your job as the group leader to help the young people in your program engage in these activities – to make peacemaking an adventure they won't forget.

How can you do this? Here are some basics...

Have fun with the activities and your group will too

Many of the activities use humor and action to engage the group. The games are playful, active and, sometimes, just plain silly. You will need to lead them this way. When playing Wizards and Gelflings, you need to be a wizard or gelfling. Have fun with the activity. Be silly. The kids will see that you are willing to play and this will certainly capture their attention.

Set the scene

Many of the activities include write-up's for "Setting the Scene." These are actually "mini-scripts" of what you might say to get the action going. It is important to pay attention to this part of the activity. This is the time to lay the groundwork: why are we playing the activity, how does it fit into a conflict resolution program, what are we trying to learn. It is this time, combined with time set aside for reflection, that makes this activity a learning experience, not just something to do.

Introduce the rules as simply as possible

Sometimes a group needs to play a practice round to understand the rules. This is often a better solution then allowing for five minutes of questions. Try to keep the instructions as simple as you can. For complex activities, you may choose to add rules or instructions as the game progresses.

Your role is facilitator, not leader

In many of the activities your group will be challenged to solve a problem that you present to them. Your role is to make sure the group understands the activity, is capable of completing it and plays safely. Your job is not to direct the group, e.g. "Sally, why don't you ask Malika to move over here." Try to refrain from telling them what to do. Instead, answer their questions with questions that will help lead them toward a possible solution. If you need to, call a time out and hold a mini-group meeting. Do whatever you can to empower the group to solve the problem themselves.

GRAB the right activity*

When selecting activities to use with your group, do a quick needs assessment. Make sure you are picking the right activity by asking the following questions:

*G*oals. What are the goals of the group? Why are you doing this activity? Does the activity fit the goals?

*R*eadiness. Is the group ready for this activity? Have they done the pre-requisite work to make the activity successful?

*A*ffect. How is the group's emotional state? Are they too wound up or too mellow for the activity? Will the activity fit their affect?

*B*ehavior. How is the group behaving? Is the activity too challenging for where they are now? Will the activity encourage the behavior you are trying to elicit?

Be prepared for the unexpected

It is never possible to predict with certainty what will happen when groups of people work together. Get used to this, it's part of what makes the program an adventure for you, the leader. If you are open to unexpected outcomes, you will not need to constantly control what the group does. Allow for a little safe experimentation. If the children want to change the rules or try something again, go with it. Encourage them to take control of their own learning.

* Adapted from *Islands of Healing, A Guide to Adventure Based Counseling* by Jim Schoel (Hamilton, MA: Project Adventure, Inc, 1984).

Don't Skip Reflection*

The activities are also written with ideas for Reflection time. This is a post-activity period that could last anywhere from two to twenty minutes. Reflection is the time when you help the children understand what they have learned from an activity. One proven way to coax your group into discussion mode is by asking the following questions:

What?   What happened during this activity? Who did what when? How did we solve the problem? This is the time to retell the story of what the group just did.

So What?   What did we learn as we were working together? For example, "What happened?" "We were frustrated." "Why and what does this teach us?" "Well everyone was talking at once. We need to learn to talk one at a time."

Now What?   This is the final step where the group takes what they have learned from a specific activity and applies it to more generic situations or to the next planned activity. For example: "So, when a large group of people are trying to work cooperatively, they need a system so everyone can give an input. How can we do this? How do you do it when you are playing a game without an adult?"

There are other ways to accomlplish your reflection time. What your's looks like – a quick thumbs up, thumbs down, a drawing project or a group discussion – may depend on the age of your group, the intent of the activity and what happened during the activity.

You will find that you need to teach your children to reflect. It may take several days or weeks before reflection time has the meaning you had hoped. Children will need to develop skills to help them think about the activities this way. Remember, though, reflection may be the most important skill you teach them, so don't give up on it.

Using the Activities

Each activity is formatted to provide you with quick and ready access to information that is helpful for your planning. A typical activity format includes:

Activity Title

Includes a short description of the activity.

The Information Corner

Icons: Icons that designate Age, Activity Type, and Activity Level have been placed at the top of the information corner for each activity. These icons can help you quickly find an activity appropriate for the age of your children, the activity level you are prepared for, and the type of activity that you would like to do. A key for the icons can be found on page 42.

---

* Adapted from *Islands of Healing, A Guide to Adventure Based Counseling* by Jim Schoel (Hamilton, MA: Project Adventure, Inc, 1984).

Age: The general age for which this activity is designed. Do not feel bound by this. Many activities can be easily modified for younger or older children. Some activities have alternate age groups indicated within parentheses – these activities include ideas about how they can be changed for various age groups. The activities have been indexed by age levels at the end of this guide.

Activity Type: The kind of activity, such as arts and crafts, storytelling, or cooking. To facilitate your use of this guide, the activities have been subdivided into 13 activity types. We hope these activity types will help you choose activities appropriate for your group and program. The activities have also been indexed by activity type at the end of this guide.

Activity Level: This describes the general level of activity required, from Very Active (i.e., running or jumping) to Quiet (i.e., talking in a circle).

Concentration Level: The level of concentration children need to do this activity. Concentration levels have been classified as Low, Medium, and High. Appropriate concentration levels are partially influenced by the environment. For example, High concentration activities may not work as well in a context with many distractions. The concentration level also expresses information helpful for scheduling the activity. For example, a high concentration activity probably shouldn't be done when children first arrive and are decompressing from a day at school.

Prerequisites: Activities children need to have completed before they can successfully do this activity.

Group Size: The optimal group size for the activity. These usually are given as a range, but feel free to experiment. If you have too large a group, you may divide the group and do the activity with two or more smaller groups simultaneously.

Space: The physical space needed to execute the activity, e.g., a large open space, kitchen, work tables, or any space available. Any space assumes that you have a room adequate for the number of children in your group.

Time: Approximately how long, in minutes, the activity takes.

Materials

The materials needed to do the activity. Materials such as activity sheets and handouts will follow the activity for which they are needed.

Set the Scene

Any necessary pre-activity set up and/or verbal set-up for the children, such as a story or explanation. Story set-ups can make the activity more meaningful and fun for children, so feel free to adapt and add on to any we have provided.

Suggested Procedure

How to do the activity. Feel free to vary this according to the needs of your group.

Reflection

Questions and discussion topics to help children think about their experience and probe what they have learned. Reflection questions are more or less based on Bloom's Taxonomy of Educational Objectives*. Sometimes reflection is presented as a list of questions; sometimes we suggest a more activity-oriented reflection. You should feel free to use the reflection strategy from one activity with another. Reflection is often difficult to pull off in an afterschool setting. Many pilot test teachers reported that they infused the reflection questions into the activity itself, so that the reflection discussion took place as children were working on a project.

---

* Benjamin S. Bloom, *Taxonomy of Educational Objectives*, (New York: Longman, 1984).

Icon Key

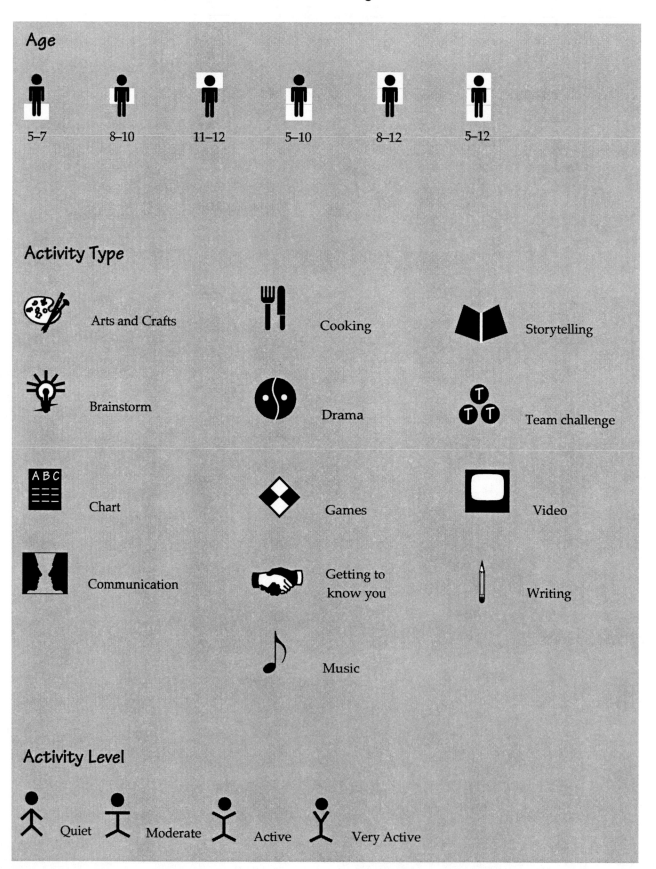

Age

5–7   8–10   11–12   5–10   8–12   5–12

Activity Type

Arts and Crafts

Cooking

Storytelling

Brainstorm

Drama

Team challenge

Chart

Games

Video

Communication

Getting to know you

Writing

Music

Activity Level

Quiet   Moderate   Active   Very Active

Part Two
Activities

5

Cooperation

Reducing conflict by helping children
work together effectively

One of the most effective ways to reduce conflict in a program is to foster a feeling of community. Cooperation skills are an integral part of fostering this feeling of community. The activities in this chapter are designed to help children acquire the skills and understandings they need to solve the common problems that come up as they work and play together.

There are four types of activities in this chapter:

1. Cooperative Skill Building

2. Getting Acquainted and Team Building

3. Cooperative Games

4. Cooperative Challenges and Group Problem Solving

Using Teachable Moments

It's not at all uncommon for children to get stuck when they try to work together. One of your roles is to help them get "unstuck." But getting unstuck is more than getting the activity going again. It's also helping children learn and develop the skills they need so that they won't get stuck in the future.

Here are some ways to help children when they are stuck:

❖ Encourage children to ask for help when they're having a problem in a group. Asking for help when the group is stuck is not an admission of failure, it's identifying that there is a problem and that it needs to be solved.

❖ Ask, "What's the problem you're having?" "What are ways you've tried to solve it?" "What help do you need from me?"

❖ Avoid saying things like, "That's not very good cooperating" or other scolding statements. These don't help the children get unstuck, and they don't help them learn new skills.

❖ Children love to look for a place to put the blame when a group isn't going well. Encourage them to look at the situation as a problem to be solved rather than as a question of who is to blame. Ask children, "How are you going to solve this problem?" or "What would get you working together again?"

❖ When children are stuck and there's lots of blaming and bad feeling, be sure to acknowledge the feeling. You might say, "Sounds like everyone is pretty angry and frustrated." Or you might ask the children to tell you how they feel, "How do you feel right now?"

❖ Suggest possible solutions when they can't think of any, but try to offer them in a respectful way that gives children choices. You might say, "If you're really stuck, I have some suggestions. Do you want to hear them?"

❖ Sometimes it happens that children must be removed from a group. When you do so, be sure there's a way for them to come back into the group. Say, "When you're ready you may rejoin the group."

❖ Sometimes the group needs a mini-break from each other. Do a group "Yes!" before starting to problem solve. Have the group stand in a circle and crouch down. Have them slowly rise together, standing and raising their hands into the air. As they do so, they say the word "yes," beginning when they are crouching and finishing when their hands are in the air.

❖ There are times when the group needs clear direction from you about what they should do. Provide guidance when it is appropriate. But try to diagnose the problem. What does it tell you about the children? What kind of skills development do they need?

Cooperative Skill Building

TOOTHPICKS

Children work to create a mutually agreed upon picture or sculpture using toothpicks.

●●●●●●●●●●●●●●●●●●●●

Age:	5–12
Activity Type:	Arts and crafts
Activity Level:	Quiet
Space:	Work tables (or open space)
Concentration Level:	High
Time:	15–20 minutes
Group Size:	4 or more
Prerequisite:	None

MATERIALS

❖ Toothpicks (at least one box for each group of three or four)

SUGGESTED PROCEDURE

1. Have the group brainstorm a list of the ways groups make decisions. Record these on chart paper or a chalkboard. Explain any that are unfamiliar to the group. If the group needs help, prompt them with some of these suggestions: voting, coming to consensus, flipping a coin, asking an expert to decide.

2. The first time you do this activity, divide the children into groups of two. When you repeat it, increase the group size to four. Explain the task to the groups. Each group is going to receive a pile of toothpicks and their task is to make something out of the toothpicks. They can make a picture, a sculpture, whatever they want. They can build up, spread out, or break toothpicks if they wish. There are only two rules. First, the group must use one of the decision-making strategies listed on the chart. (The first time you do this, give the groups the strategy to use, such as voting or everyone coming to agreement.) The second rule is that everyone gets to help make the final product.

3. Distribute the toothpicks and tell children that they may have more if needed. Let the groups begin working. Circulate among them to help with any problems.

4. When the groups finish, have them share their creations.

REFLECTION

❖ What did you build?

❖ How did you decide to build it?

❖ How did each person contribute to the sculpture?

❖ What problems came up in your group?

❖ How did you solve them?

Toothpicks

Use the "Toothpicks" activity throughout the year with all ages. By repeating it, the children not only get better at decision making, they also make better and more elaborate toothpick creations.

❖ Can you think of a way those problems could have been prevented?

❖ What would you do differently next time?

NOTES
● ● ● ● ● ● ● ● ● ● ● ●

COOPERATIVE MONSTER MAKING

Children work on creating monsters with each child assigned a specific role.

● ● ● ● ● ● ● ● ● ● ● ● ● ● ● ● ●

Age:	(5–7) 8–12
Activity Type:	Arts and Crafts
Activity Level:	Moderate
Space:	Work tables (or open space)
Concentration Level:	Medium
Time:	30 minutes
Group Size:	4 or more
Prerequisite:	None

MATERIALS

- ❖ Construction paper
- ❖ Crayons
- ❖ Scissors
- ❖ Tape
- ❖ Role cards (one set per group)

SUGGESTED PROCEDURE

1. Divide children into groups of four. Explain that the group is to create a monster and come up with a description of the monster. The rules are simple: everyone in the group helps decide what the monster will be like, and everyone in the group helps make the monster.

   In this activity the decision making is very simple because each child is in charge of a body part. The child can make the body part look however he or she wants it to look.

2. Explain that you will be giving role cards to the group. Everyone in the group will have a specific job to do. Give each group a set of cards, face down, and have the group members pick cards.

3. Give each group the materials they need to create their monsters and have them begin. Circulate to help those groups who need it.

4. When the groups have finished, have them share their monsters with the other groups.

REFLECTION

- ❖ How did having roles affect how your group worked together?
- ❖ What are some of the other roles that people play in groups?
- ❖ What kinds of group problems might be solved by assigning roles?

TIP!

Follow-up Idea

Children like to make things that they can take home. Since the cooperative monster stays in the program area and doesn't go home with anyone, a nice follow-up to this activity is to have each child make a "baby monster" for the cooperative monster. These can, of course, go home with the child who made them.

Monster Making
Role Cards

- -

Leg Maker

- -

Arm Maker

- -

Head Maker

- -

Body Maker

Getting Acquainted and Team Building

Age: 5–12

Activity Type: Circle game

Activity Level: Moderate

Space: Any

Concentration Level: High

Time: 15 minutes

Group Size: 10 or more

Prerequisite: None

MEYOULISA

Children practice each other's names.

● ● ● ● ● ● ● ● ● ● ● ● ● ● ● ● ●

MATERIALS

❖ Stopwatch

❖ A soft, throwable object that can be passed from person to person (e.g., a rubber chicken, Koosh Ball®, bean bag)

SUGGESTED PROCEDURE

1. Have everyone gather in a circle, including yourself.

2. Pull out the stopwatch and announce that you will time how long it takes for everyone to go around the circle and say his/her name.

3. Start this game by tossing the object to an unsuspecting person in the circle. That person must say three names, first the name of the person to his or her right, then the name of the person to his or her left, and then his or her own name.

4. The object then gets passed to the right.

5. This person must say the names of the people to her right and left, then her own name and pass the object to the right. Continue passing and naming until everyone has started with the object.

6. A fun variation once children have the knack of the game is to try timing it. What world record speed can the group achieve? Encourage the group to beat their own score, then try doing it eyes closed.

REFLECTION

❖ Spend a few moments marveling at the speed at which this particular group was able to go around the circle. Ask a few questions before moving on, but don't spend too much time here.

❖ Which created a better time? Eyes closed or open?

❖ Was it difficult to be the beginning person? Why?

Name Game Warm-up

This game is a great warm-up for a group that is just meeting each other for the first time. Use it as a lead-in to a name game by asking, "Okay, have you got everyone's names down now?"

IMPULSE

The group sends an impulse around a linked circle.

• • • • • • • • • • • • • • • • • •

MATERIALS

❖ None

SET THE SCENE

Use this activity as a warm-up that will get the group used to holding hands with each other. This can be one of the first steps to establishing trust in the group.

SUGGESTED PROCEDURE

1. Have the group form a circle holding hands, including yourself. There should be a comfortable amount of space between each person, so that they are neither squeezed nor stretched.

2. Explain that you are going to create a wave impulse that will circle the group.

3. Start by visibly, but lightly, squeezing the hand of one of your neighbors, moving your hands inward a bit. That person should then pass the impulse to their neighbor and so on until you receive it back again.

4. Experiment with sending the impulse in each direction and then in both directions at the same time. If they are successful, introduce a stopwatch. Establish a time and then try to better it. Try timing it with all eyes closed except the leader's.

5. If the group is not successful, try a variation such as clapping, finger snapping, or sticking out your tongue. Then bring the activity to a close.

REFLECTION

❖ How successful was the impulse?

❖ When was the impulse successful?

❖ When was the impulse not successful?

❖ What did you learn about working together from this exercise?

Age:	8–12
Activity Type :	Team challenge
Activity Level:	Moderate
Space:	Any
Concentration Level:	Medium
Time:	10 minutes
Group Size:	10 or more
Prerequisite:	None

Gauging Cooperation

It will be clear from this reflection how aware your group is about how they work together. Use it to gauge how well they understand and can practice cooperation.

Age:	8–12
Activity Type:	Getting to know you
Activity Level:	Active
Space:	Large open space
Concentration Level:	High
Time:	20–30 minutes
Group Size:	10–15 (for a larger group divide in two)
Prerequisite:	Group must be comfortable with close physical contact

Safety Note

Caution children about getting too rambunctious during this activity. As the group moves, emphasize *slowly and carefully.*

TIP!

For Younger Children

Younger children adore this game, but will find it difficult initially both to move as a group and to share something about which they're proud. With younger children skip the sharing part the first few times you do the activity.

DON'T FORGET!

The group answers questions about themselves while moving from one point to another tied together by a rope.

MATERIALS

❖ A length of rope long enough to wrap around your group snugly

SUGGESTED PROCEDURE

1. To get ready for this challenge, get the group packed together as tightly as you can. If you are starting from a circle, ask everyone to move very slowly backwards into the center until they can go no further. If you are starting randomly, ask the group to meet you at a very specific spot – all touching a piece of paper on the ground or as close to a fellow student as possible.

2. Once the group is assembled, tie a rope around them tightly enough to hold them closely together, but not so constricting that moving or breathing becomes a problem. The more loops of rope you can make the better, so that the group actually feels tied together.

3. After the rope is in place, ask the group to slowly and carefully walk from point A to point B. Pick a path with occasional physical obstacles that will offer the group a healthy challenge. For example, have the group move through a loose hedge, over a curb, around tight corners, around orange cones, etc. To make this task more difficult, ask the children to end in a sitting position. While walking, each child should share something about him or herself that is unusual or about which they are particularly proud.

4. Tell the group they've got a rope around them – like a string around a finger – so they should not forget what they hear, because you'll be asking them later what they found out about each other and what their names are.

5. When the group arrives at their destination, have them settle into a circle (untied) and reflect.

REFLECTION

- ❖ What did you learn about your group from this activity?

- ❖ Is there something you could do next time that would help the group move back together more quickly?

NOTES

● ● ● ● ● ● ● ● ● ● ● ●

Age:	5–12
Activity Type:	Team challenge
Activity Level:	Moderate
Space:	Any
Concentration Level:	High
Time:	15–20 minutes
Group Size:	6 or more
Prerequisite:	None

TIP!

Shoe Substitutions

If sharing shoes is a problem for your group, substitute something else – building blocks or tennis balls would work too.

Rainy-Day Booster

This game can be played over and over and is a great rainy-day spirit booster.

PASS THE SHOE

Students sing a rhythmical chant while trying to pass their shoes around the circle.

● ● ● ● ● ● ● ● ● ● ● ● ● ● ● ● ● ● ●

MATERIALS

❖ One shoe per person (left or right will do)

SET THE SCENE

Explain to the students, "This is a fun test of how well we can work cooperatively. We will begin by sitting cross-legged on the floor in a circle. Each one of you will have to remove one shoe."

SUGGESTED PROCEDURE

1. *Tell the children,* "We are going to pass our shoes around the circle. The goal is to get your own shoe back. The trick is we need to follow a beat."

2. Here is the chant, "We pass the shoe from me to you. We pass like this and we never, never miss."

3. As the group is chanting, they will be passing. Begin with your hand on your own shoe. The shoes get passed to the right at the beat:

   We (put your hand on the shoe in front of you)
   pass (pass the shoe to the person to your right)
   the (hand on the *new* shoe in front of you)
   shoe (pass the shoe to the person to your right)
   from (hand on the shoe in front of you)
   me (pass the shoe to the person to your right)
   to (hand on the shoe in front of you)
   you (pass the shoe to the person to your right).

4. In the second sentence, the passing pattern gets a little tricky:

   We (put your hand on the shoe in front of you)
   pass (pass the shoe to the person to your right)
   like (hand on the shoe in front of you)
   this (pass the shoe to the person to your right)
   and we (hand on the shoe in front of you)
   never (pass the shoe to your right, but don't let go)
   never (bring the shoe back in front of you)
   miss (pass the shoe to the person on your right – let go!)
   Keep chanting.

5. Try this out before you try it with the children. Have the chilren practice a few times. The goal is to continue repeating the chant until each person has his/her own shoe back or until a set time has elapsed. If someone makes a mistake, start over. You'll know when the group makes a mistake because some unsuspecting person will have a pile of shoes in front of him.

REFLECTION

❖ Did we reach our goal?

❖ If so, how did we do it?

❖ If not, what could we try next time?

NOTES
● ● ● ● ● ● ● ● ● ● ●

Age: 8–12

Activity Type: Circle game

Activity Level: Moderate

Space: Any

Concentration Level: High

Time: 20 minutes

Group Size: 6–20

Prerequisite: None

Safety Note

Caution children about getting too rambunctious during this activity. As the group moves, emphasize slowly and carefully. Also emphasize that they should lean back or forward only as far as they are comfortable.

TIP!

If the group is not taking good care of each other (too much pulling and tugging), stop the activity. Ask everyone to sit down in a circle; and use this time as a teachable moment. "What do we need to do to make this activity work?"

YURT CIRCLE

Students form a circle, alternating between leaning inward and outward.

● ● ● ● ● ● ● ● ● ● ● ● ● ● ● ● ●

MATERIALS

❖ None

SET THE SCENE

Explain to the group, "There are many times when you need to depend on the people you are with in a group and know that you can work well together. Let's see how well this group can work together."

SUGGESTED PROCEDURE

1. Ask the children to hold hands in a circle and to move outward until everyone feels some pull on their arms from the people to their left and right. Starting with any child, ask the group to count off by two's all the way around the circle.

2. Encouraging the group to move slowly and deliberately, ask all the "one's" to lean toward the center of the circle and all the "two's" to lean out (without bending at the waist). Each person should have their feet placed at about shoulder width and in line with the circumference of the circle.

3. For this activity to be successful it's important that the group members *not* bend at the waist. If the group members cooperate with one another, each person can exert quite a strong pull on their supporting partners and accomplish a remarkable forward or backward lean. It may take several tries to get to this point, as it takes a lot of trust as well as cooperation.

4. After some practice and increased proficiency, ask the "one's" and "two's" to try reversing positions (backward to forward or vice versa). This is not easy to do and will require a few attempts. Even if the group never succeeds, it's good for a few laughs and some un-selfconscious hand-holding.

REFLECTION

Ask the group how well they felt they worked together.

❖ Did they feel like they could depend on the people next to them?

❖ Did they trust each other?

❖ What things made it easier to work together?

NOTES

● ● ● ● ● ● ● ● ● ● ●

Cooperative Games

FROZEN BEAN BAG

Children move with bean bags on their heads, helping those whose bean bags fall.

● ● ● ● ● ● ● ● ● ● ● ● ● ● ● ● ● ●

Age:	5–7
Activity Type:	Team challenge
Activity Level:	Moderate
Space:	Large open space
Concentration Level:	High
Time:	15 minutes
Group Size:	8 or more
Prerequisite:	None

MATERIALS

❖ Bean bags (one per child)

SUGGESTED PROCEDURE

1. Distribute the bean bags and have children place them on their heads. Give everyone a chance to walk around a little bit, then explain the rules.

2. The goal of the game is to have everyone moving around as long as possible. If a bean bag falls, that child is frozen. The only way to get unfrozen is for someone to pick up the bean bag and put it back on the child's head. But if their bean bag falls while they are helping , they're also frozen until someone helps them.

3. Start the game, reminding the children that the goal is to keep everyone moving as long as possible. Playing the game yourself lets you demonstrate how to help others.

4. It usually only takes a few minutes for everyone to be frozen. Replay the game a few times, trying to improve the group's wandering time.

REFLECTION

❖ How could we get our bean bags to stay put longer?

❖ What other ways can/did you help people?

❖ What other ways can/did people help you?

Age:	(5–7) 8–12
Activity Type:	Team challenge
Activity Level:	Very active
Space:	Large open space
Concentration Level:	High
Time:	15 minutes
Group Size:	10 or more
Prerequisite:	Some previous experience working together.

Safety Note

This activity works best with groups that are approximately the same age and relative size. Avoid doing this activity with groups where a 10-year-old would be sitting on the lap of a 5-year-old.

GROUP LAP SIT

The entire group must work together to create a circle of laps on which everyone can sit.

MATERIALS

❖ None

SUGGESTED PROCEDURE

1. This activity is most challenging for large groups, although it will work with smaller groups as well. Introduce the activity as a group challenge that will only succeed if everyone participates and pays close attention.

2. Have everyone stand shoulder to shoulder in a circle. Ask them to turn to their left, so that they are facing the back of the person who was standing next to them. Everyone takes steps toward the inside of the circle until they are standing toe to heel, with their hands on the shoulders of the person in front of them. Make sure that the circle is as round as you can make it, not oval, square, or some other shape.

3. On the count of three, everyone slowly bends their knees and sits down on the lap of the person behind them. Encourage the students to put their whole weight down, instead of struggling to balance in a sitting position. The circle will not work unless all participants trust that the person behind them will support their weight.

4. For an extra challenge, see how long the group can hold the lap sit position or try to take small, synchronized steps and walk the circle around!

REFLECTION

❖ What was the hardest part of the activity?

❖ Did you trust the person behind you to keep you from falling down?

❖ How could the group improve its performance?

ALL KNOTTED UP

The group tries to untangle itself from a human knot without letting go of one another's hands.

● ● ● ● ● ● ● ● ● ● ● ● ● ● ● ● ●

Age:	8–12
Activity Type:	Team challenge
Activity Level:	Very active
Space:	Large open space
Concentration Level:	High
Time:	20 minutes
Group Size:	10–20
Prerequisite:	None

MATERIALS

❖ None

SUGGESTED PROCEDURE

1. Stand in a circle. Reach across to grab someone else's hand until every person in the group is holding hands with two different people. Do not hold the hand of someone directly to your right or left.

2. Try to untangle the group without letting go of hands. (When everyone is untangled, some people may be facing out and others in. You may have one or more circles.)

REFLECTION

❖ Who decided how to untangle the knot?

❖ Did you offer any suggestions out loud?

❖ Did you have any ideas that you didn't share?

❖ What was your individual role in the activity?

❖ Were you a leader? a follower? an encourager? a timekeeper?

❖ What made your group successful?

▼ TIP!

Knot First-Aid

If your group is really stuck in a mess, help them out with some knot first-aid. Allow two people to let go of their ropes and then re-connect.

Age:	8–12
Activity Type:	Drama
Activity Level:	Very active
Space:	Large open space
Concentration Level:	Medium
Time:	30 minutes
Group Size:	8 or more
Prerequisite:	None

HUMACHINES

Small groups collaborate to physically represent an everyday machine.

● ● ● ● ● ● ● ● ● ● ● ● ● ● ● ● ● ●

MATERIALS

❖ None

SUGGESTED PROCEDURE

1. Divide into groups of about five. Explain that the challenge of this game is for each group to create a "Humachine" – a machine that they see everyday, which their group will act out for others to guess. Give several examples such as popcorn maker or vacuum cleaner. Have one group volunteer to act out one for the whole group, with helpful ideas from anyone who comes up with one. For example, a popcorn maker may involve two people holding hands to create the machine, while three others slowly transform from popcorn kernels into fully popped corn, complete with sound effects.

2. Give each group ten minutes to think of their machine and practice their version of it. You may need to send a couple of groups out of the room so that there is enough distance between groups to make sure they don't overhear others planning.

3. Each group performs their Humachine while the others try to guess.

REFLECTION

❖ What were the roles that people took in your planning group?

❖ Did you work well together?

❖ Did you all make sure that everyone's opinions were considered when you decided how to act out your Humachine?

❖ How did you decide which ideas you liked best?

THE LINE FORMS HERE

The entire group must work together, without talking, to stand in order according to their birthday.

● ● ● ● ● ● ● ● ● ● ● ● ● ● ● ● ●

Age:	(5–7) 8–12
Activity Type:	Team challenge
Activity Level:	Moderate
Space:	Large open space
Concentration Level:	High
Time:	20 minutes
Group Size:	10 or more
Prerequisite:	None

MATERIALS

❖ None

SUGGESTED PROCEDURE

1. Explain that for this game there must be absolutely no talking or writing after you have finished describing the rules of play. The group goal is to line up in a certain order, such as by height, as quickly and accurately as they can. Ask the children to stand up in the middle of the room. After you have answered any questions they may have, put the no talking rule into effect.

2. Once the group has stopped all talking, tell them that the group task is to line up according to birthdays. One end of the line will be the person born closest to January 1, and the other end will be the person born closest to December 31. Tell the students that they should raise their hands in a victory sign when they think that they have lined up in order, letting you know that they are definitely finished.

3. Watch as they work it out, making sure that no one talks!

4. Once every student has raised his or her hand to show that the group is finished, let the children talk to find out if they lined up in the correct order.

REFLECTION

❖ How did you communicate without using words?

❖ How did you feel when someone didn't understand what you were trying to tell them? Were you frustrated or angry? Did it make you laugh?

❖ Did you give up or keep trying?

❖ Was there a moment when you had a communication breakthrough – when you and someone else finally understood each other?

❖ How did that feel?

❖ Did the two of you then share your new communication system with someone else?

For Younger Children

Younger children enjoy this game, but it takes them a few tries to get the knack. Start by having them line up from shortest to tallest and allow them to talk. Repeat the game and ask the group if they are ready to try it without talking.

Age: 5–10

Activity Type: Circle game

Activity Level: Moderate

Space: Any

Concentration Level: High

Time: 15 minutes

Group Size: 10 or more

Prerequisite: "Making Bean Tambourines" (p. 138).

STORMING

Using Bean Tambourines that students can make, the group recreates the sounds of a rainstorm.

● ● ● ● ● ● ● ● ● ● ● ● ● ● ● ● ● ●

MATERIALS

❖ Bean Tambourines (p. 138) (or use other tambourines or shakers)

SUGGESTED PROCEDURE

This activity can be done without using the Bean Tambourines. You can substitute other types of tambourines or shakers, or simply have children make the hand sounds in step three.

1. Stand in a circle and explain that this activity will work only if everyone participates and watches carefully. You will be making sounds which sound like a tropical rainstorm, using your Bean Tambourines.

2. You will act as the leader. Explain that you will make a motion with a sound and that the person on your left will copy that motion right after you do it. This continues until the motion has been passed all the way around the circle. Everyone continues to do the motion until the next one has been passed along. Each child will need to watch and listen carefully to see when the signal is passed to them and to notice what that motion is.

3. Begin the game. Your sound-motions should progress as follows:

   a. With the Bean Tambourine on the floor in front of you, begin by rubbing your palms together.

   b. Once everyone in the circle has done that, begin quiet finger snaps.

   c. Next, make the snaps louder.

   d. Then, start clapping softly.

   e. Clap louder.

   f. Clap your thighs.

   g. Continue clapping your thighs and stomp your feet.

   h. Keep stomping, pick up your Bean Tambourine and shake that (things are very loud at this point!).

   i. Make noises of rainforest creatures, like monkeys or birds.

j. Begin the process of having the storm subside by working backwards through steps "a" through "f," until you have reached the calm after the storm.

REFLECTION

❖ How could we make the storm sound better?

❖ What could we use instead of tambourines?

NOTES

● ● ● ● ● ● ● ● ● ● ● ●

Age:	5-12
Activity Type:	Tag game
Activity Level:	Very active
Concentration Level:	Medium
Space:	Large open space
Time:	10 minutes
Group Size:	8 or more
Prerequisite:	None

Safety Note

Before you start, make sure to talk about how everyone can have fun and stay safe at the same time. If you don't think your group is ready for such a fast pace, make it a walking tag game.

EVERYBODY'S IT

Children explore Win-Win solutions through this active, break-the-ice tag game.

● ● ● ● ● ● ● ● ● ● ● ● ● ● ● ● ●

MATERIALS

❖ Boundary markers

SET THE SCENE

Mark out a boundary that allows enough space for everyone to move around. This can be played as a running or walking tag game. If you are playing the running version, leave plenty of room within the boundary for some good jogging to take place.

SUGGESTED PROCEDURE

1. Ask the group to spread out within the boundary area.

2. In this tag game, everyone is "it." "This means when I yell 'Go' we will all run/walk around tagging each other. If you get tagged you should squat down on the ground."

3. In a matter of seconds, everyone but one person will be out. Try it again!

REFLECTION

❖ What should we do if two people tag each other at the same time?

WIZARDS AND GELFLINGS

This is a cooperative tag game for introducing or exploring the concepts of Win-Win, Win-Lose, or Lose-Lose.

● ● ● ● ● ● ● ● ● ● ● ● ● ● ● ● ●

Age:	5–12
Activity Type:	Tag game
Activity Level:	Very active
Space:	Large open space
Concentration Level:	Medium
Time:	10 minutes
Group Size:	10 or more
Prerequisite:	None

MATERIALS

❖ Boundary markers (cones, spots, ropes). For a running tag game, set off a large area. For a walking tag game, keep the boundary smaller.

SET THE SCENE

Tell the students, "We are taking a trip to the inside of the earth where there are two types of people, Wizards and Gelflings. The Wizards want everyone in the land to be like them, so they use their magic powers to freeze the Gelflings. The Gelflings like themselves the way they are. To fight off the Wizards, they must cooperate."

SUGGESTED PROCEDURE

1. Ask for two volunteers. These two will be the Wizards. Their goal is to tag all the Gelflings. Once a Gelfling is tagged, she is frozen and cannot move.

2. The rest of the group are Gelflings. The Gelflings' goal is to stay away from the Wizards.

3. If a Gelfling is tagged and frozen, she can be helped. But help can only be given if a frozen Gelfling asks for it. Once she has asked for help by calling "help me!," two unfrozen Gelflings can help by making a ring around her with their arms and saying, "Be free Gelfling!" The Gelfling is now back in the game. If a player is out of bounds, she is out of the game.

4. The game continues for as long as it is still fun for all or until all the Gelflings are frozen.

REFLECTION

❖ What is something the group did well while playing this game?

❖ What is something that you could improve when you play it again?

❖ If you were going to explain this game to younger children, how would you do it?

Safety Note

Before you start, make sure to talk about how everyone can have fun and stay safe at the same time. If you don't think your group is ready for such a fast pace, make it a walking tag game.

TIP!

Dramatizing the Game

As the facilitator, you can encourage fun by dramatizing the game when giving your instructions. If you are having fun, the kids will be, too!

Age: 8–12

Activity Type: Team Challenge

Activity Level: Moderate

Space: Any

Concentration Level: High

Time: 30 minutes

Group Size: As many as 15, fewer is better

Prerequisite: Some experience working together as a group

WARP SPEED

The group tosses a ball around the circle as quickly as they can.

● ● ● ● ● ● ● ● ● ● ● ● ● ● ● ● ● ● ●

MATERIALS

❖ Stopwatch

❖ Ball (fleece, Nerf®, Koosh®, or something soft)

SET THE SCENE

For this activity, you can move into giving instructions if the group is already gathered. If not, try a bit of subtle attention-getting. Stand quietly in the area you want the children to gather, toss the ball repeatedly in the air, and wait for someone to catch on. If the group doesn't assemble in short order, whistle a tune, spin a basketball on your finger, or juggle.

SUGGESTED PROCEDURE

1. Ask the group to form a circle and include yourself. Tell them you want to toss the ball around the circle until everyone has had it once, ending back at the first person.

2. Begin tossing the ball. To make this go smoothly, have the children who haven't had the ball yet hold their hands in a ready position.

3. Ask the group to remember who threw them the ball and who they threw it to.

4. When this sequence is done, ask them to repeat it, only this time have someone in the group be the official timer. If they have trouble remembering the order, give them a practice round before introducing the clock.

5. Once you have an initial time established (usually about five seconds per child), ask them to reduce that time by working together more closely as a team. After a few more attempts, they should be able to get their time down using more cooperation and teamwork. Tell them you think they can reduce their score even more – perhaps by another five seconds.

6. Encourage the group to brainstorm strategies and then to try one idea at a time. Remember, the two basic rules are: (1) each person must catch the ball, and (2) the ball must be tossed in the

order established. Here are some ideas they may develop: rearrange the circle so that the person you toss to is next to you; arrange everyone's hands so that the ball has a ramp to travel down.

7. Eventually the group should reduce their score to below five seconds. Congratulate the group on reaching warp speed!

REFLECTION

Ask the group to rearrange themselves in the original circle and to sit comfortably.

❖ How did the group go about cooperating and getting a better score?

❖ Did you listen to and try everyone's ideas?

❖ How did you decide which ones to try?

❖ Were there ideas that the group didn't try? Why?

❖ What were the positive ways that you worked together?

NOTES

● ● ● ● ● ● ● ● ● ● ●

Age: 8–12

Activity Type: Tag game

Activity Level: Very active

Space: Large open space

Concentration
Level: High

Time: 20 minutes

Group Size: 12 or more

Prerequisite: None

THE LILY PAD HOP

Frogs (children) hop to safety while being chased by frog-eating monsters.

● ●

MATERIALS

❖ Spot markers (enough for half of the players)

❖ Fleece balls or other soft throwable objects that will not hurt the children when they are hit with them

❖ Boundary markers

SET THE SCENE

Set up boundaries designating an area the size of a basketball court.
Divide the group in half.

Hand out lily pads (i.e., spot markers) to half of the group. *Explain,* "You are frogs. Very special, rare frogs. Unfortunately, being the special frogs that you are, you have a wonderfully delicate flavor when eaten. You're safe when you are traveling on a lily pad or when you reach Lily Land at the other end of this pond (the end of the boundary area)."

Pass the fleece balls to the other half of the group. *Explain,* "You are the frog-eating monsters. You love their delicious taste. But you have a hard time catching them. The only way you can catch a frog is to hit them with your soft, poisonous paws (the balls)."

SUGGESTED PROCEDURE

1. Frogs are trying to move from one end of the pond (boundary area) to the other. Their goal is to get all the frogs across as quickly as possible.

2. Monsters are trying to hit the hopping frogs with their fleece balls (paws), thereby slowing down the progression of the frogs.

3. Frogs can move across the pond by hopping from one lily pad (spot marker) to another. Lily pads are moved forward by flipping them. Require at least a three-foot toss. Frogs must hop (two-footed) forward onto their pads. Once on a pad, a frog can then pick up the pad and toss it forward again. Frogs are safe from monsters while standing on or throwing their lily pads.

4. If a frog is hit by a ball, she must hop back ten hops.

5. Monsters must stay outside the pond area. They cannot swim. They may retrieve any balls that fall into the pond.

6. Frogs that make it to Lily Land (the end of the boundary area) become Super Frogs. Super Frogs are immune to the poison of the monster's paws and can help their fellow frogs make it to Lily Land.

7. Start playing. Time how quickly the frogs can make it. Play a second round and allow the monsters and frogs to switch roles.

REFLECTION

❖ How did the frogs cooperate to get across?

❖ Could they have cooperated more to speed up their time?

❖ What might they do differently?

❖ How did the monsters cooperate to slow down the frogs?

❖ Did the monsters work together or was it everyone for themselves?

NOTES

● ● ● ● ● ● ● ● ● ● ●

Age: 8–12

Activity Type: Team challenge

Activity Level: Moderate

Space: Large open space

Concentration
Level: High

Time: 20 minutes

Group Size: 2 or more

Prerequisite: An ability for the group to work well together

After you describe and demostrate the activity, remind the children to go *slowly and carefully* as they do this activity. Tell them not to step back any further than they are comfortable.

A Great Follow-Up

This is a great follow-up activity to "The Very Best Part is the Bridge" (p. 287).

HUMAN BRIDGES

In pairs, children support each other by forming a balanced bridge with their bodies.

● ● ● ● ● ● ● ● ● ● ● ● ● ● ● ● ● ● ●

MATERIALS

❖ None

SUGGESTED PROCEDURE

1. It's important that the children are focused and serious for this activity, as people can get hurt if they are not paying attention. Do this on a soft surface such as a mat, carpet, or grass. You will need spotters to protect any pair that may lose their balance.

2. *Explain that this activity is for pairs,* "The goal is to create a bridge, using just our bodies. It works best if your partner is about the same height as you. One pair will spot another and then trade places, so you will need to form groups of four."

3. Have one pair demonstrate as you talk them through it. Ask for four volunteers: two for the bridge and two spotters.

   Explain to the children, "Standing face to face, put your palms up against your partner's. Hold your hands at about shoulder height. Now, very slowly and carefully, lean into your partner so that you are supporting one another's weight. Take first one small step, and then another backwards. See how many steps back you can take, so that you are really leaning into each other, forming a Human Bridge."

4. Give everyone enough time so that they get to form the bridge a couple of times and spot a couple of times.

REFLECTION

❖ Was it hard to trust your partner and spotters enough to keep walking backwards?

❖ Was anyone scared that they would fall?

GIANTS, WIZARDS, AND ELVES

A cooperative tag game to help your group think about Win-Win, Win-Lose, and Lose-Lose solutions.

● ● ● ● ● ● ● ● ● ● ● ● ● ● ● ● ●

Age:	8–12
Activity Type:	Tag game
Activity Level:	Very active
Space:	Large open space
Concentration Level:	High
Time:	10 minutes
Group Size:	20 or more
Prerequisite:	None

MATERIALS

❖ A 15 to 20-foot-long rope

Place the rope in the center of a large room/gym or on the ground outside.

❖ Four cones or other suitable markers

Place two cones approximately 20 yards from one side of the rope. Place the other two 20 yards from the other side of the rope.

SUGGESTED PROCEDURE

1. Divide the group in half. Have one half of the group stand on one side of the rope and the other half on the other side of the rope. Having everyone starting with their toes on the rope, ask them to take two steps back.

2. To play the game, the children will need to know three signs – the sign of the Wizard, the Giant, and the Elf. You will need to demonstrate the signs:

    ❖ "A Giant stands up as high as she can on her toes and with her arms raised, gives a great roar." Have the group try it.

    ❖ "A Wizard stands on one foot, puts her hands straight ahead and wiggles her fingers while saying 'Shazaam!'"

    ❖ "An elf squats down, puts her hands behind her head and yells 'Tweedle, tweedle, tweedle' in her little elfish voice." Show them, then have them try it.

3. Now that everyone knows the signs, explain that Giants chase Wizards, Wizards chase Elves, and Elves chase Giants. This is important. Have the group repeat it back to you.

4. The goal is for each group to win members from the other group. Whichever group shows the "stronger" sign becomes the chasers. The group with the "weaker" sign becomes the runners. The runners try to run past their cones to safety

Set Up

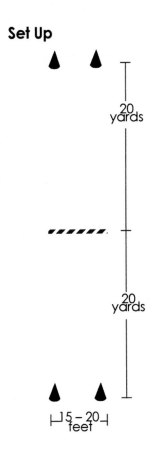

without being tagged. Those people who are tagged return to the other side for the next round.

5. Ask each group to huddle up behind their cones and pick which sign they will show first. Have each group pick two in case both sides pick the same sign. This will be a practice round. Give the group 45 seconds to choose signs.

6. Have the groups return to the rope (two steps away). On the count of three have the groups simultaneously give their signs. If one side does the Giant sign and the other side does the Elf sign, the Elves are the chasers and the Giants try to run back towards their cones without being tagged. Anyone tagged becomes a member of the other group. Have the groups reassemble at their cones and pick another two signs.

7. Continue the game until there is only one group left.

REFLECTION

❖ What did we do well in playing this game?

❖ What would make the game go more smoothly?

❖ Can you think of a way to change the game to make it more fun?

❖ If you were going to explain this game to younger kids, how would you do it?

MAKING GROUP ROLE HATS

Children create hats to help them play different roles.

● ● ● ● ● ● ● ● ● ● ● ● ● ● ● ● ● ● ●

MATERIALS

- ❖ Paper bags
- ❖ Markers, crayons, paints
- ❖ Construction paper
- ❖ Scissors
- ❖ Glue
- ❖ Tape

Age:	8–12
Activity Type:	Arts and crafts
Activity Level:	Moderate
Space:	Large open space
Concentration Level:	Medium
Time:	30 minutes
Group Size:	Any
Prerequisite:	None

SET THE SCENE

Tell the children, "Cooperation and conflict resolution often rely upon well-functioning groups. One way to work well in small groups is to practice playing specific roles. These decorative, silly hats will help us remember our responsibilities to the group."

SUGGESTED PROCEDURE

1. Decide on roles for which your group will create hats. Some roles that are helpful to teach children are *timekeeper* (makes sure the group finishes on time), *encourager* (gives positive feedback), *checker* (makes sure everyone understands and is okay with group decisions), *summarizer* (keeps summarizing what the group has said or decided thus far), *reporter* (reports back to the large group), *scribe* (takes notes or writes), and *jester* (keeps the group laughing and having fun). Feel free to create roles which seem particularly useful for your group.

2. Break students into work groups of three or four. You may decide to have the children work in groups where everyone in the group is creating a hat for the same role. This way, they can collectively brainstorm words, symbols, and designs that fit a certain role. For example, one group may work on timekeeper hats, pooling together all their ideas (e.g., draw clock faces on it, write "five minutes left" around the brim, etc.).

3. When they have finished making the hats, have children model them, saying a few key phrases that someone in that role might say. Store the hats for future use during group work.

REFLECTION

❖ Why might it be important to have people play roles when we work together in groups?

❖ Which role do you usually play when you are in a group? Do you like that role? Are you good at it?

NOTES

● ● ● ● ● ● ● ● ● ● ● ●

Cooperative Challenges and Group Problem Solving

Age: 8–12

Activity Type: Team challenge

Activity Level: Moderate

Space: Any

Concentration Level: High

Time: 20 minutes

Group Size: 15 or more

Prerequisite: None

THREE-LETTER WORD

Each person tries to match with two other people to spell three-letter words.

● ● ● ● ● ● ● ● ● ● ● ● ● ● ● ●

MATERIALS

❖ Alphabet Cards

Create your own alphabet cards on index cards by writing one letter per card. A good guideline is to make many cards with the most common letters and fewer of the less-used letters. For instance, make 6 A's and O's, 9 E's, 6 I's, 3 L's, 2 M's, 2 N's, 2 P's, 4 R's, 4 S's, T's and U's, and one of everything else. Throw in a few wild cards to add to the fun.

SUGGESTED PROCEDURE

1. Depending on the number of children in the group, divide up the alphabet cards so that each person gets at least one card, preferably two or three. You might have them pick out a few of their favorite letters or give them out randomly.

2. Tell the group that at the signal, they will have 45 seconds to form a three-letter word with one or two other people. Once they form the word, they should sit down and watch the rest of the group.

3. If at the end of the time anyone has not joined a group in forming a word, they become observers until it is time for a new round.

4. Increase the stakes by asking for four, five, and six-letter words in subsequent rounds. Create rules about allowable words (Scrabble® rules work well).

5. As a variation, have the group try to spell as long a word as possible. Alternately, have teams compete to see how many different words they can make from their group of letters.

▼ **TIP!**

Modeling the Game

Don't set yourself up when asking for four-letter words. Caution them about inappropriate words ahead of time, but don't exaggerate this negatively. Model the game how you wish it to be played – the group will follow your lead.

REFLECTION

In closing, congratulate the group on their spelling prowess and
ability to create so many combinations.

❖ What conflicts took place while playing?

❖ How could the group have worked together more
successfully?

NOTES

Age: 8–12

Activity Type: Writing

Activity Level: Quiet

Space: Work tables

Concentration
Level: High

Time: 20 minutes

Group Size: 4 or more

Prerequisite: None

HUMONGOUS POEMAMONGUS

The entire group writes a conflict resolution poem together.

● ● ● ● ● ● ● ● ● ● ● ● ● ● ● ● ● ●

MATERIALS

❖ Newsprint (one sheet per group)

❖ Markers (one per group)

SUGGESTED PROCEDURE

1. Fold a piece of newsprint accordion-style, in as many pleats as there are people in your group.

2. Describe the process of writing a "Humongous Poemamongus." One person will begin the poem by writing one line of a poem about conflict resolution on the first fold of the pleated newsprint sheet. The second person in the circle will read the first line, write a second line, and fold the poem so that the third person can read only the second line. The third person writes a line and refolds the paper again, so that only her third line shows. Continue until every person has contributed one line to the poem.

3. Read the poem out loud and hang it up on the wall.

REFLECTION

❖ Is the poem very different from one that you would have written by yourself? If so, how?

❖ How can we share this poem with the group?

A PICTURE IS WORTH A THOUSAND WORDS

Small groups write a story, inspired by a painting.

Age:	8–12
Activity Type:	Writing
Activity Level:	Quiet
Space:	Work tables
Concentration Level:	High
Time:	30 minutes
Group Size:	6 or more
Prerequisite:	None

MATERIALS

❖ Books from the library with reproductions of paintings

❖ Paper and pens

SUGGESTED PROCEDURE

1. Split into groups of three. Introduce the activity by reminding students of the cliché "A picture is worth a thousand words." The task for each group is to choose a picture from one of the books and then write a story about it together.

2. Once the groups have written their stories, have them read them to the large group, while passing around the original picture.

REFLECTION

❖ How did you decide which picture to use?

❖ Who wrote your story? Were all three of you co-authors? Did you write cooperatively? How did you do that?

Age: 8–12

Activity Type: Team challenge

Activity Level: Quiet

Space: Any

Concentration Level: High

Time: 40 minutes

Group Size: 5 or more

Prerequisite: Previous experience working on problem-solving activities

COOPERATIVE PUZZLE

Children complete their puzzles by sharing pieces with others.

● ● ● ● ● ● ● ● ● ● ● ● ● ● ● ● ●

MATERIALS

❖ Cut five, five-inch squares from poster board for each team. Cut each square into five pieces. You need to create sets of five square puzzles where no one of the puzzles has the same shaped pieces – i.e., five different puzzles made of different pieces. Make all the puzzles the same color.

SET THE SCENE

For this activity, children will need to be grouped into small teams of five. Once you have created a set of five puzzles, you will need to mix up the pieces. Create one envelope per person. Each envelope should have five pieces.

Explain to the group, "This is a cooperative problem-solving activity. You will be working in a small team of five. Each person on the team will have an envelope. Inside that envelope will be some puzzle pieces. Your goal is for each person on your team to have a complete puzzle. When complete, the puzzle is in the shape of a five-inch square."

SUGGESTED PROCEDURE

1. Have each team of five find a comfortable location. Present the rules.

   ❖ Students may not talk to each other during the activity.

   ❖ The children will need to share; however, no one may ask anyone else for a piece. They may give a piece away, but they may not ask (nonverbally or otherwise) for a piece. Be sure everyone understands this rule before you go on.

   ❖ The team's goal is to help each person complete a puzzle. The team is finished when they have five, five-inch square puzzles completed.

2. Pass out the puzzle pieces.

Problem Solving

This can be a difficult problem to solve. What usually causes problems is (1) not talking and (2) not asking for a piece that you see you can use. If groups are having a lot of difficulty, give a few hints. There is no one solution to this problem. The trick is for children to be aware of what their teammates are doing and to be willing to pass their pieces.

REFLECTION

There are several themes to pursue when reflecting on this activity:

❖ *Sharing and helping*. In this activity, children were not allowed to ask for what they needed. How did this make sharing and/or helping hard? Was there any frustration associated with only being able to give pieces away?

❖ *Cooperation*. The group's goal was for everyone to have a completed puzzle.

  ❖ Did everyone concentrate on the group goal or were individuals focused on getting their own square complete?

  ❖ What did people do once their own square was complete?

  ❖ Did they help or "check out"?

  ❖ What happens to cooperation when not everyone is committed to the group goal?

NOTES

● ● ● ● ● ● ● ● ● ● ● ●

Age:	5–12
Activity Type:	Team challenge
Activity Level:	Active
Space:	Large open space
Concentration Level:	High
Time:	20 minutes
Group Size:	10–16
Prerequisite:	None

Set Up

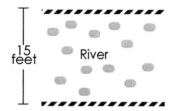

15 feet — River

For Younger Children

Set the marshmallows up in the river. The goal is still to get across without anyone falling in, but everyone must hold hands. For the first try, you be the leader. Let them try again on their own.

MARSHMALLOWS

The group navigates a "river of chocolate" (marked-off area) by stepping only on "marshmallows."

● ● ● ● ● ● ● ● ● ● ● ● ● ● ● ● ● ●

MATERIALS

❖ Wooden blocks, carpet sections, or ethafoam squares (one per person)

❖ Two ropes Create a riverbank with the rope. Place one rope on the ground and the second rope about 15 feet away.

SET THE SCENE

Tell the children, "You are little ants. Your goal is to work together to cross this river of chocolate to get to your family picnic. You can use these marshmallows to get across, but be careful because the river of chocolate is flowing quickly. Remember, you have only these 'marshmallows' (wooden blocks or carpet sections), which have the power to hold anyone safely above this river of hot cocoa. Don't lose touch of any marshmallow, or it will sink into the chocolate void, never to be seen again! You must get safely from one riverbank to the other, using the marshmallows as stepping stones."

SUGGESTED PROCEDURE

1. Line the group up at one bank of the river. Give the group a stack of marshmallows (equal to the number of people in their group minus one). Tell them that their goal is to get across the river without falling in.

2. There are a few rules. No one may touch the river. The only safe way to cross the river is on the marshmallows. If someone falls off a marshmallow, he/she must start over.

3. It is critical that there always be one point of physical contact with each marshmallow. For example, if a marshmallow is left on the floor without anyone touching it, it will quickly float down the river and be lost. Take away any marshmallows that "sink into the chocolate."

REFLECTION

❖ Did the group collaborate while embarking on their journey? Why?

❖ Did the group create a plan? Was it followed through?

❖ Was it hard to keep touching all the marshmallows? Why?

TWELVE HOURS OF COOPERATION

In a circle, the group moves as quickly as possible "12-hours" (one rotation) in one direction and back again.

● ● ● ● ● ● ● ● ● ● ● ● ● ● ● ● ●

Age:	(5–7) 8–12
Activity Type:	Team challenge
Activity Level:	Very active
Space:	Large open space
Concentration Level:	Medium
Time:	20 minutes
Group Size:	10 or more
Prerequisite:	None

MATERIALS

❖ One spot marker

❖ Stopwatch

SUGGESTED PROCEDURE

1. Have the group stand in a circle. *Ask the group,* "Do you think we can cooperate for twelve hours? Let's give it a try!"

2. Place the spot marker in front of one person. "This marker is 12 o'clock."

3. The group begins by holding hands and squatting down. The goal is to stand up and move as quickly as possible 12 hours in a clockwise direction (so that the person starting at 12 ends up back at twelve) and then to rotate all 12 hours back in a counterclockwise direction. This must be done without breaking the chain of hands.

4. If the chain of hands is broken, the group starts over.

5. Time the group's progress using a stopwatch. Allow for some brainstorming and a second, third, and fourth try.

REFLECTION

❖ What was the group's first time? What was the group's final time?

❖ How did you get from time one to this final time? What strategies worked best?

For Younger Children

Younger children will need to do this activity in stages, with you directing them at each stage. First have the group move one hour, then more. Finally, have them move counterclockwise.

Age:	5–12
Activity Type:	Team challenge
Activity Level:	Very active
Space:	Large open space
Concentration Level:	High
Time:	30 minutes
Group Size:	10 or more
Prerequisite:	None

ALL TOGETHER NOW

The group must work together to pass through a jump rope.

● ● ● ● ● ● ● ● ● ● ● ● ● ● ● ● ● ●

MATERIALS

❖ One rope at least 20 feet long

SET THE SCENE

Ask the group, "Who here can jump rope? Do you think you can all jump this rope together?"

SUGGESTED PROCEDURE

1. Ask for two volunteers. These two will swing the rope. Give them a minute to practice and get the hang of it.

2. While the swingers are practicing, tell the group that their goal is to have the entire group pass through the rope without (1) missing a beat or (2) touching the rope. They will have 20 minutes to try.

3. What does missing a beat mean? It means that each time the rope hits the ground, at least one person must pass through. If the rope makes a rotation without someone passing through, two people return to the starting side.

4. If someone touches the rope while passing through, that person returns to the starting side.

5. Help the group work together to get the whole group through.

6. Substitute new rope swingers every so often.

REFLECTION

Give each person a 5" x 7" index card. Have each child in the group rank, from 1 to 5 (5 is excellent and 1 is poor), how well the group cooperated in this activity. The object is to get everyone's ranking.

Discuss as a large group:

❖ Why did people rank the way they did? What did they use as criteria?

❖ What did we do well as a group?

❖ How could we do this activity better if we had a second chance?

EVERYBODY'S UP

The group works in pairs to pull up from a sitting to standing position, then tries it as an entire group.

● ● ● ● ● ● ● ● ● ● ● ● ● ● ● ● ●

Age:	(5–7) 8–12
Activity Type:	Team challenge
Activity Level:	Moderate
Space:	Any
Concentration Level:	Medium
Time:	15 minutes
Group Size:	6 or more
Prerequisite:	None

MATERIALS

❖ None

SUGGESTED PROCEDURE

1. *Explain*, "We're going to try some simple cooperative stunts. We'll start in pairs."

2. Ask two people of approximately the same size to sit on the floor facing one another. Their toes should be touching, their knees bent, and their bottoms on the floor. Ask the pair to pull themselves up to a standing position.

3. Have everyone find a partner and give it a try.

4. Once most everyone is successful, ask the pairs to find another pair and see if they can do the same with four people. If they can do it with four, try five, six, or more.

5. If your group is having some fun with this physical cooperation, add some variations to the basic pull up – start sitting back to back, standing side to side, etc.

REFLECTION

Have each person find his initial partner. Ask each pair to think of one thing they did together that helped them to cooperate. Bring the group back together in a circle and have each pair report back. Use the report to begin a short discussion on what strategies help us cooperate.

Safety Note

Do not allow interlocked arms; this could lead to shoulder injuries.

Age:	8–12
Activity Type:	Team challenge
Activity Level:	Very active
Space:	Large open space
Concentration Level:	High
Time:	15 minutes or more
Group Size:	8–15
Prerequisite:	None

SAVE THE CITY

Children use ghost shields (plastic milk containers) to transport ghosts (balls) to a safe area.

● ● ● ● ● ● ● ● ● ● ● ● ● ● ● ● ● ● ●

MATERIALS

❖ Milk jugs, one per person. Cut the spout section out of one gallon, plastic milk containers, leaving the handle intact to create a carrying jug – you may add a short craft project here and have each child decorate his own jug.

❖ Two balls (e.g., tennis balls)

❖ Objects to create two boundaries (you may use tape on the floor)

❖ Stopwatch

SET THE SCENE

Explain to the children, "There has been an accident in town and some pesky ghosts have escaped from the safety containers where they are kept. The city is calling on us, the ghost experts, to capture and return the sneaky spirits before we are all infected with their bad moods."

SUGGESTED PROCEDURE

1. *Tell the children,* "The city has provided some ghost-safe jugs in which to carry the ghosts. The goal is to carry the ghosts from the beginning boundary to the safety area (marked by a second boundary a good distance away) as quickly as possible."

2. No person can touch the ghosts (i.e., the balls). The ghosts can only touch the jugs. The ghosts cannot be dropped. If a ghost is dropped, the group must return to the beginning.

3. Each ghost must touch the inside of each jug. By the time the ball reaches the end of the boundary area, each person should have had the ball at least once.

4. Time is crucial. Use a stopwatch to time the activity.

5. Once the group has tried once, brainstorm ideas for doing it faster. Try it again. Let the group continue trying as long as they maintain interest. Encourage ongoing brainstorming and problem solving.

▼ TIP!

Facilitating Fun

As in many Adventure activities, you, the facilitator, create the fun. Set the scene in a funny, silly way and everyone will enjoy the game so much they'll forget they are cooperating.

REFLECTION

- ❖ What happened? Ask for many different interpretations.

- ❖ What is something the group did well?

- ❖ What could the group do better the next time they play?

NOTES

Age: 8–12

Activity Type: Team challenge

Activity Level: Quiet

Space: Any

Concentration Level: High

Time: 20 minutes

Group Size: 8 or more

Prerequisite: None

CAN'T WE COUNT TO TEN?

The group tries to count to ten (or twenty).

● ● ● ● ● ● ● ● ● ● ● ● ● ● ● ● ● ●

MATERIALS

❖ None

SET THE SCENE

Tell the students, "We are going to have a quick CAT test today. What's a CAT?, you ask. Well, a Cooperation Achievement Test."

SUGGESTED PROCEDURE

1. Have the group settle down into a comfortable spot. Ask everyone to close their eyes.

2. Tell the group their challenge is to count to ten as a group, but they must obey the following rules. Everyone must keep their eyes shut. No two people may speak at the same time. The group may not speak except to say a number. If two people talk at the same time, the group must start over at one. When you say "go," they may start.

3. Give the group 10 or 15 minutes to try this. As they'll soon see, this is not as easy as it sounds.

4. The occasional group can do this on the first try. If this happens, congratulate the group on a job well done. If your group is like most, however, they may not be able to do it at all. Allow the group to continue trying for another 10 to 15 minutes.

REFLECTION

❖ What made it hard to cooperate in this activity?

❖ How did your group cooperate without using your eyes or mouths?

Number Patterns

One way to solve this is by falling into a pattern. For instance, each person could take ownership of a number, moving to the right or left of the person who begins.

GO FISH

Students attempt to retrieve a bucket of "fish" (balls) from the center of the "lake" (marked-off boundary area).

● ● ● ● ● ● ● ● ● ● ● ● ● ● ● ● ●

Age:	11–12
Activity Type:	Team challenge
Activity Level:	Moderate
Space:	Large open space
Concentration Level:	High
Time:	30 minutes
Group Size:	8 or more
Prerequisite:	Other Team challenges

MATERIALS

- ❖ One bucket, with a handle

- ❖ Three pieces of rope, each approximately 15 feet long

- ❖ Three pieces of bicycle inner tube (cut to approximately 6 inches long)

- ❖ Enough plastic fish or tennis balls to fill the bucket

- ❖ Spot marker

- ❖ Masking tape or a large rope to mark off a 10-foot diameter circle

SET THE SCENE

You'll need to get this ready before the group arrives. Create the lake by laying down masking tape or rope to mark off a circle ten feet in diameter. Place the rubber spot marker in the center. Place the bucket with the fish (balls) on top of the spot marker.

Explain to the children, "Today we're going fishing. But no one may enter the lake. It's filled with evil little creatures who will eat anyone who enters the water or leans over the boundary rope. You'll need to work together to figure out how you'll fish using this."

Children use the three pieces of rope and the inner tube pieces to "catch" the bucket and retrieve it from the lake.

SUGGESTED PROCEDURE

1. Explain the rules to the group. No one may touch or cross the boundary.

2. No fish may be lost. If any fish are dropped into the lake, the group must begin again.

3. The group will have 25 minutes or four tries, whichever is quicker.

4. The props may be used to get the fish. The props may touch the lake.

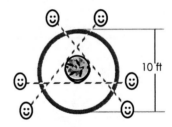

Threading Solution

One solution to this problem is to thread the inner tubes over the ropes. This leaves the group with three long ropes, each with a piece of inner tube on it. One person takes each side of a rope and the ropes are stretched across the diameter of the circle. The rope guides move cooperatively to wrap their inner tube-encased ropes around the bucket. The bucket is then lifted out of the circle.

REFLECTION

This is a hard problem to solve. The group must think creatively and work cooperatively to execute the solution. It is not uncommon for a group to have a tough time moving from solution to execution. If this happens with your group, expect some frustration. Frustration is not bad, it's part of the learning process.

Start the reflection time by having the group share with each other what happened.

- ❖ What did we just do?

- ❖ How did we do at working cooperatively? Give me some examples – both positive and negative.

- ❖ If we had the chance to do this activity again, what might we do differently?

- ❖ If we were going to do this activity with younger kids, how would we need to change it?

NOTES

● ● ● ● ● ● ● ● ● ● ● ●

HIGHWAY SHUFFLE

Two groups meet and try to pass each other without stepping off a narrow "highway."

Age:	5–12
Activity Type:	Team challenge
Activity Level:	Moderate
Space:	Large open space
Concentration Level:	High
Time:	20 minutes
Group Size:	6–20
Prerequisite:	None

MATERIALS

❖ One highway: a 30-foot strip of thick felt or canvas about four to six inches wide (depending on the age of the children)

You can substitute masking tape or, if your group is really good, several 2" x 4" boards laid end to end.

SET THE SCENE

Tell your students, "The population of the world is getting tremendously large. Soon, it may be so crowded that we have only narrow sidewalks on which we can move around. Imagine if we had only enough room around us to shuffle forward. There's no danger just yet, but I think maybe we should practice balancing on a thin highway and walking around with only a small space before we actually have to do it all the time."

SUGGESTED PROCEDURE

1. As a warm-up, have the entire group walk from one end of the "highway" to the other, being careful not to touch the ground. If they touch, ask them to return and try again. Ask the group to monitor themselves about stepping off.

2. To begin, divide the group in half and ask each group to line up on each end of the highway. Explain to them that they'll be timed as they walk from one end of the highway to the other, passing the other group along the way. Each time they touch the ground, a penalty of fifteen seconds will be added.

3. After a completed attempt, encourage the group to talk things over and give it another try. It is important to attempt the problem more than once. The first attempt establishes a time to beat. Additional attempts invariably result in a faster attempt as the result of cooperation, planning, individual effort, etc.

For Younger Children

Younger children enjoy this activity, but it needs to be adapted for them. They will experience more success with this challenge if the highway is six to eight inches wide and if they work with small groups of no more than ten. To start with, have them work with groups of four (two and two), then increase the size of the groups.

REFLECTION

Ask the group to tell you what happened during the first attempt.

- ❖ How did they change their procedure after that?
- ❖ Were there things that the group as a whole did differently?
- ❖ What did each person do individually?
- ❖ Do they think the group could get an even better time?
- ❖ How might they do it?
- ❖ What were the key parts of getting past each other quickly?

NOTES
● ● ● ● ● ● ● ● ● ● ● ●

JUMPING STARS

Children move from "star" (ropes tied in a circle) to "star" in an increasingly starless sky until the whole group fits on one star.

Age:	5–12
Activity Type:	Team challenge
Activity Level:	Moderate
Space:	Large open space
Concentration Level:	High
Time:	15–20 minutes
Group Size:	15 or more
Prerequisite:	None

MATERIALS

❖ One 10 to 24 foot rope per person (offer a variety of sizes), tied into circles

Hoops may be substituted for ropes.

SET THE SCENE

Explain to the group, "Each one of us is unique. We have a lot to offer each other. We are stars! I'd like each one of you to take a rope. Find a spot on the floor to stand, spread your rope out, and stand inside of it. This is your very own star in our after-school sky."

Once your group has their stars in place, you're ready to play.

"Now, don't get too comfortable in your star. In order to be safe, we are all going to need to work together and share our stars because the universe is constantly changing."

SUGGESTED PROCEDURE

1. Tell the group that when you give the word ("Go!"), they will need to find a new star. In order to be "safe," you must have your feet totally inside a star. There's no need to run; give the group as much time as they need to find a safe place.

2. Once everyone is safe, play a second round. This time, remind the group that the universe is constantly changing and remove one of the stars from the floor. Some confusion might occur. Two people will need to share a star. "Is this OK?" they'll ask. Don't answer, just repeat the instructions, "In order to be safe you must have your feet totally inside a star."

3. Repeat several more rounds, each time removing more and more stars.

4. For the final round, leave only one star. To end the game, everyone must be safely in this star. Be sure to leave one of the bigger stars, but don't underestimate the creativity of the group and leave too large a star. If they ask for clarification, give whatever hints you think are necessary. They will most likely come to the

For Younger Children

Younger children enjoy this game but you need to adapt it. Change step four so that there are a few stars left, not just one.

realization that they can sit on the floor and hold their feet over the circle. Or, they may discover another more adventurous solution!

REFLECTION

Ask each person to find a partner. Have the pairs find a comfortable spot in the room. Get them settled and quiet. Now ask the partners to:

❖ think of one reason why this activity was hard;

❖ describe one thing the group did to solve the problem (you may need to give some hints or an example).

Bring the group back together. Have each pair report their answers. Write the problem-solving steps on a large piece of paper. Give a brief summary and move on. Leave the steps hanging on the wall to use as a reference for future cooperative activities.

NOTES

Communication

Helping children acquire observation, listening, and other communication skills to reduce conflict and handle it effectively

All conflicts are rooted in some kind of communication problem – a misunderstanding, an inability to communicate, or hurtful and aggressive communication. Likewise, all conflict resolution involves communication to address the problems that gave rise to the conflict. Communication is a process that involves a number of skills: observing accurately, speaking clearly, listening reflectively, and responding appropriately.

There are four kinds of activities in this chapter:

1. Skill Building

2. Observation, Memory, and Point of View

3. Exploring Communication

4. Listening and Speaking

Using Teachable Moments

❖ When you are dealing with conflicts between children, give each child a chance to talk and assure them that you will listen. Not being listened to is one of children's main concerns in a conflict. Prove to them that you will listen and the problem's resolution will often go much more smoothly.

❖ Model good listening yourself. Reflect back to children what they tell you.

❖ Encourage children who are having a conflict to reflect or paraphrase what the other has said. This gets them in the habit of listening and making sure that they've understood the information correctly before they proceed.

❖ Many conflicts children have are rooted in misunderstandings. As you help them untangle these conflicts, also help them identify ways to avoid such misunderstandings in the future. Ask, "What could you do to keep from having this kind of misunderstanding again?" If you need to, be very explicit, as in, "Next time, what could you say when she doesn't want you to play?"

❖ Pay attention to nonverbal communication. Only about ten percent of communication is the actual words we use. Another 25 percent is conveyed in the tone, the volume, and the inflection we give those words. The other 65 percent is in the body language we use, such as stance, posture, facial expression, and so on. Help children become aware of what they are communicating with their bodies.

❖ Post a "Communication Potholes" chart (see p. 105) and point out when children are using one of the potholes and its negative effects. Don't do this in an accusing way, but simply point out the behavior. For example, say, "That's name-calling and it's a communication pothole. Do you see how name-calling makes this situation worse?"

❖ Avoid using the communication potholes yourself. Also try to avoid these common communication stoppers: asking too many questions, giving unsolicited advice, directing when it's not appropriate, and so on.

❖ Identify good communication habits when you see them. If you do the "Communication Potholes" activity you will have a chart of positive communication behaviors to which you can refer. Even if you don't complete the activity, try to develop a habit of identifying good communication habits when you see and hear them. This can be as simple as saying, "Good job saying what you need" or "I like the way you said you were angry without yelling or trying to hurt her."

Communication
Skill Building

Age:	5–12
Activity Type:	Chart
Activity Level:	Quiet
Space:	Any
Concentration Level:	High
Time :	25 minutes
Group Size:	Any
Prerequisite:	None

Talking Chips

Here's a way to give all the children in a group a chance to participate and to prevent one or two from dominating the group. Give all the children in the group an equal number of chips. Ten chips is a good number to start. Each time a child speaks, he or she puts a chip into the pot. Once they run out of chips, they cannot speak. When everyone runs out of chips, they may ask for more.

GOOD LISTENING

Through demonstration, role play, and brainstorming, children identify the skills of "good listening."

MATERIALS

❖ None

SUGGESTED PROCEDURE

1. Discuss with the group why listening is important. For example, by listening we get information, identify dangerous situations, learn how others feel, get enjoyment, etc. Arrange ahead of time for one child to assist you in demonstrating poor listening and good listening. Call that child up for the demonstration. *Say the following to the child:*

   "_____ (Child's name), I just got a message from the principal. You just won a contest and you get a million dollars and a free trip anywhere you want to go. But you have to go down to the office right away and call the contest people or they will give the prize to someone else. And you have to say these special words to them or they will give the prize to someone else. You have to say 'I'm a great listener.' Do you understand?"

   As you talk to him or her, have the child look around the room, fidget, interrupt you, hum, and show other signs of "poor" listening. Ask the children to describe what they saw.

2. With the same student, repeat the speech, this time with the child demonstrating good listening, i.e., paying attention, looking at you, nodding occasionally, not interrupting, repeating the key information when you have said, "Do you undertand?"

Mini-Reflection

◆ What did you see the second time?

◆ How was it different from the first time?

◆ Which was good listening?

◆ What did _____ miss because of poor listening?

3. Make a "T-Chart" of Good Listening with the class. Write the following diagram on a piece of chart paper:

What Good Listening Looks Like	What Good Listening Sounds Like

Have children identify specific behaviors for each side of the chart.

REFLECTION

❖ How can good listening make our program a better place?

❖ Who can give an example of a time good listening helped them?

❖ How can good listening help you in a conflict?

NOTES

● ● ● ● ● ● ● ● ● ● ● ●

Age:	8–12
Activity Type:	Getting to know you
Activity Level:	Quiet
Space:	Any
Concentration Level:	High
Time:	20 minutes
Group Size:	6 or more
Prerequisite:	None

PETE AND REPEAT*

Children practice active listening skills by paraphrasing what others say.

● ● ● ● ● ● ● ● ● ● ● ● ● ● ● ● ●

MATERIALS

❖ None

SUGGESTED PROCEDURE

1. Begin by explaining what paraphrasing is. Give the children some practice by helping them paraphrase some simple sentences, such as:

    ❖ The book I'm reading is exciting.

    ❖ I saw some boring TV shows last night.

    ❖ I'm excited about the field trip we're taking.

2. Have children work in pairs. Designate one child as Pete and the other as Repeat. Explain that whenever Pete says something, he or she will stop for a moment and Repeat will paraphrase it. Pete should nod or say "uh-huh" if it is an accurate paraphrase. Have all the Petes address the topic, "The things grown-ups do that make me mad." After a few minutes, have students switch roles, then continue as above.

REFLECTION

❖ What was it like to paraphrase the other person's sentences?

❖ What made it difficult?

❖ What was it like hearing someone else repeat what you said?

❖ How would this paraphrasing help when listening to other people?

---

* Adapted with permission from William J. Kreidler, *Creative Conflict Resolution* (Geneva, IL: Scott, Foresman and Company, 1984).

COMMUNICATION POTHOLES

Children brainstorm Communication Potholes as guidelines for types of communication to avoid.

● ● ● ● ● ● ● ● ● ● ● ● ● ● ● ● ● ●

Age:	8–12
Activity Type:	Brainstorming
Activity Level:	Quiet
Space:	Any
Concentration Level:	Medium
Time :	20 minutes
Group Size:	5–20
Prerequisite:	None

MATERIALS

❖ Chart paper and markers

SUGGESTED PROCEDURE

1. *Explain to the children,* "We want to set some group guidelines for how to communicate. We don't want people's feelings to be hurt and we don't want to communicate in a way that leads to fights. What should we do to have positive communication?"

2. Label one sheet "Communication Helpers." Record children's suggestions for positive communication behaviors on the chart. When a child suggests something negative, like "Don't call people names," ask them to hold that suggestion for a moment. Right now none of the suggestions should begin with "don't."

3. Label the second sheet "Communication Potholes." Discuss what potholes are and why people want to avoid them.

   Ask the children:

   ❖ What are some of the ways of communicating that are like potholes that we should avoid in our program?

   ❖ What kinds of communication make people feel bad?

   ❖ Record children's suggestions for negative communication.

4. Post the charts where others can see them. Have children who weren't part of the discussion give their reactions and allow them to add to the lists.

5. You might want to present the charts at a group meeting and get the group's consensus about abiding by the suggestions on the chart.

Setting Standards

Use the "Communication Potholes" activity as a way to set standards for communicating in your program. You could call the positive chart 'Positive Communication Power' and the negative one 'Communication Potholes.' To get the kids used to it, have them identify one behavior a day from each chart and ask them to work on it that day. For example, on a particular day they might choose 'Say Please' (one of the positive communication behaviors) and 'Not say Shut Up.' (one of the negative behaviors) as the behaviors to work on. It is important to help them identify alternatives to the negative behaviors. How do you tell someone to 'shut up' without saying 'shut up?'

REFLECTION

❖ How might following the suggestions on these charts help our program?

❖ What could we do to encourage others to follow the suggestions?

❖ What are some reasons people might not follow the suggestions?

❖ How could we help them with that?

NOTES

● ● ● ● ● ● ● ● ● ● ●

Observation, Memory, and Point of View

Age:	8–12
Activity Type:	Circle game
Activity Level:	Quiet
Space:	Any
Concentration Level:	Medium
Time :	20 minutes
Group Size:	5–20
Prerequisite:	None

CROSSED & UNCROSSED

Children learn about the importance of observing body language when they try to replicate a pattern established by the leader.

● ● ● ● ● ● ● ● ● ● ● ● ● ● ● ●

MATERIALS

❖ Two dowels, sticks, or pencils

❖ Chairs (one for each child)

SUGGESTED PROCEDURE

1. Gather chairs in a circle and sit together with the children.

2. Begin this puzzle by asking a child to pass you two sticks (or whatever two items you choose). Then pass the sticks to the child sitting next to you. Tell the group, "I got these sticks crossed, and I'm passing them crossed." Cross your legs as you receive the sticks and pass them along. Do not tell the groups that this is what you are doing.

3. Indicate to the group that each person is to receive the sticks and then pass them on either crossed or uncrossed. As they do this, they should state both how they received the sticks and how they are being passed (crossed or uncrossed).

4. The "key" to this puzzle is the leg position of the person doing the passing and the leg position of the person to whom they are being passed. For example, the person receiving the pencils says, "I am getting these pencils crossed." (Are the passer's legs crossed or uncrossed?) and "I am passing them on uncrossed." (Are the receiver's legs crossed or uncrossed?) Tell each passer if they are correct or incorrect in the passing.

5. As the group passes the sticks, hopefully some will catch on and answer correctly. If they do not, when the sticks come to you again, obviously cross your legs as you pass the sticks on. That should do the trick.

REFLECTION

Briefly explain the premise of the activity. Ask the students how they were able to discover the pattern.

- ❖ How did it feel not to know the pattern?

- ❖ Did you give up trying to find the pattern when you couldn't get it in the first few tries?

- ❖ What have you learned about your observation skills today?

- ❖ How attuned to body language are you?

NOTES

● ● ● ● ● ● ● ● ● ● ● ●

Age:	8–12
Activity Type:	Circle game
Activity Level:	Quiet
Space:	Any
Concentration Level:	Medium
Time :	20 minutes
Group Size:	5–20
Prerequisite:	None

DUCK AND CHICKEN

Children try to guess how one becomes a chicken by observing clues given by the leader.

●●●●●●●●●●●●●●●●●●

MATERIALS

❖ None

SET THE SCENE

Say to the group, "Duck, Duck, Duck, Duck, Chicken. Guess who is the chicken!"

SUGGESTED PROCEDURE

1. Gather the children together sitting comfortably in a circle.

2. The goal is to identify "the chicken" each time after you, the game leader, chant the phrase, "Duck, Duck, Duck, Duck, Chicken. Guess who is the chicken."

3. *Say,* "Duck, Duck, Duck, Duck, Chicken. Guess who is the chicken" and wait for a response from someone in the group. After a few guesses, begin again. The frustration level will rise as they try to guess the chicken. Whoever speaks the first word after your question is the chicken (The first person to talk – even if he/she is talking to a friend).

4. Other clues for variations of this game could be to use body or limb positions. As you ask "Who's the Chicken?" cross your legs or fold your arms, mimicking the position of one of the children. This child will then be the chicken.

REFLECTION

Briefly explain how you were choosing the chicken. Ask the children how they discovered the answer.

❖ How did it feel not to know the answer?

❖ If you gave up trying to find the answer, when did you give up and why?

HANDS DOWN

Children try to guess numbers illustrated by the pattern in a set of sticks.

● ● ● ● ● ● ● ● ● ● ● ● ● ● ● ● ●

Age:	8 –12
Activity Type:	Circle game
Activity Level:	Quiet
Space:	Any
Concentration Level:	High
Time :	20 minutes
Group Size:	5 or more
Prerequisite:	None

MATERIALS

❖ Five dowels, sticks, or pencils

SET THE SCENE

Tell the children, "I've got a way of indicating numbers from one to ten, and I'll show you. Guess which number I'm making and I'll tell you if you're right. If you figure out how I'm making the patterns, don't tell. Let everyone try to figure it out for themselves."

SUGGESTED PROCEDURE

1. Gather the children together sitting comfortably on the floor in a circle.

2. Place five pencils or sticks on the ground in front of you so that a pattern is formed. Any pattern will do. Ask the group to indicate the number from one to ten that this arrangement demonstrates. Set up two or three different patterns so that the group gets to see and guess additional numbers that you are depicting.

3. The number is not indicated in the sticks at all, but in your hands beside them! Set down whatever pattern of sticks you want, placing your hands, palms down, on the floor next to the sticks with the number of fingers exposed showing the number you have in mind (two fists is zero, two hands with all fingers extended is ten).

4. Someone will eventually figure out what you are doing. Use that person to maintain group interest by asking him or her to name the number in each new pattern. If no one catches on after a few patterns, place your hands closer to the sticks or lay them down more obviously.

REFLECTION

Briefly explain how you were forming the numbers. Ask the students to describe how they were watching what you did, but also how they were listening to what you said. (You never said the pattern was in the sticks.) Ask the group to share other situations where the answer wasn't obvious, for example, when a friend says one thing, but their body language or tone of voice says another.

NOTES

● ● ● ● ● ● ● ● ● ● ● ●

I'VE GOT THE BEAT

Children try to repeat a rhythmic pattern, established by the leader, practicing observation skills.

Age:	5–12
Activity Type:	Circle game
Activity Level:	Quiet
Space:	Any
Concentration Level:	Medium
Time :	20 minutes
Group Size:	5–20
Prerequisite:	None

MATERIALS

❖ None

SUGGESTED PROCEDURE

1. Sit together with the children in a circle.

2. Using an object or your hand, tap out a rhythm, sigh deeply (but not too obviously), and say, "I've got the beat." There should be no more than seven to nine movements to the beat. For instance, you may tap the table twice quickly, draw an imaginary circle, tap again, pat the table with your hand, etc. Any rhythmic pattern will do.

3. After you've repeated the pattern a few times, ask someone in the group to try.

4. The trick is that they must do everything *exactly* as you do, including taking a deep breath beforehand saying, "I've got the beat" afterward, or any other motion that you would like to add (shifting in your seat, etc.).

5. Predictably, children who try to repeat the pattern will miss something at first. Repeat it as many times as they need, slowing down if necessary. If they become frustrated, tell them they are focusing on the wrong thing and guide them subtly in the right direction. This puzzle will have more value if they discover the answers themselves.

6. As a variation, ask a member of the group to make up a rhythm.

REFLECTION

Ask everyone to repeat the last sequence together.

❖ How were they able to discover the answer? Talk to the group about focusing and observing carefully.

For Younger Children

With younger children, this can be played as a "repeat the beat" game with no hidden difficulties.

Age: 5–10

Activity Type: Observation game

Activity Level: Quiet

Space: Any

Concentration Level: High

Time : 20 minutes

Group Size: 6 or more

Prerequisite: None

DETAILS, DETAILS

This observation activity is a good lead-in for role playing.

● ● ● ● ● ● ● ● ● ● ● ● ● ● ● ● ●

MATERIALS

❖ None

SET THE SCENE

Tell the group, "I'd like everyone to close their eyes. Raise your hand if you can remember what color shirt I have on today. OK, open your eyes."

Talk about how many people could answer this question. Predictably, not many will answer correctly.

Continue by explaining, "Recognizing or noticing little details, like the color of a shirt or the words in an argument, takes some practice. To help resolve a conflict, it is often important for us to be able to remember the details. We will be doing some role playing to practice understanding what makes conflict escalate. Before we do this, let's test our observation skills."

SUGGESTED PROCEDURE

1. This activity can be done in pairs or as a large group. The large group format works better with younger children who need more supervision and coaching. If you are working with a large group, ask for one volunteer. If you are working with pairs, have the children find a partner.

2. *Explain to the group,* "This is an observation game. We will examine visually this volunteer (or our partner) for 30 seconds. Once that time is up, the volunteer will leave the room."

3. Ask the volunteer (or one of the partners) to leave the room. While they are gone, have them change one thing on themselves. This thing will be observable. Once they return, have the others guess what has been changed.

Note: Be clear about what can be changed – allow only observable changes such as removing a watch.

4. Ask for a new volunteer or have the partners switch roles. Another variation when working with a large group is to have two or more volunteers.

REFLECTION

❖ What did it feel like to observe someone for 30 seconds?

❖ What did it feel like to be observed?

❖ Do we normally look at each other so closely?
Why or why not?

❖ How did you do at guessing the changes? Did you get better as
the game went along? What made you better?

❖ What do you have to do to be an expert observer? Make a list
for reference while observing the role plays.

NOTES

● ● ● ● ● ● ● ● ● ● ● ●

Age: 8–12

Activity Type: Communication

Activity Level: Active

Space: Any, preferably outside

Concentration Level: Medium

Time : 30 minutes

Group Size: 10–25

Prerequisite: Experience being blindfolded

HUMAN CAMERA

Students explore point of view by becoming cameras and photographers.

● ● ● ● ● ● ● ● ● ● ● ● ● ● ● ● ● ●

MATERIALS

❖ None

SUGGESTED PROCEDURE

1. Divide the group into pairs. Explain that they'll be using their partners as cameras. Tell the group that the camera is like a human eye – it sees things from a certain perspective, depending on how the photographer focuses, frames, and shoots the picture.

2. Have one partner act as the photographer and the other as the camera.

3. The partner who is the photographer then chooses a picture to shoot. He must decide and take note of the subject he intends to photograph ahead of time.

4. The partner who is the camera closes his eyes, allowing himself to be led around by the photographer. The photographer sets up his partner's head (the camera) in such a way that his eyes are directly in front of the chosen subject. Then, gently pulling an ear lobe, he activates the shutter. With this encouragement, the "camera" opens and closes his eyelids (shutter) very quickly in order to record the scene.

5. Have the partners take five or six "pictures." Have them vary the scenes from close-ups to distant landscapes.

6. Ask all the camera/photographer pairs to talk about what they have jointly recorded.

Mini-Reflection

◆ What did the photographer intend to photograph?

◆ What did the camera record or see?

◆ Why does the camera think the photographer chose his or her subject?

◆ Why did the camera, in fact, choose that subject?

7. The pairs should switch roles after having talked about the experience, and follow-up with another debriefing using the questions above.

REFLECTION

Have the group come back together and share their experiences.

❖ What did the photographers decide to photograph?

❖ What were the challenges of being a camera?

❖ Did any surprises turn up when you talked about what was recorded?

❖ Did the photographers succeed in capturing what they wanted on film?

Close by asking the group to think about how people see different details when looking at the same thing.

❖ What are the values of differing perspectives?

❖ What are the potential pitfalls?

NOTES
● ● ● ● ● ● ● ● ● ● ●

Age: 8–12

Activity Type: Storytelling

Activity Level: Quiet

Space: Any

Concentration
Level: Medium

Time : 30 minutes

Group Size: 10–15

Prerequisite: Some group
experience

BIG PICTURE

Children together recount the events of a story to explore differing perspectives.

● ● ● ● ● ● ● ● ● ● ● ● ● ● ● ● ●

MATERIALS

❖ A subject or past event for the group to remember

❖ Chart paper and markers

SUGGESTED PROCEDURE

1. Have the group sit together in a circle. Select as your subject something the group has done together recently. Tell the children that they must recount every detail about the event. They must tell exactly what happened, how people felt, what time it was, what the weather was, anything that they recollect about the event.

Note: This simple storytelling process may be difficult to accomplish smoothly because certain children will want to speak often. Before beginning, establish that children must listen to one another and not interrupt.

2. Ask a volunteer to begin telling what happened. When another child observes that a detail has been left out, or remembers something else in the sequence, they share that detail and then take over telling the story.

3. In order to make the event concrete for children, record the events on a large web chart, adding everything that is said. This allows the children to move backward to add details or to account for two different things happening at once.

4. This activity can be applied to many situations. Recount an activity, a discussion, or a disagreement. Another option is to add goals beyond simply recounting the event. For example, the activity could be varied so that everyone must add something during the story or one person could tell the story while the others solicit details by asking questions.

Illustrating Viewpoints

This is a good activity for illustrating differing points of view. It might be most profitable following an episode where working together was difficult. The event of working together can then become the subject for this activity.

REFLECTION

In closing, congratulate the group on their ability to remember so many details about things. They have created the "big picture" with everyone's input!

Post the web chart and tell the children that details can be very important both in solving problems and in getting your point across clearly.

❖ Looking at the web chart, what were the different perspectives that were raised?

❖ How do the different perspectives help to give a complete and clear account of the event? How do they prevent a complete and clear account?

NOTES

● ● ● ● ● ● ● ● ● ● ●

Age:	5–12
Activity Type:	Storytelling
Activity Level:	Quiet
Space:	Any
Concentration Level:	Medium
Time :	20 minutes
Group Size:	Any
Prerequisite:	None

UNDERSTANDING OTHER PERSPECTIVES

Children use picture books to explore other points of view.

● ● ● ● ● ● ● ● ● ● ● ● ● ● ● ● ●

MATERIALS

❖ *Two Bad Ants* by Chris VanAllsburg

❖ *The True Story of the Three Little Pigs* by Jon Scieska

SUGGESTED PROCEDURE

1. Encourage children to be playful in looking at points of view that are different from their own. Pass around the picture book *Two Ants* by Chris VanAllsburg, which shows how a kitchen looks from the perspective of two ants. Children of all ages are fascinated by this book.

2. When everyone has had a chance to look at the book, have the children draw pictures showing how the afterschool room would look from an ant's perspective. The ant might be on the floor, inside a desk, on the ceiling, etc.

3. Continue to help children appreciate that there is more than one point of view on any situation. First read or retell the story of "The Three Little Pigs." Follow this by reading *The True Story of the Three Pigs* by Jon Scieska, which tells the story from the wolf's point of view.

4. With older children, have the group write or tell their own "Point of View Tales" by retelling fairy tales from the point of view of the villain. These tales can be expanded into skits to present to the group.

REFLECTION

❖ If you were the ant, what would be your point of view on the activities in our program?

❖ What do you think of the wolf's point of view?

❖ How did you decide what the point of view would be in your story?

STANDING IN THEIR SHOES

Children practice identifying differing points of view by "standing in someone else's footprints."

Age:	8–12
Activity Type:	Chart
Activity Level:	Quiet
Space:	Any
Concentration Level:	Medium
Time :	20 minutes
Group Size:	Any
Prerequisite:	None

MATERIALS

❖ Sets of footprints made from colored construction paper

SUGGESTED PROCEDURE

1. Show the group two pairs of footprints made from different colors of construction paper. Explain that these are point of view footprints. When you stand in them, you see someone else's point of view – you look at the world the way they do.

2. Set the footprints on the floor. Present the group with situations such as those that follow. Ask a volunteer to stand on one set of footprints and summarize one point of view, then stand on the other set of footprints and give the other point of view. Encourage children to identify both the point of view and the feelings the people might have about the situation.

Sample situations:

❖ Ms. Chang says no one in afterschool can use a computer until their homework is done. Reginald doesn't like this idea.

❖ Ruth wants to watch a video she just rented. Her sister Naomi wants to watch a show on TV at the same time.

❖ Marcus wants to sit by himself and read a book. His best friend Raphael keeps asking him to play a game.

REFLECTION

❖ What was it like trying to identify with different points of view?

❖ How might different points of view lead to conflict?

❖ What other points of view might there be in these situations?

Exploring Communication

MOOKIE

Children explore avoidance as a conflict resolution technique.

● ● ● ● ● ● ● ● ● ● ● ● ● ● ●

Age:	5–10
Activity Type:	Drama
Activity Level:	Active
Space:	Large open space
Concentration Level:	Medium
Time :	20 minutes
Group Size:	10–20
Prerequisite:	None

MATERIALS

❖ None

SET THE SCENE

Explain to the group, "We've been thinking about conflict and some of the factors that lead up to it. Can you tell me some of these things (not listening, etc.)?" "Usually, not listening might be a way to get into a fight with someone, but sometimes not listening can keep you out of trouble. When someone is trying to provoke you, not getting drawn in when they call you a name can stop the fight."

SUGGESTED PROCEDURE

1. Have the group practice saying the word "Mookie" in different voices and manners. Have them say it as a sergeant would, then a grandma. How about a cow, or a cat, a vampire, or a rapper? Develop as many different and playful ways as possible.

2. Then announce that they must try to say "Mookie" without laughing. This will take some doing.

3. Have the group form two parallel lines, facing each other (a gauntlet). Ask for a volunteer to walk slowly down the gauntlet without cracking a smile. All the while the gauntlet will be doing their best Mookie calls, trying to distract the walker and get him to smile. Repeat this many times, encouraging variation of Mookie calls.

REFLECTION

Ask each person to find a partner. Have the pairs find a comfortable spot in the room. Get them settled and quiet. Now ask the partners to think about:

❖ one reason why this activity was hard;

❖ a similar situation that might happen at school;

❖ how it felt to be part of the gauntlet;

❖ how it felt to walk down the center of the gauntlet.

Bring the group back together. Have each pair report their answers.

Age: 6–12

Activity Type: Communication

Activity Level: Active

Space: Large open space

Concentration
Level: Medium

Time : 20 minutes

Group Size: 10 or more

Prerequisite: None

**Safety
Note**

Before using this activity, be certain
that your group is ready to play
safely. Be clear that intentional
crashing is not acceptable behavior.
Set a challenge not to crash.

BUMPER CARS

Children practice communication skills by directing
others with verbal instructions.

● ● ● ● ● ● ● ● ● ● ● ● ● ● ● ● ●

MATERIALS

❖ Boundary markers to mark a large rectangular space that will
fit everyone but will force everyone to walk around each other

SET THE SCENE

Ask the students, "Has anyone here ever driven a car? Now is your
big chance. But, since we are making this special chance available
to you, you will need to be very careful with your car. Your car
trusts you to drive carefully and not crash her into any other cars.
You have a very expensive, sporty car. Be careful!"

SUGGESTED PROCEDURE

1. Everyone will need to find a partner. In each pair, one person is
   the car and one person is the driver. The car will keep her eyes
   closed while the driver drives her around.

2. The driver's goal is to drive around during an allotted time period (two minutes) without any crashes. The driver will tell the
   car to move forward by placing both hands on her shoulders.
   To stop, the driver will remove her hands. To go right, she will
   tap lightly with her right hand. To go left, she will tap lightly
   with her left hand. The driver and car may not talk (of course,
   cars do not talk!).

3. Once the time period is up, have the partners switch roles.

REFLECTION

Bring the group back together in a comfortable space. Ask each
person to complete the sentence, "I liked being the _____ (car or
driver) best because…"

Go around the group getting their responses.

❖ Did anyone find it difficult being the car? Why?

❖ What did your driver do that made you feel safe? unsafe?

❖ Did the cars trust their drivers? Why?

❖ Did anyone who was a car keep their eyes open?

ORBIT

One child guides a blindfolded partner to form a circle out of rope as a way to explore issues of trust.

● ● ● ● ● ● ● ● ● ● ● ● ● ● ● ● ● ●

Age:	8–12
Activity Type:	Communication
Activity Level:	Active
Space:	Large open space
Concentration Level:	High
Time :	20 minutes
Group Size:	10–15
Prerequisite:	None

MATERIALS

❖ Blindfolds (enough for half the group)

❖ 8-foot lengths of rope (enough for half the group)

SUGGESTED PROCEDURE

1. Have the group divide into pairs by forming a straight line. "Fold" the line in half. Each person will be standing in front of another person. These two people are now partners.

2. Give each team a blindfold and a piece of rope.

3. Ask the children to decide who will be blindfolded first. The partner who can see is the "earth." The earth should stand in an open area close to the blindfolded person.

4. The other partner is a "rocket ship." The rocket ship needs to create a perfect orbit around the earth, laying down a trail of rope as it goes. The blindfolded rocket ship will receive verbal directions from the earth. The earth may not touch the rocket ship.

5. Let the groups work at their own pace, deciding when they have completed a circle and then removing blindfolds to see their results.

6. Have the partners switch roles and try again. After each partner has made a circle, try more complicated shapes. Squares, triangles, ovals, or letters will prove more challenging. Let the children think of their own variations.

7. Close by having all the children come together and form the ropes into a large circle to sit inside.

REFLECTION

Sitting inside the circle, conduct a discussion about creating orbits.

❖ What was the most difficult thing about trying to make the orbit?

❖ Did it get easier as you tried different shapes?

❖ Did anyone peek? Why?

❖ Was there any pair that didn't complete the orbit?

❖ What are some of the things it takes to communicate well?

Focus on discovering how they communicated or failed to communicate.

NOTES

● ● ● ● ● ● ● ● ● ● ●

THE QUIET HIGH RISE

Without talking, teams must communicate and cooperate in order to build a tower.

● ● ● ● ● ● ● ● ● ● ● ● ● ● ● ● ● ●

Age:	6–12
Activity Type:	Team challenge
Activity Level:	Moderate
Space:	Work tables
Concentration Level:	Medium
Time :	30 minutes
Group Size:	6 or more
Prerequisite:	None

MATERIALS

❖ A set of Tinker Toys®

Building blocks, Styrofoam cups, or assorted stuff can also be used as a substitute. (Legos® do not work well for this activity, as they are less likely to topple and roll.)

SET THE SCENE

Explain to the group, "OK, we're going to test our communication skills here. In many of our communication exercises we have spoken about listening skills. Usually this means being attentive and quiet while someone else is talking. In this activity, you are going to have to figure out a new way of listening, because no one can talk!"

SUGGESTED PROCEDURE

1. Break the group into smaller teams of three or four. Distribute building materials evenly. Each group must build on a similar base (desk top, set of floor tiles, etc.). Establish a height you want each tower to be.

2. *Tell the children the following rules:*

❖ Each group is going to try to build a tower to a specific height.

❖ Tower sections that fall or roll off the base or out of the base area may not be used again.

❖ Group members may not talk while assembling their tower.

The goal is for every group to complete their tower to the required height by working quickly and cooperatively, following the rules just named.

REFLECTION

Come back together in a large circle. Talk about how the groups communicated.

❖ Can someone describe how they built their tower?

For Younger Children
For younger children, use a group size of 2 or 3.

❖ What strategy for communication did you use?

❖ Did not being able to talk make it harder or easier? Why?

❖ What would you do differently next time?

NOTES
● ● ● ● ● ● ● ● ● ● ● ●

SLOT MACHINE

Groups invent sounds and motions, then try to communicate their intent to other groups.

● ● ● ● ● ● ● ● ● ● ● ● ● ● ● ● ●

Age:	8–12
Activity Type:	Team challenge
Activity Level:	Moderate
Space:	Any
Concentration Level:	Medium
Time :	30 minutes
Group Size:	12 or more
Prerequisite:	None

MATERIALS

❖ None

SET THE SCENE

Say to the group, "We are going to make a human slot machine. Does anyone here know what a slot machine is? Can you describe it to me?"

"Great. We are going to build our own slot machine. We will divide into three groups. Each group will take some time to develop a sound and a motion. Once this is done, we'll come together in the shape of a triangle, I'll pull the handle of the machine, and we'll see what we get. Our goal is for everyone to come up with the same sign – then we'll win the bonus prize. It sounds easy? Well, getting it to work may be a little harder than you think."

SUGGESTED PROCEDURE

1. Divide your group into three teams. Arrange each team to form the three sides of a triangle.

2. Ask each group to find a private space (within the space you're using) and take a couple minutes to create a *sound* and a *motion* that they think will make the other two teams laugh. The sound and motion they invent should not last more than two or three seconds and should be something everyone can do without risking injury.

Note: If necessary, discuss appropriate vs. inappropriate sounds and motions.

3. Allow three to five minutes for the three teams to create their humorous presentations.

4. Once the groups are ready, re-form the triangle and ask each team – one by one – to demonstrate its sound and motion. After each demo, ask the two observing teams to reproduce what they saw so that the creators can have a chance to see what they looked like.

When Cooperation is Difficult

Sometimes a particular team may get locked into their own sound and motion combination and refuse to change despite what the other two groups do. This refusal to compromise can cause confusion and conflict. Remind people what the objective is – to have fun and to cooperate – then try a few more rounds. If the desired result doesn't emerge, use this as a teachable moment to talk about what happened and what can happen when small groups anywhere – in school, neighborhoods, etc. – choose not to cooperate.

5. After viewing and practicing all three sound and motion inventions, here's the challenge: the three teams must meet separately (no communication between teams other than telepathy and mindmelding) and determine what they think the other two teams will do.

6. Re-form the triangle. The goal is for all three teams to stand in the triangle and, on the count of three (when you pull the "handle"), have all three teams do the same sound and motion together. Each team has to reproduce one of the three sounds and motions demonstrated. The creation of any new motions or sounds is not allowed.

7. The group can have as many rounds (each team privately selecting a sound and motion and then all three showing their selected sound and motion together) as they need. Three to five rounds is normally sufficient to reach consensus. Most groups will intuitively decide that one of the three presentations is funnier and choose to reproduce that one and everyone will be amazed at the power of the group.

REFLECTION

❖ How did this make people feel? Letting go of our own motion and sound can sometimes feel frustrating. Why?

❖ How did the group whose motion/sound was used feel?

❖ How did the other two groups feel about the third group?

❖ Often the two compromising groups feel that the third group is superior or feels they have won. Talk about the fact that someone needed to emerge as the leader.

❖ How do we feel when one person or group is the leader? How are these leaders selected?

BALL LINE-UP

Pairs search for a ball with their number on it, then line up in numerical order.

● ● ● ● ● ● ● ● ● ● ● ● ● ● ● ● ●

Age:	5–12
Activity Type:	Team challenge
Activity Level:	Moderate
Space:	Large open space
Concentration Level:	Medium
Time :	30 minutes
Group Size:	10 or more
Prerequisite:	Comfort with blindfolds

MATERIALS

❖ One fleece or tennis ball per pair

❖ One blindfold per pair

SET THE SCENE

Before the group arrives, number the balls sequentially with a marker or masking tape. Spread the balls around the room.

Have each person find a partner. Ask one person in each pair to put on the blindfold. Assign each team a number.

SUGGESTED PROCEDURE

1. Each twosome must find the ball with their number on it. The sighted partner cannot touch the ball.

2. The sighted partner may touch the blindfolded partner, but may not physically direct the movements of the blindfolded partner. The sighted partner's job is to keep the blindfolded partner safe.

3. The blindfolded members may not talk.

4. The sighted partners may talk and give directions.

5. Once the partnerships have found the balls, all the blindfolded members must line up in order of their numbers.

6. Time the activity. Once it is completed, have the partners switch roles and try it again. See if the activity is completed in less time.

REFLECTION

Ask the children to share how they found their balls.

❖ How did you go about helping your partners find the balls?

❖ How did the blindfold partners know where to line up?

For Younger Children

Give each child a number. Skip the blindfolds. The goal is then to find your ball and line up in order as quickly as possible.

Now, talk about what happened.

❖ Was it quicker the second time?

❖ What made it easier the second time?

❖ If we were to do it again, how could we be even faster?

Use the answers to the "so what" questions to talk about "now what" – generalizing their learning and applying it to other communication problems.

❖ What did we learn about communication? Give some examples.

NOTES
● ● ● ● ● ● ● ● ● ● ●

CAN YOU GUESS?

The group tries to communicate using only clapping.

● ● ● ● ● ● ● ● ● ● ● ● ● ● ● ● ● ● ●

Age:	8–12
Activity Type:	Communication
Activity Level:	Moderate
Space:	Any
Concentration Level:	Medium
Time :	15–30 minutes
Group Size:	Any
Prerequisite:	None

MATERIALS

❖ None

SET THE SCENE

Ask the children, "Who here is good at figuring out directions? Can I have two volunteers? The volunteers will leave the room. While they are gone, the rest of us will think of a simple direction for the volunteers to follow when they return. "

SUGGESTED PROCEDURE

1. Tell the group the rules. The group will not be able to talk to the volunteers when they return. The group can communicate only by clapping – loud clapping when the volunteers are close to following the direction and no clapping if they are not close at all. Give a standing ovation when they've got it!

2. The directions for the volunteers must be simple. Help to guide the group to an appropriate selection. For example, the volunteer could be directed to come into the room and pick up a piece of paper. Set a time limit for selecting the direction.

3. The volunteers may need some prompting. The best way to figure out the directions is to start doing things around the room. Encourage the volunteers to stay active. If they seem stumped, give a hint.

4. Try several rounds.

REFLECTION

Talk about the different rounds.

❖ What made some volunteers more successful at finding the solution than others?

Work with the group to identify those things that made communication easier. Conclude by talking about the relationship between the volunteers and the group. Tell the children that communication cannot rely on one person. It is a relationship between two people or groups.

Age: 5–12

Activity Type: Team challenge

Activity Level: Active

Space: Large open space

Concentration Level: Medium

Time : 30 minutes

Group Size: Any

Prerequisite: None

FIND YOUR PARTNER

Partners try to find one another while blindfolded.

MATERIALS

❖ Blindfolds

SET THE SCENE

Ask each person to find a partner. If there is one extra, you can play too.

Say, "I'd like you and your partner to find matching names. For example, if your partner is peanut butter then you are jelly, if your partner is French then you are fry. Once you've got the names, come over here and line up."

SUGGESTED PROCEDURE

1. Ask each twosome to share their names. Enjoy the fun and creativity!

2. Have one person from each pair stand at one side of the open area and the other person stand at the other end. Ask everyone to put on their blindfolds (or close their eyes).

3. The pairs must now try to find each other by calling out their partner's name. Have the children walk with their "bumpers up" (hands up at chest level with palms forward).

REFLECTION

Once they have found their partners, have the teams find a space and sit down. Ask them to think about communication.

❖ How were you communicating with your partner? What worked? What didn't?

❖ What are two other ways you can communicate with someone without talking?

Have the teams report back to the large group.

Listening and Speaking Activities

Age: 5–12

Activity Type: Arts and crafts

Activity Level: Moderate

Space: Large open space

Concentration Level: High

Time : 30 minutes

Group Size: 2 or more

Prerequisite: None

OPERATOR, PLEASE CONNECT ME

Children make telephones and have conversations, keeping track of miscommunications.

MATERIALS

❖ Clean tin cans with the tops carefully cut off (or paper cups)

❖ String or nylon thread

❖ Hammer and nail (or paper clips)

❖ Scissors

SUGGESTED PROCEDURE

1. In pairs, have the children make telephones by poking a hole through the bottom of two cans or cups and then knotting string so that it will not slide through. Leave forty feet of string between the two cans and knot the string at the other end, so that the two are now connected. Decorate them!

2. Once the phones are complete, give a copy of the Silly Phone Story handout to one partner in each group. Explain that the other partner cannot look at the handout.

3. Have the students walk apart until the string is taut. Students should turn so as not to see the person on the other end of the telephone. Give them some time to practice before starting on the Silly Phone Story.

4. Have the partner who was given the script read the Silly Phone Story handout. He must make up a story, starting with the first line of the Silly Phone Story, and read it clearly to his partner. Partners may ask questions to clarify what they heard. Have the listeners in each team report back to the group on what they heard.

REFLECTION

❖ Did you get frustrated because your partner didn't understand you correctly?

❖ Does this ever happen to you in real life? When?

❖ How did it feel to be a listener? What obstacles were there to communication?

❖ What do you do when you feel like you are not being understood correctly by someone?

Silly Phone Story

You are the Silly Phone Story writer. Make up a story and tell it to your partner over the phone, as clearly as you can. Your partner can ask you questions if he does not understand something you said. Remember how your story goes, because your partner will have to tell it back to you.

Here's the first line of your story...

Firstly, Finny Foniapolis dialed his friend Francine...

Now you finish the story!

Age:	5–10
Activity Type:	Arts and crafts
Activity Level:	Moderate
Space:	Work tables
Concentration Level:	Low
Time :	20 minutes
Group Size:	Any
Prerequisite:	None

MAKING BEAN TAMBOURINES

Students make bean-filled tambourines.

● ● ● ● ● ● ● ● ● ● ● ● ● ● ● ● ● ●

MATERIALS

❖ Paper plates

❖ Dried beans (kidneys, peas, pintos, whatever)

❖ Markers, crayons

❖ Stapler

SUGGESTED PROCEDURE

1. Have the children make bean-filled tambourines by stapling a handful of dried beans between two paper plates.

2. Decorate the tambourines.

3. Store the Bean Tambourines in a special place in the room to use in other activities.

REFLECTION

❖ How could we use these Bean Tambourines to communicate?

FOLLOW-UP

Use the Bean Tambourines in "It's Bean Great Hearing You!" (p. 139) or "Storming" (p. 66).

IT'S BEAN GREAT HEARING YOU!

Children practice listening to one another using the bean-filled tambourines they have made.

●●●●●●●●●●●●●●●●●●●●

Age:	5–10
Activity Type:	Getting to Know You
Activity Level:	Moderate
Space:	Any
Concentration Level:	High
Time :	15 minutes
Group Size:	Any
Prerequisite:	"Making Bean Tambourines" (p. 138)

MATERIALS

❖ Bean Tambourines, from "Making Bean Tambourines" (p. 138).

SUGGESTED PROCEDURE

1. Gather with the children in a circle.

2. Tell the children following the rules.

   ❖ Only the person who holds the bean tambourine may speak.

   ❖ Everyone else must listen quietly.

   ❖ If someone would like to respond or add something to what was said, they must make the "bean tambourine sign," which looks like a lower case "b" formed by placing the pointer finger and thumb together, with the other fingers pointing up.

   ❖ The speaker decides who can speak next by passing the bean tambourine.

   ❖ The next speaker begins her turn by saying, "It's *bean* great hearing from you," and addressing the previous speaker by name.

3. Tell the children the topic you would like to discuss and ask for a volunteer to begin. Play continues until the conversation has ended or time runs out.

REFLECTION

❖ Was it difficult to wait for your turn to speak?

❖ Was there ever a moment when you really wanted or needed to say something, but the person with the bean tambourine didn't pass the speaking responsibility on to you? How did that feel?

❖ When you are talking at other times, do you always wait for one person to finish talking before you say your idea? Why or

Use with Any Topic

You can use this speaking and listening game at any time, for any topic you need to discuss with your group. It may be particularly useful for making decisions where everyone's opinion needs to be heard.

why not? How do you know when it is okay to interrupt someone else? Is it ever okay?

❖ How did it feel to say, "It's bean great hearing from you"
all the time? Do we ever say anything like this in everyday
conversations? Should we? When or why?

NOTES

● ● ● ● ● ● ● ● ● ● ●

LISTENING ROLE PLAYS

Children practice listening and speaking skills by role-playing conflict situations.

Age:	8–12
Activity Type:	Drama
Activity Level:	Moderate
Space:	Any
Concentration Level:	High
Time:	15–20 minutes
Group Size:	5 or more
Prerequisite:	Listening skills work

MATERIALS

❖ Role-play Cards

SUGGESTED PROCEDURE

1. Ask for volunteers to role play a conflict that involves listening. Give the players the role-play cards and have them present the conflict. They should not show how the conflict is resolved. Stop the role play, discuss the conflict, and ask students to give the characters advice on how to be better listeners. Reflect with the children:

   ### Mini-Reflection

   ◆ What's the conflict here?

   ◆ How do they feel right now?

   ◆ How are they not being good listeners?

   ◆ How could they be better listeners? What could they do differently?

2. After a short discussion, have the role players continue, using the suggestions to help resolve the conflict. Have the players complete the role play, incorporating the suggestions from the class. The goal is to show how good listening can make a difference when solving problems. Encourage the students to talk from their own perspective. Suggest that they begin their sentences with the word "I."

REFLECTION

❖ How did the conflict change once the actors started listening to each other?

❖ What did they do to be better listeners?

❖ What difference did it make when the characters started with the word "I"?

Listening
Role Play Cards

Child 1 heard that Child 2 was making fun of her. Now Child 1 has decided she's not speaking to Child 2. Child 2 has just asked Child 1 if she wants to play.

Child 1 promised Child 2 he would join the drama club afterschool. Now Child 1 wants to play games in the gym instead.

Children 1 and 2 were making chocolate chip cookies. Child 1 wanted to stir in the chips. But when Child 1 went to get a towel, Child 2 stirred in the chips.

LISTENING FOR FEELINGS

Children practice listening for the emotional content of sentences.

Age:	8–12
Activity Type:	Drama
Activity Level:	Quiet
Space:	Any
Concentration Level:	High
Time :	20 minutes
Group Size:	Any
Prerequisite:	None

MATERIALS

❖ None

SUGGESTED PROCEDURE

1. Explain that when we listen to people in a conflict, we need to listen for two things. One is what they say. The other is how they feel about it.

2. Read the following sentences to the group and have them identify the feelings in the sentences. Explain that there can be more than one feeling at a time and that different people can have different feelings about the same thing.

   For ages 10 to 12:

   ❖ I just can't figure it out. I give up.

   ❖ Wow! Eight days until vacation!

   ❖ Will you be calling my parents?

   ❖ Look at the picture I drew.

   ❖ I can do this part by myself. I don't need your help.

   ❖ I guess it was pretty mean. I shouldn't have said it.

   For ages 7 to 9:

   ❖ I don't have any friends.

   ❖ She let me cut in line.

   ❖ The teacher said we should share.

   ❖ I got here first.

   ❖ That's mine!

   ❖ No one will play with me.

   ❖ I don't want to. It's dark in there.

3. Have volunteers say and act out the sentences in a way that communicates the feeling. When each volunteer is finished, ask if someone has a different way to say the sentence.

REFLECTION

❖ What makes it easy or hard to identify the feelings in these sentences?

❖ How do people's feelings affect their behavior in conflicts?

NOTES

● ● ● ● ● ● ● ● ● ● ● ●

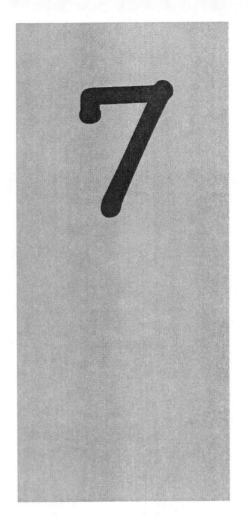

Expressing Feelings

Helping children understand and discuss their feelings related to conflict and other situations

There are always feelings in any conflict. Anger is the feeling usually identified with conflict, but most conflicts involve a whole range of feelings, from fear and frustration to anger and remorse. When people are in a conflict that is escalating, their feelings escalate as well. And people in conflict are more likely to act based on their feelings than reason. The activities in this chapter are designed to help children identify their feelings and express them in ways that are constructive, rather than destructive and hurtful.

There are four types of activities in this chapter:

1. Emotional Skill Building

2. Group Trust and Emotional Safety

3. Expanding Feeling Vocabularies

4. Expressing and Managing Anger

One way to reduce conflict in a program is to increase the feeling of trust and emotional safety. In addition to the activities on Group Trust and Emotional Safety included here, you may want to start with activities from the other chapters, particularly *Cooperation*. Also look at the "Ground Work" suggestions in Chapter 2.

The skill-building activities that follow are designed to help you enrich children's feeling vocabularies and introduce the basics of anger management.

Using Teachable Moments

❖ Make a feeling chart as recommended in the emotional skill-building activity "Creating a Feelings Chart" (p. 148). Post this chart where it is easily seen. If you have several rooms, make one for each room. Use the chart to help children name their feelings as they participate in activities. For example, if you are dealing with a conflict, ask, "How do you feel right now?" or "Is there a word on the chart that describes how you feel?" These questions need not be limited to conflicts, however. You can stop in the middle of a game and ask the same questions.

❖ When there's a conflict, always ask children how they feel. This reinforces the understanding that feelings are an integral part of any conflict situation.

❖ Don't force children to talk about feelings. If they don't respond to your prompting questions, don't worry about it.

❖ Supply words for feelings when the children lack them, but do so in a way that is respectful of those feelings. For example, try saying, "Would 'frustrated' be a good word to describe how you feel?" or "It sounds to me like you are outraged about this. Is that right?"

❖ Point out when children are expressing anger and other feelings in appropriate ways. For example, you might say, "I know you're angry, and I like the way you told her that without yelling at her."

❖ Have anger management procedures and skills in place before you need them. If you want children to use cool-off techniques, for example, teach them before you are breaking up a fight between two angry children. But do refer to and help children use anger management in actual conflict situations. For example, say, "I'm going to ask you what happened in this situation, but first I want you to cool off by taking three slow breaths."

❖ One way to encourage children to talk about their feelings is to do it yourself. Start by talking in a matter-of-fact way about your own feelings about various events and activities in the day. Your goal is both to model the use of affective vocabulary and to give children permission to talk about their feelings. Take advantage of opportunities to model use of affective vocabulary.

❖ As you go through the day, ask children how they feel about different events and activities. Encourage them to go beyond "I feel good about it," and "I like it," neither of which is really affective. Asking children how they feel doesn't have to be artificial or invasive. Try to ask about feelings in a way that is natural and matter-of-fact. You're simply acknowledging that most aspects of daily life have a feeling component.

❖ For group meetings try doing a "Feelings Check-In." Simply go around the circle with children saying how they feel at that moment. If children are stuck for words, make some suggestions from the feelings chart.

Emotional Skill Building

Age:	5–12
Activity Type:	Chart
Activity Level:	Quiet
Space:	Any
Concentration Level:	Low
Time:	20 minutes
Group Size:	2 or more
Prerequisite:	None

TIP!

Post Your Feelings Chart

A Feelings Chart is a very useful thing to have posted prominently in the program space. This activity is a very structured and instructional way to develop this chart with the children in your program. If this type of activity doesn't fit your program style, one alternative is to have adults in the program make a Feelings Chart and post it. Children will get used to using it as they see and hear adults use it.

CREATING A FEELINGS CHART

Children create a chart of feeling words for later reference.

● ● ● ● ● ● ● ● ● ● ● ● ● ● ● ● ● ●

MATERIALS

❖ 4" x 6" index cards

❖ Chart paper (blocked with headings for each letter of the alphabet)

SUGGESTED PROCEDURE

1. Explain that the group will be making a Feelings Chart to be posted in the program area. Have the children brainstorm feeling words. Write or have a volunteer write each word on an index card.

2. When the group has at least ten words, organize the words alphabetically. You can do this with the group or have volunteers do it. (With young children, simply alphabetize the words yourself.) Record the words alphabetically on the chart paper under the appropriate letter labels.

3. Expand the chart by reading the following sentences and having volunteers identify the feeling for the particular "trigger":

   ❖ When someone pushes me, I feel _____ .

   ❖ When I make a mistake, I feel _____ .

   ❖ When I do a good job, I feel _____ .

   ❖ When I help someone and they say thanks, I feel _____ .

   ❖ When someone calls me a name, I feel _____ .

   ❖ When someone won't share with me, I feel _____ .

   ❖ When someone will share with me, I feel _____ .

   ❖ When someone smiles at me, I feel _____ .

   ❖ When I get a snack I didn't expect, I feel _____ .

4. Refer to the chart often during the program day. Use and add to the chart to help children name their feelings. To add to the chart suggest more feeling words and ask children to bring in words (e.g., if there are no words under "S," ask the children for possible contributions.).

REFLECTION

❖ Which feeling words do you hear most often?

❖ Which words were brand new to you?

NOTES

● ● ● ● ● ● ● ● ● ● ●

Age:	5–12
Activity Type:	Chart
Activity Level:	Quiet
Space:	Any
Concentration Level:	Medium
Time:	15 minutes
Group Size:	Any
Prerequisite:	None

THE ANGER THERMOMETER

Children learn a metaphor to help them identify how angry they are in specific situations.

● ● ● ● ● ● ● ● ● ● ● ● ● ● ● ● ● ● ●

MATERIALS

❖ Anger Thermometer Chart (based on the model on page 152).

❖ Thermometer

SUGGESTED PROCEDURE

1. Show a thermometer to the group and ask children to describe what a thermometer does. *Ask,* "What happens to the thermometer when the air gets hotter?"

2. Show the Anger Thermometer and explain that when people get angry, it's as if they get hotter. Their anger can be measured on this Anger Thermometer. Review each term on the Anger Thermometer and discuss its meaning.

3. Discuss how different triggers lead to different degrees of anger by reading the following set of questions aloud. As students name their feelings, point to the appropriate word(s) on the Anger Thermometer.

How would you feel if:

❖ someone took something that belonged to you?

❖ someone smooshed your snack?

❖ someone kept bothering you while you tried to draw?

❖ someone called you a bad name?

❖ a boy on the bus said, "You can't sit here. I own this seat"?

❖ a girl in the hall said, "You little children should go to a daycare center instead of after-school"?

❖ you want to swing but the children who are on the swings won't get off?

❖ you see some children picking on a new child in our group?

Post Your Anger Thermometer

The Anger Thermometer is another chart that is very useful to have posted prominently in the program space. When children are angry, it gives them a way to talk about that anger by saying where they are on the Anger Thermometer. This activity is a very structured and instructional way to introduce the Anger Thermometer to the children in your program. If this type of activity doesn't fit your program style, an alternative is simply to post the chart and begin referring to it when children are angry. Children will get used to using it as they see and hear adults use it.

REFLECTION

- ❖ What things make you angriest?

- ❖ What word on the Anger Thermometer describes how angry you get?

- ❖ What things didn't bother you that much?

- ❖ What word on the Anger Thermometer describes those feelings?

- ❖ What can you do to cool off if you are "hot" on the Anger Thermometer?

FOLLOW-UP IDEA

Children sometimes enjoy making their own Anger Thermometers. Have them copy the pattern on a piece of oak tag or other cardboard. Help them cut slits in the cardboard at the top and the bottom of the thermometer. For "mercury" in the thermometer, give each child a length of white ribbon that is of a width that fits comfortably into the slits cut in the cardboard. Have the children color half of the ribbon with a red marker and allow the ribbons to dry. Then thread the ribbon into the thermometer so that the white is at the top of the thermometer and the red is at the bottom by the bulb. By pulling on the white end of the ribbon, the red "mercury" will rise in the thermometer as the "Temper-ature" rises. By pulling on the red end, the "mercury" will lower and the temper will cool.

The Anger Thermometer

Enraged

Furious

Angry

Irritated

Annoyed

BALLOONING AND DRAINING*

Children are introduced to two simple techniques to help them cool off their anger.

Age:	5–12
Activity Type:	Drama
Activity Level:	Moderate
Space:	Any
Concentration Level:	Low
Time:	15 minutes
Group Size:	Any
Prerequisite:	"The Anger Thermometer" (p. 150)

MATERIALS

❖ None

SUGGESTED PROCEDURE

1. "Ballooning" is basically deep breathing. Have the children stand, then tell them to take slow (*not* deep) breaths and fill themselves up with air as if they were balloons. Then, they should slowly let the air out of the "balloons." Repeat a few times and have the children note how they feel.

2. "Draining" is consciously tensing and relaxing the muscles in the body. Again, have the children stand. Ask them to tighten all the muscles in their bodies and hold them tight until you say to let go. After a few seconds, say, "Now relax slowly and let all the anger drain out of you. Imagine a puddle of anger at your feet."

REFLECTION

❖ How did you feel when you finished ballooning/draining?

❖ When might you use them?

❖ How could you balloon or drain in a less obvious way?

* Adapted with permission from William J. Kreidler, *Creative Conflict Resolution* (Glenview, IL: Scott, Foresman and Company, 1984).

Group Trust
and
Emotional
Safety

I TRUST YOU, BUT...

With the help of spotters, children close their eyes and run toward a goal.

● ● ● ● ● ● ● ● ● ● ● ● ● ● ● ● ● ● ●

Age:	8–12
Activity Type:	Team challenge
Activity Level:	Very active
Space:	Large open space
Concentration Level:	High
Time:	20 minutes
Group Size:	12 or more
Prerequisite:	Previous teambuilding experience together

MATERIALS

❖ None

SET THE SCENE

Explain to the children, "As in all trust activities, the set-up of this is important. Being a spotter in this activity is a very important, serious job. Joking around or not paying attention is not acceptable." Be sure your group understands this and can commit to the serious nature of this activity before you try it.

SUGGESTED PROCEDURE

1. Ask for two volunteer runners. The runners will line up at one end of a boundary area. They will be jogging *slowly* across the boundary area with their eyes closed and their hands (palms out) in front of their chests.

2. Line the rest of the group up around the perimeter of the boundary area. For a boundary area the size of a basketball court, it is best to have four people down each side and four people across the end.

3. The role of the spotters is to keep the runners safe. Spotters hold their hands up in front of their chests. If a runner is coming towards them, the spotters meet their hands to the hands of the runner, thus telling the runner to stop.

4. Repeat with as many rounds as necessary to allow whoever wants to go a chance.

REFLECTION

Bring the group together in a sitting circle. Ask everyone to close their eyes. Allow one minute for each person to think of one emotion/feeling they had while playing this game. The feeling can be associated with being a spotter or a runner. Once everyone has had time to think, go around the group hearing responses.

❖ Follow up with questions about why the children had the feelings they had. Encourage the group to think about how

Safety Note

The spotters at the end of the boundary area will need to be alert as the runners will be jogging right at them. The spotters should move laterally to line themselves up with a runner. As the runner approaches, the spotter in line with the runner will hold up her hands to the runner's hands and the runner will stop. This is a trust activity and it is important to keep everyone safe. Remind the runners to jog *slowly*.

they feel in risky situations as compared with safe situations.

❖ How was running across the floor and trusting the spotter like expressing your feelings to someone?

NOTES
● ● ● ● ● ● ● ● ● ● ● ●

PASS THE CHICKEN

A tag game for introducing the idea of "asking for help."

● ● ● ● ● ● ● ● ● ● ● ● ● ● ● ● ● ●

Age:	5–12
Activity Type:	Tag game
Activity Level:	Very active
Space:	Large open space
Concentration Level:	Medium
Time:	10 minutes
Group Size:	10 or more
Prerequisite:	None

MATERIALS

❖ Five or six rubber chickens or substitute chickens (e.g. knotted towels, stuffed toys) – allow one bird per four players

❖ Boundary markers

SET THE SCENE

Say to the group, "To stay safe in this tag game, you'll need to be able to ask for a little help from your friends. This is a tag game, so remember, move carefully."

SUGGESTED PROCEDURE

1. Set out a boundary area. Allow a large open area so the group can do some running. Ask for two or three volunteers to be "it."

2. Like most tag games, the goal of the people who are "it" is to tag those who are "not it." The goal of those who are "not it" is to avoid being tagged.

3. Unlike most tag games, those "not it" have a strategy for helping each other. If a "not it" is holding a chicken, he or she cannot be tagged.

4. A player man not move with a chicken. Two players may not pass a bird back and forth – the bird must pass to a third player. To get a chicken, players should yell loudly "Pass me the bird!" (To encourage enthusiasm and fun, demonstrate calling wildly.)

REFLECTION

❖ What did we have to do to stay safe in this game? Let me hear it! … Pass the Bird!

❖ Sometimes we need to be able to ask for help. How can we ask for help when we are involved in a conflict? Who might we ask for help?

Expanding Feeling Vocabularies

FEELING COLLAGES

Children explore feeling words by creating collages.

● ● ● ● ● ● ● ● ● ● ● ● ● ● ● ● ●

Age:	5–12
Activity Type:	Arts and crafts
Activity Level:	Quiet
Space:	Work tables
Concentration Level:	Low
Time:	30 minutes
Group Size:	Any
Prerequisite:	Feeling vocabulary

MATERIALS

❖ Magazines

❖ Paste

❖ Scissors

❖ Paper

SUGGESTED PROCEDURE

1. Each child or group of children chooses a feeling word. They "write" the word on a piece of drawing paper by cutting the appropriate letters out of magazines and pasting them to the paper.

2. Have children illustrate the feeling by cutting out and pasting pictures that show faces expressing that feeling.

3. When the collages are finished, have children share them. Repeat the activity if there is time.

REFLECTION

❖ How did you decide which feeling words to illustrate?

❖ What words were easiest to illustrate?

Age: (5–7) 8–12

Activity Type: Drama

Activity Level: Moderate

Space: Any

Concentration Level: Medium

Time: 20 minutes

Group Size: 4 or more

Prerequisite: None

FEELING PANTOMIMES

Children act out feeling words.

MATERIALS

❖ Sheet or blanket

SUGGESTED PROCEDURE

1. Have the group stand and watch as you pantomime a feeling word. Ask them to mimic what you are doing, then guess what feeling you are miming. After you have done the first feeling, have a student volunteer come to the front of the room and mime another feeling, which the other students first mimic, then try to guess.

2. Vary the activity by asking for a volunteer who is willing to be covered with the sheet or blanket. Have the volunteer sit in a chair and cover his or her head and body with a sheet or blanket. Only the legs should show.

3. Whisper a feeling word into the volunteer's ear. He or she should pantomime the feelings you name using only his or her legs and feet.

REFLECTION

❖ What did you learn about feelings from the pantomime?

❖ How do feelings affect our bodies?

❖ What are some of the ways we know what other people are feeling?

 TIP!

For Younger Children

Younger children enjoy this activity even if they are not part of a drama club. It's a good way to loosen them up and introduce other feeling activities.

SPEEDY THREESOME

Three people together develop and practice gestures to represent different feelings.

● ● ● ● ● ● ● ● ● ● ● ● ● ● ● ● ●

Age:	(5–7) 8–12
Activity Type:	Circle game
Activity Level:	Active
Space:	Any
Concentration Level:	Medium
Time:	20 minutes
Group Size:	9–21
Prerequisite:	None

MATERIALS

❖ None

SUGGESTED PROCEDURE

1. With the entire group, develop a list of different feelings. The feelings may or may not be associated with conflict. Make the list as long as possible; think of it as an opportunity to introduce a larger vocabulary for feelings.

2. The idea behind this game is to demonstrate the body language that accompanies many feelings. Working from the list, have the children work together in groups of three to develop gestures that represent specific feelings. For example, love could be represented by three children hugging each other tightly, or sadness could be represented by the center child wiping her eyes while the children on the left and on the right lean way over like willows. Enjoy this part, the more dynamic the gestures are, the more fun they'll have. Remember, the gestures need to have three people.

3. Once the smaller groups have each created and named gestures for several different feelings, have the entire group form a circle. Stand in the center. Explain that when you point to the center person in a group of three they will form the gesture for the feeling you call out.

4. The three children must produce the gesture before you call out, "Speedy Threesome." After a few practice rounds announce that if they fail, you'll take the place of the center person and they'll go in the center. Continue in this manner as long as the group interest is high.

5. Bring the activity to a close by having the group link hands and take a deep bow. Tell them they've done a great job.

TIP!

For Younger Children

With younger children, choose three feelings. Develop gestures with the whole group, then practice them.

REFLECTION

Have everyone sit comfortably in a circle to talk about the game. Ask the students to recount the list of feelings and gestures they came up with and ask if they can think of new ones now. Point out that often a student may need the help of their peers in order to express himself or herself more effectively.

Also talk about the game:

❖ Was it difficult to work together to create the gestures?

❖ How did it feel when you had to go into the center?

❖ Were you part of a group that didn't make a gesture well? How did that feel?

NOTES

● ● ● ● ● ● ● ● ● ● ●

SING THAT TUNE

Children win points for singing two lines of a song that uses a "feeling word."

● ● ● ● ● ● ● ● ● ● ● ● ● ● ● ●

Age:	8–12
Activity Type:	Music
Activity Level:	Moderate
Space:	Any
Concentration Level:	Medium
Time:	30 minutes
Group Size:	6 or more
Prerequisite:	None

MATERIALS

❖ Paper and pencils (one for each group of three or four)

SUGGESTED PROCEDURE

1. Break the group into teams of three or four. Give each a team piece of paper and pencil.

2. Give each team ten minutes to brainstorm all the songs they know that use words that express feelings. In order to get points for the song, they must be able to sing two lines and identify the feeling word and what it means.

3. Once the ten-minute time limit is up, have the groups sit in a circle. Begin with one group. Have them name their song, sing the lines, and talk about the feeling words. For each song for which this is successfully accomplished, they earn a point. Once a song has been sung, no other group can use that song.

4. Move on to the second group, and so on, until there are no new songs.

5. The team with the most points wins.

REFLECTION

❖ What new feelings words did people learn?

❖ Was it hard/easy to find songs that expressed feelings? Why?

Age:	(5–7) 8–12
Activity Type:	Getting to Know You
Activity Level:	Moderate
Space:	Any
Concentration Level:	High
Time:	30 minutes
Group Size:	6 or more
Prerequisite:	Feelings vocabulary

WHAT IS THIS?

Children try to guess a feeling by touching an object while blindfolded.

● ● ● ● ● ● ● ● ● ● ● ● ● ● ● ● ● ●

MATERIALS

❖ Set of assorted materials and objects from which children can choose

❖ Feelings Cards

❖ Blindfolds (strips of old sheets or bandannas work well)

SUGGESTED PROCEDURE

1. Have each person find a partner.

2. Pass each person three Feelings Cards. Explain that they are to find something from the materials gathered to represent the feeling so that their partner, when blindfolded, will be able to identify it.

3. Give the children ten minutes to search for their objects.

4. Ask children to find their partners and a comfortable spot in the room. Once they are settled, begin with one partner blindfolding herself and feeling the other partner's objects. Have them guess which Feeling Cards their partner has.

5. Have the partners switch roles.

REFLECTION

This activity can be used to talk about the different ways we each define emotions. For one person, a ball of goop may be "scary"; for another this goop may be "comfortable." To one person "angry" may be a jagged, rough piece of wood. For another person "angry" may be a smooth and solid rock.

Begin by asking partners to share their objects and words.

Move on to talk about the "misunderstandings."

❖ Why weren't we always able to guess correctly?

❖ What makes it hard to guess how people are feeling?

❖ Is it easy to know how someone feels just because he tells you?

❖ What else might you ask to find out how someone is really feeling?

▼ **TIP!**

Feeling Cards

These cards can be purchased as a set or you can make your own. To make you own, use 4 x 6 index cards. Each card has a feeling word on it.

For Younger Children

Younger children will experience more success with this game if you limit the number of feeling words available to them. Also, it sometimes helps if you let the child who is trying to guess ask "yes" or "no" questions.

KING FROG

Children play a game with gestures that represent feelings about conflict and its resolution.

● ● ● ● ● ● ● ● ● ● ● ● ● ● ● ● ● ●

Age:	8–12
Activity Type:	Circle game
Activity Level:	Moderate
Space:	Any
Concentration Level:	High
Time:	30 minutes
Group Size:	8–12
Prerequisite:	None

MATERIALS

❖ None

SET THE SCENE

Say to the group, "Think of the many gestures or body positions that people make when they are involved in a conflict. Sometimes these are positive signs, like holding out a hand. Other times these are signs of frustration, like sticking out a tongue."

Demonstrate several gestures or positions and ask for more examples (two thumbs up, rolling your eyes, crossing your arms, offering a hand shake, etc.). "Can each of you go around and think of a gesture?"

SUGGESTED PROCEDURE

1. Sit with the group in a circle. Go around and have each child introduce their gesture. Encourage them to have very expressive signs. When everyone has introduced their sign, go around once more to practice signs. Tell them they must remember and be able to repeat everyone's sign.

2. As the leader, you are "King Frog." King Frog's sign is a fist punched into an open hand.

3. When you feel that everyone is comfortable with the signs, announce that the group will begin to talk to each other using only signs. Communication goes as follows: King Frog starts by making her own sign (a fist punched into an open hand), then the sign of someone else in the group. That person responds by first making their own sign, then the sign of someone else, and so on.

4. Allow the group a few rounds to practice.

5. The object of the game is to climb the ladder to the King Frog seat. The lowest seat is to The Frog's left and so on around the circle. If you make a mistake while communicating, you must move to the lowest seat. Everyone else shifts one seat to the left,

as well, and inherits the sign of the person whose seat they take. There are several ways to make a mistake:

❖ making the wrong sign;

❖ signing in the wrong sequence;

❖ creating a sign that doesn't exist;

❖ not responding when your sign is made;

❖ not responding quickly enough.

Once play begins there should be no talking.

This game will start off slowly, but as everyone catches on, it can move quite quickly. Play as long as you have time, ending it by crowning the person in the lowest seat as King Frog for next time.

REFLECTION

Take a moment to reflect on the gestures the group developed:

❖ Which ones were fun, or easier to make?

❖ Which did the group use the most, and why? Did the group make mainly positive or negative gestures?

❖ Are there other gestures that the group can think of now?

❖ Are there gestures that are both positive and negative?

Talk about playing the game as well:

❖ When you signed to someone else in the group, did you try to climb the ladder or did you stick with a sign that was comfortable for you?

❖ What were the advantages of the lowest seat? Of the highest?

FEELER SOUP

Children act out feelings, pretending to be ingredients in a "Feeler Soup."

● ● ● ● ● ● ● ● ● ● ● ● ● ● ● ● ● ● ●

Age:	(5–7) 8–10
Activity Type:	Drama
Activity Level:	Moderate
Space:	Large open space
Concentration Level:	Medium
Time:	20 minutes
Group Size:	15 or more
Prerequisite:	None

MATERIALS

❖ Alphabet Cards

❖ Feelings Cards

❖ Large circle of rope to form the soup pot

❖ Chart paper and markers

❖ Apron and chef's hat (optional)

SUGGESTED PROCEDURE

1. Tell the group you are going to cook a soup using feelings for ingredients. Have one child start as the cook by standing on a chair holding the Feelings Cards.

2. Give everyone an Alphabet Card (more than one each if the group is small) and tell them to press it against the top of their head without looking at it. Have them get into the soup pot (stand within the rope circle) and start "mingling around."

3. The cook calls out a feeling from one of the Feelings Cards, and the group acts it out spontaneously for a few seconds, all the while mingling in the soup pot.

4. After a few of rounds of this play, the cook reads out another word from a Feeling Card, holding it up for everyone to see.

5. The children then look at their letters and move together to spell the word as quickly as possible. Once they've spelled the word, everyone must act it out for a few seconds. A member of the group records the word on a pad of paper and play continues.

6. After play has created a list of several feelings words, bring the group together to go over each one to make sure the group has a clear understanding of each word. Ask them to come up with a definition, and then have them act it out briefly or give an example of when they felt that way.

For Younger Children

With younger children, omit the spelling aspect of the game if you think it will be too challenging for them, and instead simply do the pantomime.

REFLECTION

❖ Why is it important to know how you feel when you are in a conflict?

❖ What were some of the actions you used to express the feelings? Why?

❖ How were your actions unique? How were they similar to others?

NOTES

● ● ● ● ● ● ● ● ● ● ●

SAVE AN EGG

Children build a device to allow an egg to fall eight feet without breaking.

● ● ● ● ● ● ● ● ● ● ● ● ● ● ● ● ● ●

Age:	8–12
Activity Type:	Team challenge
Activity Level:	Moderate
Space:	Any
Concentration Level:	High
Time:	30 minutes
Group Size:	4 or more
Prerequisite:	None

MATERIALS

❖ Chair

❖ Drop cloth (or large piece of plastic)

Per team of four students:

❖ One egg

❖ 25 straws

❖ Six feet of masking tape

❖ One poster-size sheet of paper

❖ Colored markers

SUGGESTED PROCEDURE

1. Break the group into teams of four, with each team finding their own space in the room.

2. When everyone is quiet and settled, *explain the directions*, " Each one of you is going to be given your group 'feelings.' Remember what we have learned about feelings. Feelings are delicate. Feelings need to be taken care of. Feelings are sometimes hard to protect."

3. Pass one egg to each group, *saying*, "We have been learning how to express our feelings during a conflict. This is not always easy. We have learned some strategies. I want each group to think about what we need to do to keep our feelings (hold up the egg) safe, because our feelings are going to encounter a conflict."

4. Each team has twenty five minutes to create a device that will keep their egg safe when dropped eight feet. They may draw only from their set of supplied resources (25 straws and six feet of masking tape).

5. Each team must also prepare a three-minute ad for their egg-saver device to be aired on prime time during this afterschool program. The ad must explain what the straws represent. For example, "Our straws are going to keep our feelings safe

because they are willing to listen." Encourage the group to be creative in their presentation – a skit, a poster, whatever! Any resources available in the room may be used for the presentation.

6. While the group is working, set up a chair with a large plastic covering on the floor beneath. This is where you will drop the eggs.

7. Once the group is finished working, come back together in a large group. Have one group at a time present their advertisement and then stand on the chair to drop their egg.

REFLECTION

This activity relies on the use of metaphor. The egg represents feelings. The straws represent strategies for keeping our feelings safe during a conflict. This activity can teach many points – communication, cooperation, problem solving, etc.

❖ What challenges did you face in keeping your eggs safe (e.g., lack of resources, needing to work together)? What makes it hard to keep our feelings safe during a conflict or argument?

❖ How were you able to keep your egg safe? If you didn't keep your egg safe, what might you try next time? What can you do to keep your feelings safe during a conflict?

❖ What would a safe conflict look like? What would a safe conflict sound like?

FEELINGS RELAY

Teams compete to act out the most Feelings Cards.

● ● ● ● ● ● ● ● ● ● ● ● ● ● ● ● ●

Age:	5–12
Activity Type:	Tag game
Activity Level:	Very active
Space:	Large open space
Concentration Level:	High
Time:	20 minutes
Group Size:	8 or more
Prerequisite:	None

MATERIALS

❖ Feelings Cards (five cards per group, or one per person)

SUGGESTED PROCEDURE

1. Divide the group into teams of four or five. Have each group stand at equal distances away from you. Explain that each team will be shown a set of Feelings Cards. They must discover what these cards are by having one person in the group act out the feeling on their card for the others. No talking will be allowed. The first group to guess all their cards wins.

2. The group then sets up an order they will act in so that each person in the group gets a chance to act.

3. When everyone is ready, say "go." One person from each team runs to you and gets a card. They then read the card and leave it on the floor by your feet, returning to their group to act out the feeling for the group. Once the group guesses the feeling correctly, a new group member can come to you for a new card. This relay continues until one team guesses five feelings, or until each person's card has been guessed.

Note: If a group gets really stuck on a word or the person acting does not know what the word is, pull that card out and substitute a new one.

REFLECTION

❖ Think of a time when you couldn't describe how you felt. What happened?

❖ To whom were you trying to describe how you felt?

❖ How did you eventually resolve the conflict?

Age:	5–12
Activity Type:	Chart
Activity Level:	Quiet
Space:	Any
Concentration Level:	Medium
Time:	15 minutes
Group Size:	Any
Prerequisite:	Completion of an activity

REFLECTING ON FEELINGS

Feelings Cards are used to reflect on any activity in this chapter.

● ● ● ● ● ● ● ● ● ● ● ● ● ● ● ● ●

MATERIALS

❖ Feelings Cards

SUGGESTED PROCEDURE

1. Upon completion of an activity, ask the group to form a circle. Place a set of Feelings Cards in the center of a circle.

2. Give the children five minutes to each find three cards that represent how they felt at the beginning of the activity, how they felt at some point in the middle, and how they feel now. For younger groups, have each child choose only one card.

3. Once each person has their cards, go around the group. Allow each person to share their cards and say why they chose each card.

REFLECTION

As the group is sharing, look for common themes or interesting comments. Return to these themes or comments once each person has shared their ideas.

HOW DID IT FEEL?

Children use Feelings Cards to describe any role play.

Age:	6–12
Activity Type:	Drama
Activity Level:	Quiet
Space:	Any
Concentration Level:	Medium
Time:	20 minutes
Group Size:	Any
Prerequisite:	Use with a role play

MATERIALS

❖ Feelings Cards

SUGGESTED PROCEDURE

1. After observing a role play, divide students into teams of three or four.

2. Give each team a set of 15 Feelings Cards.

3. They must develop a set of cards to describe how each "actor" in the role play felt at (1) the beginning, (2) the middle, and (3) the end.

4. Students may trade cards with other groups if they see a card they need or want.

5. Ask each group to present their cards to the group and describe why they chose their particular cards.

REFLECTION

❖ What happened in the role play that made the group choose a particular feeling?

❖ Where in the role play did the feelings change? Why? What exactly was said to cause the feelings to change?

Age:	5–10
Activity Type:	Arts and crafts
Activity Level:	Moderate
Space:	Work tables
Concentration Level:	Low
Time:	30 minutes
Group Size:	Any
Prerequisite:	None

MASKING OUR FEELINGS

Children make masks to illustrate a range of feelings.

● ● ● ● ● ● ● ● ● ● ● ● ● ● ● ● ● ●

MATERIALS

- ❖ Construction paper
- ❖ Markers
- ❖ Felt and other scraps of material
- ❖ Glue and clear tape
- ❖ Yarn, string, or ribbon

SUGGESTED PROCEDURE

1. Ask students to think of as many different feelings as they can. Make a list.

2. Have students pick one feeling and create a mask that shows what this feeling looks like using the materials provided. Encourage students within the group to pick a variety of feelings.

REFLECTION

- ❖ How did you choose what to put on your mask?
- ❖ Did you think of a time when you felt the feeling you chose?
- ❖ Did you picture what someone looks like when they feel that way?
- ❖ Did you choose certain colors to mean something?
- ❖ Do you ever "wear a mask" that *doesn't* show what you are feeling?
- ❖ When and why might people do this?

EMOTION MOTIONS

Children silently act out an emotion using the mask they developed in "Masking Our Feelings."

● ● ● ● ● ● ● ● ● ● ● ● ● ● ● ● ● ●

Age:	5–10
Activity Type:	Drama
Activity Level:	Active
Space:	Any
Concentration Level:	Medium
Time:	25 minutes
Group Size:	Any
Prerequisite:	"Masking Our Feelings" (p. 174)

MATERIALS

❖ Masks from "Masking Our Feelings" (p. 174)

SUGGESTED PROCEDURE

1. Wearing the masks they created for "Masking Our Feelings," ask students to act out silently the feelings for the group, using only "emotion motions" (no talking or other sounds).

2. Have the other children guess what feeling each student's mask represents.

3. Hang the masks on the wall to use in future role plays, games, and discussions.

REFLECTION

❖ How did you guess which feeling other students were acting out? Which gave you the biggest hint: their masks or the way they moved?

❖ Describe how you came to portray your feeling the way you did. Did you think of a time when you felt like that? What else influenced your performance?

❖ In what ways can our body language communicate our feelings? Describe a time when you knew how someone was feeling, even though she didn't tell you directly.

Age: 5–10

Activity Type: Arts and crafts

Activity Level: Moderate

Space: Work tables

Concentration Level: Medium

Time: 60 minutes

Group Size: Any

Prerequisite: None

MOOD GLASSES

Children create eyeglasses to represent different emotional moods.

● ● ● ● ● ● ● ● ● ● ● ● ● ● ● ● ●

MATERIALS

❖ Pipe cleaners

❖ Cardboard

❖ Feathers, glitter, yarn, material scraps

❖ Markers, paint, crayons

❖ Glue, scissors

❖ Mood Glasses pattern (p. 177)

SUGGESTED PROCEDURE

1. Make the forms for the Mood Glasses ahead of time by tracing the pattern onto cardboard and cutting the shape out. Make enough forms for every child in your group.

2. Explain to the children that they will be making Mood Glasses, magic eyeglasses that make the person who wears them feel a certain way. Each student will make one pair, and everyone will choose his or her own emotion to represent.

3. Brainstorm a list of many different feelings. If you have already done the "Masking Our Feelings" activity, you may want to return to the list you generated on that day or look at the masks that the children made for ideas. Try to get a varied list of emotions.

4. Have each child choose an emotion which they will express with their Mood Glasses.

5. Each child makes Mood Glasses by decorating a cardboard form with whatever arts and crafts supplies you have available. Encourage the children to think about creative ways to express the emotion they have chosen, using color, form, and pattern. Have everyone label their Mood Glasses with the word for their emotion.

6. Display the glasses in the room. Use them in future activities as a concrete way to discuss different feelings and how our moods affect our actions.

REFLECTION

❖ Can you think of times in your life when you have felt like you
were wearing the Mood Glasses that you made today? How
did you feel? What made you feel that way?

Mood Glasses
Pattern

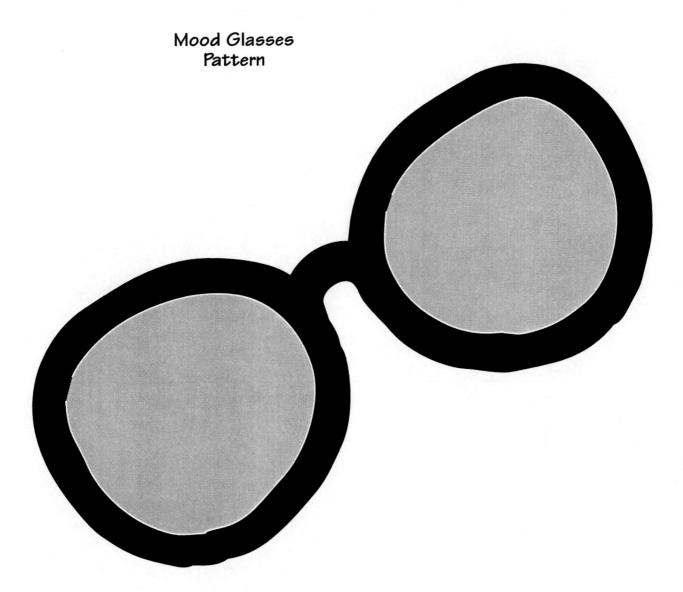

Age:	5–10
Activity Type:	Drama
Activity Level:	Moderate
Space:	Any
Concentration Level:	Medium
Time:	20 minutes
Group Size:	Any
Prerequisite:	"Mood Glasses" (p. 176)

IT DEPENDS ON HOW YOU LOOK AT IT

Using decorated Mood Glasses, students play act responses to different scenarios.

● ● ● ● ● ● ● ● ● ● ● ● ● ● ● ● ●

MATERIALS

❖ Mood Glasses (see p. 176)

SUGGESTED PROCEDURE

1. Introduce the activity by discussing how our emotions affect the way that we act. Ask the students for examples from their own lives when their mood made them react to a situation in a certain way.

2. Display the Mood Glasses that the children made, giving everyone a chance to look at all of them and ask questions about emotions with which they may not be familiar.

3. Explain that the children will use the Mood Glasses to demonstrate a person's emotional reaction to a situation. Ask for a volunteer to be the first Mood Glasses model. Explain that you will describe a situation, and the volunteer will act out how she would react to the situation, using three different sets of Mood Glasses.

4. Suggest situations to the actor which could be acted out in many different ways, such as, "You just remembered that to–day is your friend's birthday," or "Your mom just told you that she's going to have a baby," or "You have just found a stray cat at your window."

5. Have the audience members take turns choosing which Mood Glasses the actor will use for a particular skit.

6. Rotate the roles of actor and choice of the Mood Glasses, so that everyone gets a chance to participate.

▼ **TIP!**

Checking in on Feelings

Reinforce feelings vocabulary by creating Feeling Slots. Have each child write his or her name on a tongue depressor, popsicle stick, or cardboard strip. Collect five or six coffee cans or empty milk cartons. Label each can or carton with a feeling word: happy, sad, angry, lonely, contented, satisfied, proud. At the beginning of the program day, have children put their names into the can that represents how they feel. Repeat after lunch, at the end of the day, and at any other time you choose.

REFLECTION

❖ If you were an actor, how did you decide to act out the different feelings? Did you think about a time when you felt angry, or sad, or happy, or crabby?

❖ What did you use to express the mood? Did you use your tone of voice, your body language, or certain words?

❖ What clues tell us how other people may be feeling?

❖ Why might it be important to be aware of our own feelings and moods? Why might we want to be aware of how other people with whom we interact are feeling?

NOTES

● ● ● ● ● ● ● ● ● ● ●

Expressing and Managing Anger

SCULPTOR, MODEL, & CLAY

One student is a blindfolded sculptor who must try to place a second student (the clay) in the same position as a third (the model).

Age:	5–7 (8–12)
Activity Type:	Drama
Activity Level:	Active
Space:	Large open space
Concentration Level:	Medium
Time:	20 minutes
Group Size:	9 or 12
Prerequisite:	None

MATERIALS

❖ Blindfolds

SET THE SCENE

Explain to the group, "When you get angry, how do you show it with your body? Let's come up with some body movements that the whole group can do." Spend some time developing different anger gestures and practicing them. Ask the group to think of ones that they've seen other people do as well. "If you can recognize these gestures, you might be able to know when someone is angry just by how they look."

SUGGESTED PROCEDURE

1. After you've created several anger gestures, have the children break into groups of three. Give them one blindfold per group.

2. Explain that one person will be the blindfolded sculptor, one person will be the clay, and one person will be the model. Since we've been practicing looking for anger gestures, the model will pick an anger gesture and hold that pose. The blindfolded sculptor will use her hands to figure out the pose of the model and shape the clay into the same shape as the model.

3. Explain that the clay and model will have to be patient while the sculptor works. They will each have a turn at each role.

REFLECTION

Gather the children together to talk about the different roles in the activity, as well as their new vocabulary of anger gestures.

❖ What was the most difficult for you to be: the clay, the model, or the sculptor? Why?

❖ Do you think you can recognize anger gestures more easily now? What were some of the ones we came up with today? Are there any more that you can think of?

Safety Note

Talk to the children about being gentle when touching the model and clay. Tell the children it is all right if a child doesn't feel comfortable in one of the roles. They can be an observer for this activity.

 TIP!

For Older Children

Older children may find this game too "babyish" and may be more uncomfortable with the touching aspect than younger children. It varies depending on the group, so use your knowledge of the group and, if necessary, substitute another feelings activity, giving it an anger slant.

Age:	6–12
Activity Type:	Circle game
Activity Level:	Active
Space:	Large open space
Concentration Level:	Medium
Time:	20 minutes
Group Size:	6 or more
Prerequisite:	None

GROUP ANGER JUGGLE

The group tries to juggle several objects labeled with different anger feelings.

●●●●●●●●●●●●●●●●●●●●

MATERIALS

❖ More tossable objects than there are group members (soft balls, soft toys, rings, wads of paper – make them varied and humorous)

❖ Tape

❖ Markers

❖ Large pad of paper

SET THE SCENE

Ask the students, "What are the words we use to describe how we feel when we're in a conflict with someone? Let's spend a few minutes coming up with as many different words as we can."

SUGGESTED PROCEDURE

1. Gather the group into a circle and begin to generate a long list of different anger words. If the group branches off into other feelings they associate with conflict, write those words as well. The idea is to see what kind of vocabulary the group has for their anger feelings and to give them new words to use.

2. When the list is long, hand everyone an object and have them choose a word with which to label it. They may choose a word from the list or one of their own. Give them tape and markers to write their words.

3. Now you are ready to begin juggling. Divide the group into smaller groups of six to ten children. Take all the words/objects and have each group stand in a circle. Give each group one object. One person begins by tossing the ball to a second person. That person now throws to a third. This continues until everyone has had the ball once. They must toss it to a person across the circle from them who has not yet had it, until everyone has had the object once.

4. Ask each person to remember who they threw to and who threw them the ball. Have the group repeat the pattern and each person says the name on the object as they toss it.

5. Begin the sequence again, this time adding a second object shortly after the first. With each new object that you add, say that word as you toss it.

6. If the group drops an object they must start over. After you've had a few objects in play, suggest a goal and encourage the group to beat it.

7. If you find that you have a few extra minutes at the end, try this variation. Ask the group to reverse the pattern! In other words, toss the ball to the person from whom you were receiving it.

REFLECTION

When the group reaches its goal or time grows short, have the children pair off and spend a few minutes talking about two words from the list. Ask them to make sure they are clear on what each word means by checking with each other. Then have them return to the circle and share their definitions.

In closing, explain how being able to communicate exactly how you feel can help in a conflict.

NOTES

● ● ● ● ● ● ● ● ● ● ●

Age: 5–10

Activity Type: Drama

Activity Level: Moderate

Space: Any

Concentration Level: Medium

Time: 25 minutes

Group Size: Any

Prerequisite: None

THE ANGER SUIT

Children wear an old suit to act out what it looks and feels like to be angry.

● ● ● ● ● ● ● ● ● ● ● ● ● ● ● ● ●

MATERIALS

❖ Old suit (or dress, or T-shirt)

❖ Chart paper and markers (optional)

SUGGESTED PROCEDURE

1. Explain that the first step in learning how to control anger is being able to identify it when we see or feel it.

2. Hold up the Anger Suit and explain that a tailor friend of yours made this suit especially for this group. *Explain to the group,* "This suit makes the person who wears it act very, very angry. We will use it to help each other learn to recognize some of the clues that show other people are angry and some techniques to use to help other people and ourselves calm down when we're feeling angry."

3. Ask for a volunteer to try on the Anger Suit. Warn him or her that it may feel strange at first, to be so angry with no apparent reason. You may need to pull the volunteer aside to prompt her to really exaggerate the emotion.

4. Ask the audience to suggest something that might happen to the volunteer to make her angry. Ask the volunteer to show the group how she might react to that situation in a really angry way.

   Optional: Draw three columns on a piece of newsprint. At the top of the first column, write, "Anger looks like..." On the top of the second, write, "Anger sounds like..." And for the third column write, "Anger feels like..." Fill in the chart as a group, considering what the volunteer did, said, and felt like in the Anger Suit.

5. Hang the anger chart up, and store the Anger Suit for later use. Follow up with the "Hanging Up the Anger Suit" activity (p. 186).

REFLECTION

❖ Why might it be important to be able to tell what anger looks and sounds like?

❖ Why do we need to know how anger feels?

NOTES

● ● ● ● ● ● ● ● ● ● ● ●

Age: 5–10

Activity Type: Drama

Activity Level: Moderate

Space: Large open space

Concentration Level: Medium

Time: 30 minutes

Group Size: Any

Prerequisite: "The Anger Suit" (p. 184)

HANGING UP THE ANGER SUIT

The group tries to help someone wearing the Anger Suit calm down.

MATERIALS

❖ Anger Suit (p. 184)

❖ Chart paper and markers

SUGGESTED PROCEDURE

1. Have a volunteer wear the Anger Suit. Remind the group that this suit has magical powers and makes those who put it on instantly and intensely angry.

2. Review the anger chart that your group created in "The Anger Suit" activity (p. 184), identifying the way that anger looks, sounds, and feels.

3. Explain that the task for the group today is to help the volunteer who has put on the Anger Suit figure out how to get out of the suit and hang it back up. The only way that he can do this is by following the advice of the audience – anger management experts – who will each offer tips that can help him calm down.

4. You may need to help the "experts" come up with anger management techniques. You can do this by reminding them about how anger looks, sounds, and feels. For example, you might refer to the anger chart, where it says that "anger feels like...your heart is beating really fast" and suggest that taking deep, slow breaths will change this.

5. Make a list of the anger diffusion techniques that the group of experts develops. As they suggest things, have the volunteer act them out, slowly taking off the Anger Suit as he calms down, until he has taken it off, hung it up, and returned to normal.

6. Give other children a chance to try on and take off the Anger Suit as the experts suggest techniques from the list.

REFLECTION

❖ How did it feel to wear the Anger Suit? How did you feel when you were calming down?

❖ When might we need to remember the list of things to do to hang up the Anger Suit in our daily lives?

8

Appreciating Diversity

Reducing conflict by helping children see all types of differences as positive and valuable

All types of differences, not just racial and ethnic diversity, can lead to conflict. But this need not happen. Children can learn to appreciate human differences as enriching, not threatening. Research shows that if children are in an environment in which differences are actively appreciated, they will themselves be more appreciative of diversity. Similarly, the more children understand about prejudice and discrimination, the more they will be able to resist prejudice themselves.

There are four types of activities in this chapter:

1. Appreciating Diversity: Skill Building

2. Looking at Our Differences and Similarities

3. Exploring Other Cultures

4. Understanding Stereotyping, Prejudice, and Discrimination

Using Teachable Moments

❖ Assess your program space. There are a number of simple steps you can take to create a climate that affirms diversity. For example, check the materials in your program. When you use pictures for bulletin boards or for discussion starters, be sure they reflect a variety of cultures and skin colors. Include pictures showing disabled people performing everyday tasks.

❖ Review the children's books you have to be sure that they accurately represent different cultures. Check, too, to see if you have books that show women and men performing nontraditional jobs and tasks. Try to include books that depict all kinds of families. The goal here is not to eliminate books and materials that are more traditional in their depictions of American life, but rather to round out those depictions by providing a more diverse, more inclusive, and more accurate picture of our society.

❖ Look at the toys, play props, and manipulatives in your room. For example, have you integrated the doll corner with multiracial dolls? Does your housekeeping corner have chopsticks, clay pots, baskets, woks, etc. Do you include among your games some that are rooted in other cultures?

❖ Model an appreciation for diversity throughout the program day. As important as the environmental considerations are, don't neglect the importance of the example you set. Take opportunities to discuss similarities and differences among children. Help them see specific ways in which differences benefit the group. If children see that you appreciate diversity yourself, this both gives them permission to talk about differences and helps encourage their appreciation for diversity.

❖ Give children opportunities to share their uniqueness with the group as one way to affirm the values of diversity. But remember to point out commonalties as well as differences. Appreciating diversity is a balance between seeing what we have in common and showing how we are different.

❖ Deal with name-calling on several levels. Don't lecture or scold children, as this is more likely to lead to resentment than to change. Instead, try to help children come up with alternatives. For example, you might say, "In this program we don't call people racial names no matter how angry we are. What's another way you could have told her you were angry?"

❖ As a staff, have clear policies about name-calling and prejudiced remarks. Try to come to a general agreement about how everyone will handle such incidents when they occur.

❖ Challenge stereotypes and misconceptions about different cultures or groups when you hear children express them. Don't lecture, but do treat these as teachable moments. Sometimes children make these statements instead of asking questions, and sometimes stereotypical statements are a reflection of developmental levels. For example, a light-skinned child may say that dark-skinned children are dirty. He or she may be, in fact, asking if they are dirty. Or the child may be expressing confusion – rooted in the static thinking of this age group – about the permanence of some physical characteristics. You can challenge this stereotype by having children wash their hands and demonstrate that skin color doesn't wash off.

Appreciating Diversity: Skill Building

Age: (5–7) 8–12

Activity Type:: Getting to know you

Activity Level: Moderate

Space: Large open space

Concentration Level: Moderate

Time: 15–20 minutes

Group Size: 10 or more

Prerequisite: None

PICK YOUR CORNER

Children explore differences and similarities in the group by identifying groups to which they belong.

● ● ● ● ● ● ● ● ● ● ● ● ● ● ● ● ● ●

MATERIALS

❖ None

SUGGESTED PROCEDURE

1. Designate two corners of the room or sides of the gym as "belong to this group," and "don't belong to this group." Explain to the children that you will be reading statements to them and you want them to go to the appropriate corner, depending on whether they feel they belong or don't belong to the group mentioned.

2. Have the children stand. *Say*, "If you belong to the group that likes broccoli, move to this corner of the room. If you don't belong to that group, move to that corner of the room." As you speak, indicate the appropriate corners and have the children move.

Mini-Reflection

◆ What are some of the good things about belonging to this group?

◆ What are some of the disadvantages to not being part of the broccoli-liking group?

◆ What kind of conflict could occur between these two groups?

3. Continue the activity with other groups, such as:

❖ girls, not girls;

❖ tall, not tall;

❖ bike riders, not bike riders;

❖ Latino, not Latino;

❖ can tie own shoes, can't tie own shoes;

❖ brown eyes, not brown eyes;

❖ Catholic, not Catholic;

▼ TIP!

For Younger Children

Younger children enjoy this activity. It helps them become more comfortable talking about differences and commonalities.

❖ speak more than one language, don't speak more than one language;

❖ etc.

4. The groups you name can be as controversial or non-controversial as you wish, but try to present a mix of choices based on groups formed by choice, interests, personal tastes, ethnic and cultural group, etc.

REFLECTION

❖ How did you become a member of this group? Were you born into it?

❖ Did you choose to be a member?

❖ Did you learn something that made you a member?

❖ What could you learn from someone in another group?

❖ How could different groups be in conflict?

❖ How could they resolve those conflicts?

NOTES

● ● ● ● ● ● ● ● ● ● ●

Age: (5–7) 8–12

Activity Type: Chart

Activity Level: Moderate

Space: Any

Concentration Level: Moderate

Time: 15–20 minutes

Group Size: 10 or more

Prerequisite: None

EACH ONE TEACH ONE

Children identify the advantages of diversity by identifying things they can teach others.

● ● ● ● ● ● ● ● ● ● ● ● ● ● ● ● ● ●

MATERIALS

❖ Chart paper and markers

SUGGESTED PROCEDURE

Note: This activity may necessitate making some scheduling changes since the goal is to have children lead small group activities themselves. If you want to use this activity, decide how to best schedule and support children in teaching their activities.

1. Make a chart with each child's name listed. Next to the names make two columns, one labeled "I can teach" and another labeled "I want to learn." Show the chart to the group. Explain that there are many people in the group who have skills they could teach others.

2. Ask children to think of something they might teach to others in the group and to write that in the first column next to their names. It is helpful if, before you have this discussion with the class, you meet two or three children ahead of time and explain the chart to them. They can then act as models for the rest of the group. Also, there will be some children who need help in thinking of something they can teach to the other children.

3. Once the first column is filled in, children can read the chart and, if they find something they would like to learn, they should write their names in the second column, next to the skill being offered.

4. Once the chart is complete, have children look it over and reflect on it. Also, discuss with them how the activity scheduling will take place. Once children have been introduced to this activity, it can make a nice, ongoing component to your program for the rest of the year. (See **Tip**.)

TIP!

For Younger Children

Younger children may not seem to have much to offer in terms of teaching others. However, give them the opportunity to offer activities. They may be able to offer more than you expect!

Scheduling Child-led Activities

Use this activity to introduce child-led activities, as well as to affirm that everyone has something to offer. When children volunteer to teach something, first find out if anyone is interested in that activity. Then schedule the activity. Consider creating a weekly time slot and insist that the child-led activities be completed in one session.

REFLECTION

❖ Are there any surprises on this chart? Any talents you didn't know people had?

❖ Look at how different the offerings are. Why is that a nice thing for our program?

❖ What's something you have learned from people who are different from you?

NOTES

● ● ● ● ● ● ● ● ● ● ●

Age: 8–12

Activity Type: Storytelling

Activity Level: Moderate

Space: Any

Concentration Level: High

Time: 15–20 minutes

Group Size: 10 or more

Prerequisite: None

GREEN POISON DARTS

Using storytelling, children are helped to identify the hazards of name-calling.

MATERIALS

❖ Chart paper and a black marker and green crayon (or chalkboard with white chalk and green chalk)

SET THE SCENE

This story helps children see the effect of put downs on the afterschool community by comparing such remarks to "green poison." Draw seven circles with the black marker or white chalk, with dots for eyes.

SUGGESTED PROCEDURE

1. Discuss the meaning of the word "put downs," that is, remarks or comments about other people that make them feel bad, hurt, or like they are not worthwhile. Examples of put downs are name-calling, dissing, making fun of how others look, or the things they do. Ask for other slang words that mean "put downs," then explain that you'll be reading a story that describes how put downs can affect other people.

2. Read the following story to the class. As you do, use the green crayon or chalk to illustrate how the "green poison" is spreading. Color in the drawings with green at appropriate intervals in the story.

"One day Roger [point to one of the circles] was doing his math homework in afterschool and he was having a lot of trouble. He was getting really frustrated, and he started putting himself down. 'I'm so stupid,' he said to himself. 'I never get anything right.' He was so mad at himself, it was as if he filled up with a green poison. [Color in the Roger circle.] Maria, who sat next to him [point to another circle] asked, 'Hey Roger, can I borrow a pencil?'

'Shut your big mouth,' Roger said. 'I'm trying to work.' It was as if he shot a poison dart at Maria. [Draw a line from Roger to Maria.] Maria felt hurt, and she felt like she was filled with green poison. [Color in the Maria circle.] 'You shut up,' she said.

"Tanesha came up to Maria. 'Can you help me with this spelling?' she asked. Maria shot a green poison dart at Tanesha. 'You're so stupid, you always need help,' she said [draw a line from Maria to Tanesha], 'Do it yourself.' 'You're the stupid one,' said Tanesha. She filled up with green poison herself. [Color in the "Tanesha" circle.]

"Tanesha sat down. Two boys near her were talking to each other. Tanesha shot green poison darts at them. They filled up with green poison. [Draw lines from Tanesha to two new circles, then color these circles green.]

"Then they shot green poison darts at people by putting them down. They called names and said unkind things. Soon the whole group was filled with green poison and everyone was shooting green poison darts at each other over and over. [Draw more circles and color them in.]"

REFLECTION

❖ Have you ever been in a place that was filled with put downs?

❖ How did it feel to be there?

❖ Did you feel emotionally safe there? (If children have done emotional safety activities from Chapter 7, refer to those now.)

❖ The story compares put downs to green poison. What are some other ways to describe put downs?

❖ What can we do to keep our program free of put downs?

Looking at Our Differences and Similarities

HOOP DELIGHT

Children explore groups to which they belong by playing this "musical hoop" game.

● ● ● ● ● ● ● ● ● ● ● ● ● ● ● ● ● ● ●

Age:	5–10
Activity Type:	Getting to know you
Activity Level:	Very active
Space:	Large open space
Concentration Level:	Medium
Time:	15–20 minutes
Group Size:	10 or more
Prerequisite:	None

MATERIALS

❖ 10 hula hoops

❖ Cassette player; tape of fun, age-appropriate music

SET THE SCENE

Before the group arrives, you will need to set up a large circle of hoops. Allow six feet between hoops. *Say to the group:*

"Who here has played musical chairs? Well, we're all much too old for that, but this is a fun variation of musical chairs called Hoop Delight. To begin, I'd like everyone to find a hoop and take a seat. We'll need to have more than one person in some hoops.

"Hoop Delight is a game that will help us learn more about diversity. Does anyone here know what the word diversity means?" Spend a couple of minutes getting the children's ideas.

"There are many ways we are diverse – the way we look, the way we act, what we like, etc. We are going to call these our categories. Now we are ready to play."

SUGGESTED PROCEDURE

1. Ask the children to stand up in their hoops.

2. Once the music starts, the children will hop from hoop to hoop. When the music stops, everyone should stop where he or she is.

3. Once everyone has stopped, you (the facilitator) will yell out a category.

4. Children will find all the other people who are in the same category as they are and get in a hoop together before you turn the music back on.

5. Do several rounds.

6. Here are some possible categories:
   Height – find all the people that are within an inch of your height.
   Favorites – find all the people that have the same favorite sport, food, etc. as you.

Introduction to Diversity

Use this game as an introduction to diversity. It offers an active opportunity to get children thinking about how we are the same and how we are different.

Language – find all the people who speak the same language at home as you.

REFLECTION

Take a few moments at the end of the activity to talk about why understanding diversity is important.

❖ Why are we all so different? Talk about diversity categories we inherit such as our "looks" versus those we acquire. If we acquire them, where do they come from?

❖ How can diversity make our activities more fun? What would this activity have been like if we had no diversity? Are there other activities you have played or can think of which diversity has made more fun?

❖ How can diversity cause conflicts or misunderstandings?

NOTES

● ● ● ● ● ● ● ● ● ● ● ●

MY VERY OWN TREASURE MAP

Students individually create maps of their lives and then share them with the group.

Age:	11–12
Activity Type:	Arts and crafts
Activity Level:	Quiet
Space:	Work tables
Concentration Level:	Medium
Time:	30 minutes
Group Size:	Any
Prerequisite:	None

MATERIALS

- ❖ Construction paper
- ❖ Crayons, markers
- ❖ Pastels, water colors
- ❖ Pipe cleaners
- ❖ Ribbon, yarn
- ❖ Tissue paper
- ❖ Glue, tape

SUGGESTED PROCEDURE

1. Start by describing the project – creating treasure maps that describe our whole lives, up to this very moment, so that we can learn more about each other. Explain that each child will do his own map individually and that he can use any of the materials you have available. This will be like a treasure map, because the finished product will help someone else learn how you got to the treasure – YOU! Encourage students to include people, events, objects, places, or other things that have been important to them in their maps.

2. Have the children work individually on their maps for about 20 minutes.

3. Share your treasure maps with each other, explaining what you drew.

REFLECTION

- ❖ Was it hard to decide what to put in your map? How did you eventually decide? Was there anything you wanted to include but didn't? What was it and why did you leave it out?

- ❖ Did you learn anything new about someone in the group?

- ❖ Was your map similar to anyone else's in the group? Whose map was the most different from yours? What was different about it?

- ❖ What would you like your map to look like in five years? In ten years? In twenty years?

Age:	6–12
Activity Type:	Hunt game
Activity Level:	Moderate
Space:	Any
Concentration Level:	Medium
Time:	20 minutes
Group Size:	10 or more
Prerequisite:	None

THUMB HUNT

Children search the room for thumb prints of other children who meet specific criteria.

MATERIALS

❖ Several washable ink pads (Be sure they use *washable* ink.)

SET THE SCENE

Explain to the group, "Each one of us is born with many unique characteristics. One of these characteristics is our thumb print. No one thumb is like any other. In this activity, we are going to find the thumb prints of as many different people in the room as we can.

"In order to collect someone's thumb print, he or she must answer yes to one of the questions on the Thumb Hunt List."

SUGGESTED PROCEDURE

1. Create a list of questions to use as the Thumb Hunt List. These are questions that help the children to learn about each other. Be creative in developing this list. One way to structure the list is to offer a set of "I" statements. For example, "I like to eat with chop sticks." "I speak English at home."

2. Make one copy of the list for each child. When formatting the list, allow room for a thumb print next to each statement.

3. Ask each student to find people who can answer "yes" to any one of the statements. The goal is to try and get as many different thumb prints as possible.

REFLECTION

During the reflection time, talk about what the children learned about each other. Bring the group back together in a circle. Get everyone sitting comfortably.

Explain, "I am going to give you two minutes to think. I'd like to think of one thing you learned about someone today that you did not know. As soon as you know what it is, raise your hand."

Once everyone has an idea, go around the circle letting each person share his or her thought.

IF

Children share what they would be if they were a machine (or an animal, or a musical instrument).

Age:	8–12
Activity Type:	Getting to know you
Activity Level:	Quiet
Space:	Any
Concentration Level:	High
Time:	20 minutes
Group Size:	Any
Prerequisite:	None

MATERIALS

❖ None

SUGGESTED PROCEDURE

1. Have the group sit in a circle and explain that this game is called "If." The rules are very simple: you will ask a question, and everyone has a chance to give their personal answer. There are no right or wrong answers.

2. Questions can include things like, "If I were a *color*, I would be _____." Try other things too, like: animal, mood, type of food, musical instrument, toy, piece of furniture, smell, or song. Be creative!

3. For variety, have students answer the question for the person sitting on their left.

4. Watch out for put downs and cruel jokes here. This activity is ripe for teachable moments.

REFLECTION

❖ Did anybody's answers surprise you? Did you learn anything new about anyone?

❖ Was it difficult to answer these questions? Did you ever not want to say something because you were afraid of what other kids might say or think of you? Did you say that thing anyway? Why or why not?

❖ Was it easier to answer for someone else or for yourself? Why?

Age: 8–12

Activity Type: Team challenge

Activity Level: Quiet

Space: None

Concentration Level: High

Time: 20–30 minutes

Group Size: 6 or more

Prerequisite: None

COMMONALITIES

Small groups compete to find the most hidden commonalities.

● ● ● ● ● ● ● ● ● ● ● ● ● ● ● ● ●

MATERIALS

❖ One pencil and one piece of paper per team

SET THE SCENE

Divide the group into small teams with four or five children on each team.

Say to the children, "As you look at the other children in your group, what do you see that you have in common with them?" Allow for answers like – "we're both boys," "we have the same hair color," "we all have on yellow shirts," etc.

"So, as you have shown me, you have a lot of visible commonalties. In this game we are going to try and find out what our hidden commonalties are. A hidden commonality is something we have in common with someone that we cannot see. For example, we both live on Oak Street, or we both live with our grandparents."

SUGGESTED PROCEDURE

1. Give each team a piece of paper and a pencil.

2. Allow each team 15 minutes to find as many *hidden* commonalties as they can. A commonality is something two or more team members have in common.

3. Each team is trying to reach the highest score.

4. Points are awarded as follows – one point for a two-person commonality, two points for a descriptor common to three or four people, and three points for something common to the whole team.

REFLECTION

Once the time is up, have each team share their lists. Start with the threepoint commonalities. Ask groups to share what they think is their most unique or interesting commonality.

❖ What was one thing you had in common with someone in the group that surprised you? Go around the room and have each person answer.

NOTES

● ● ● ● ● ● ● ● ● ● ●

Age: 8–12

Activity Type: Getting to know you

Activity Level: Quiet

Space: Any

Concentration Level: High

Time: 20 minutes

Group Size: 5 or more

Prerequisite: None

PICTURE ME

Each child shares three things about themselves.

MATERIALS

❖ Paper and pencils, enough for each child

SUGGESTED PROCEDURE

1. Give each child a piece of paper and a pencil and have them move to a comfortable spot where they can write.

2. Tell them you want them to write down three things. The first should be something very important to them. The second is someone whom they like and who is important to them. The third is something about themselves.

3. When everyone has had a chance to complete their writing, have the group get up and start moving around in a small area.

4. After a few moments, ask them to stop and share something from their paper with another person, telling why they wrote it. Give them enough time to make a connection with that person, and then repeat the process.

5. This is a good way for a group to become more familiar with each other quickly.

REFLECTION

❖ Did you have anything in common with those with whom you shared? If so, what?

❖ What did you find interesting about the person(s) you spoke to?

FIND YOUR PLACE

A diversity version of the cooperative activity "Line Up." Children line up based on categories.

Age:	6–12
Activity Type:	Getting to know you
Activity Level:	Moderate
Space:	Any
Concentration Level:	Medium
Time:	20 minutes
Group Size:	10 or more
Prerequisite:	other line ups

MATERIALS

❖ None

SET THE SCENE

You will need to decide upon the line-up categories before the group arrives. The best categories allow children to line up along a spectrum: for example, from one to ten. Some possibilities include:

❖ number of siblings;

❖ number of years living in this community;

❖ first letter of middle name.

Tell the children, "This is a short activity that will help us to learn something new about each other. We will need to use our problem-solving skills because a strange flu has hit all of us and we can no longer speak!"

SUGGESTED PROCEDURE

1. Tell the group their task is to line up in order from X to Y (depending on the category you have chosen) without talking. Let them know where the beginning and end of the line will be.

2. Remind the group there should be no talking.

3. Allow five or ten minutes for the group to get in order.

4. Once an order has been established, check to make sure the line-up is correct. As you are doing the checking, encourage the children to share. For instance, if you are using number of years in the community as the category, ask, "Where did you live before you came here? When did you move?"

5. Repeat the activity with a new category.

TIP!

Use for Early Diversity Discussions

This activity is useful for the early stages of discussions about diversity. It is a quick and fun way to look at our many differences and to help children learn a little more about each other.

VARIATION

If you have a group that is really good at problem solving, try adding blindfolds. This will add to the time it takes to solve the problem. It will also require the children to touch each other.

REFLECTION

❖ Raise your hand if you learned something new about one of your groupmates. What did you learn?

NOTES

● ● ● ● ● ● ● ● ● ● ●

HAVE YOU EVER . . . ?

The group explores differences by shifting positions in response to questions.

● ● ● ● ● ● ● ● ● ● ● ● ● ● ● ● ●

Age:	5–7
Activity Type:	Getting to know you
Activity Level:	Moderate
Space:	Any
Concentration Level:	High
Time:	20 minutes
Group Size:	10 or more
Prerequisite:	None

MATERIALS

❖ One spot marker per person in the group (toys or rings work too)

SET THE SCENE

Ask the group, "Have you ever gone barefoot in the snow? Have you ever held your breath for twenty seconds or more? Have you ever driven a car? Have you ever held a bird on your finger? Have you ever cut your own hair? Your friend's hair? Have you ever worn your mother's clothes? Your father's? Have you ever eaten six donuts? Fifty eggs?"

SUGGESTED PROCEDURE

1. Gather the group into a circle. *Ask them,* "Have you ever been in a circle in this classroom?" Place a spot marker at the foot of each person (not including yourself) and explain that for the time being, this is their humble home.

2. This humble home is located on Have-You-Ever Avenue. The students should take a minute to meet their neighbors, by turning to each neighbor and saying, "Hello, Neighbor!" in the most welcoming way.

3. After meeting each other, the group is ready to begin play. Step into the center of the circle and ask your best "Have You Ever . . ." question. Everyone in the circle will respond either "yes" or "no." People answering "no" will stay at their humble home. Those answering "yes" must look for a new home on another part of the street (not just next door).

4. Having answered "yes" to your own question, you move into one of the empty homes. This will leave one child without a home for the time being. They remain in the center to ask the next "Have You Ever. . ." question.

5. Record the "Have You Ever" questions on a list to be used for subsequent activities.

TIP!

Facilitating Questions

If the questions become inappropriate or embarrassing, or if the group is stuck thinking of questions, move slowly enough on the next question that you are caught in the middle. Use this opportunity as facilitator to redirect the questioning.

REFLECTION

❖ How many different Humble Homes did you get to live in?

❖ Is there anyone who never moved?

❖ What were the questions to which everyone said "yes"?

NOTES

● ● ● ● ● ● ● ● ● ● ● ●

HAVE YOU EVER . . . ?
YES/NO ROPE

Teams answer "Have You Ever" questions.

Age:	8–12
Activity Type:	Team Challenge
Activity Level:	Moderate
Space:	Any
Concentration Level:	High
Time:	20 minutes
Group Size:	10 or more
Prerequisite:	"Have You Ever . . . ?" (p. 207)

MATERIALS

❖ Copies of the "Have You Ever" list (created in "Have You Ever . . . ?" on page 207)

❖ Pencils and paper for each team

❖ A length of rope to form a line on the ground

SUGGESTED PROCEDURE

1. Divide the group into smaller teams (of four or five children) and have them each settle into a corner.

2. Hand each group a list of "Have You Ever" questions and a pencil. During the next ten minutes they are to figure out how many people in their group can say "yes" to each question.

3. When the groups are finished finding out about their teams, have them generate a list of their own "Have You Ever" questions. At least one person must be able to answer "yes" to the questions.

4. After five minutes, collect the lists and move everyone to a central location. Lay down the Yes/No rope, explaining to the children which side is "yes" and which side is "no."

5. Read the lists the groups have written aloud and have the children cross the rope from the Yes to the No side depending on their response. Once they cross the rope they should greet at least two other people by shaking hands and saying, "Oh, how nice to see you!"

6. Close by having the entire group try to sit together inside a circle they make from the Yes/No rope.

REFLECTION

Keep the lists of "Have You Ever" questions for other days or grand competitions. Return to this game by seeing if there are any children who can answer "yes" to all or most of the questions. Speak to the group briefly about how diverse the group is, noticing all the different questions they came up with and reminding them that this is a strength and a resource of the group.

Age: 8–12

Activity Type: Getting to know you

Activity Level: Quiet

Space: Any

Concentration Level: High

Time: 30 minutes

Group Size: 5–12

Prerequisite: None

INTERVIEWING

Children use interviewing to discover more about each other.

● ● ● ● ● ● ● ● ● ● ● ● ● ● ● ● ●

MATERIALS

❖ Pencils and paper

SET THE SCENE

Explain to the group, "We are all individual people. Sometimes it may appear that we have nothing in common, while at other times we find that we share several experiences or feelings. We are going to spend time today interviewing each other to discover these similarities and differences."

SUGGESTED PROCEDURE

1. Gather the group into a circle and do a quick temperature check by asking everyone to state one word that tells how they felt as they were on their way there today.

2. Start the interviewing with a "safe" subject, for example, yourself! This may sound like a risky idea at first, but it will give the group a wonderful feeling of access to you, knowing that they can ask you questions just as you ask them.

3. If you feel the need to set up guidelines beforehand, spend a few moments with everyone working up a list of topics that the group wants to find out about each other. Options for focus include family (numbers of siblings, parents at home), cultural background, favorites (food, colors). Find more subjects listed in the "Have You Ever . . . ?" activities (p. 207).

4. Using these established subjects or letting the group follow their own curiosity, allow yourself to be interviewed for a period of time. After this, you can have the children interview each other or have them invite in someone to interview.

5. If you use this activity to interview everyone around a specific topic, take the time to record the range of answers and post them somewhere in the room.

Other Uses of Interviewing

Interviewing can be used repeatedly as a tool to discover how the group is feeling about a subject or to increase their awareness of each other. Once the group is familiar with interviewing, you may want to move to more difficult, personal, or controversial topics, depending on what the group can handle.

Follow-up Idea

If you have access to videotape equipment, these interviews can be followed up by conducting videotaped versions. Children can interview, on videotape, as many people as possible in the program. Once the video project is complete, have a premier showing of the tape.

REFLECTION

In closing, tell the group you are going to interview *them* for a moment.

❖ What things did they share in common? What were some differences they discovered?

Take the time to portray all the differences in a positive light, as another resource for the group.

NOTES

● ● ● ● ● ● ● ● ● ● ●

Age:	5–10
Activity Type:	Arts and crafts
Activity Level:	Moderate
Space:	Any
Concentration Level:	Moderate
Time:	15–20 minutes
Group Size:	4 or more
Prerequisite:	None

FAMILY BAG PROJECTS

Children explore differences by creating "bag projects" about their families.

● ● ● ● ● ● ● ● ● ● ● ● ● ● ● ● ● ●

MATERIALS

❖ Brown paper bags

❖ Crayons

❖ Collected objects

SUGGESTED PROCEDURE

1. Have the children create "bag projects" that represent their families. On the front of the bag have them draw pictures of their families. If the bags have printing on them, children can draw the pictures on drawing paper and paste the drawing to the front of the bag. Inside the bags they should place various objects representing aspects of their family life. Give the group three to five types of objects to collect. For example, they may collect objects representing:

   ❖ something your family likes to do together;

   ❖ a tradition in your family;

   ❖ a way you help your family;

   ❖ a trip your family took;

   ❖ a story that your family likes to read.

2. Give children a few days to work on their projects, then have them present their bag projects to the group. They should describe the picture on the front of the bag, then show each object and describe what aspect of their family's life it represents. As children present their bag projects, discuss how families can be very different, but they have many things in common.

REFLECTION

❖ How did your family develop its traditions?

❖ How are our families different?

❖ How are they the same?

TELL ME YOUR STORY

Children write short descriptions of a family tradition, then share them with the group.

● ● ● ● ● ● ● ● ● ● ● ● ● ● ● ● ● ● ●

Age:	8–12
Activity Type:	Team challenge
Activity Level:	Quiet
Space:	Any
Concentration Level:	Medium
Time:	40 minutes
Group Size:	6–15
Prerequisite:	None

MATERIALS

❖ Paper and pencil, one per person

❖ Basket, bowl, hat, etc. to collect the stories

SET THE SCENE

Say to the group, "I'd like each one of you to think of a special tradition that your family does. Sometimes family traditions are based on our cultural background. For example, many Irish-American people celebrate St. Patrick's Day by eating corned beef. Other family traditions are unique to families – how we celebrate birthdays or what happens when we lose a tooth.

"Once you have thought of your family tradition, write it down on your piece of paper. When you're done, fold up the paper and put it in this basket. Now we are going to divide into teams of three or four people each. Each team is going to try to 'win' other people by correctly guessing the author of each story."

SUGGESTED PROCEDURE

1. One team begins the game by picking a story from the basket. The team has two minutes to guess whose story it is.

Note: Tell children that if their group draws their own story, they must pretend it is not theirs. This adds to the fun.

2. If the team guesses correctly, they "win" this person to their team and get to draw a second story. The person whose story was guessed joins the team.

3. If the team guesses incorrectly, the story gets passed to the next group. The story continues to be passed around until someone guesses correctly.

4. The game ends when all the stories have been guessed. The team with the most people wins!

REFLECTION

Use this activity to build on children's understanding of cultural and family diversity. The reflection time for this activity can be brief, since as the stories are guessed, children typically share more.

Age:	8–12
Activity Type:	Hunt game
Activity Level:	Moderate
Space :	Any
Concentration Level:	high
Time:	45 minutes
Group Size:	5 or more
Prerequisite:	None

HUMAN BINGO

Students learn about the diversity in their group by finding others who answer certain questions differently from themselves.

● ● ● ● ● ● ● ● ● ● ● ● ● ● ● ● ●

MATERIALS

❖ Human Bingo card (see next page), one per person.

SUGGESTED PROCEDURE

1. Hand out a Human Bingo card to every person in the group and explain the rules of the game. Each person looks for someone who can answer the questions on the Human Bingo card differently from the way they would answer them. For example, if a child's response to the question "Do you come from a small family?" were yes, then he would need to find someone who would answer "no."

2. When you find someone whose answer does not match your own, have them sign their name in that box. The goal is to fill the entire card with people's names, without using any one person's name twice. If you have fewer than sixteen people in your group, you will need to change this rule, as there are sixteen different spaces on the card.

3. The first person who fills her card yells, "Human Bingo!" and reads her answers to the group, explaining how each person who signed is different from her.

REFLECTION

❖ Was it difficult or easy to find people in this room who are different from you?

❖ Were you surprised by anyone's answer?

❖ Does anyone think that it would be impossible to find people to answer every question differently than you would? (If yes, try to prove to that person that this can be done.)

Human Bingo Card

Make a BINGO (5 across, 5 down, or 5 diagonally) by interviewing and discovering *people who are contrasting matches to you* for each category. When you find a contrasting match, have that person write his or her name in the box. You may not use anyone's name twice.

Favorite TV show _____	Ethnic background _____	Favorite holiday _____	Country you would most like to visit _____	Right handed/ left handed _____
Most typical meal that our family eats _____	Eye color _____	Favorite cereal/ breakfast food _____	Country you would least like to visit _____	Favorite sport _____
Typical summer activity _____	Favorite place to visit in the U.S. _____	Favorite subject in school _____	Favorite music group _____	An ethnic group you know very little about _____
Own a pet/ don't own a pet _____	Favorite hobby _____	City and state of birth _____	Walk to school/ ride the bus to school _____	Neighborhood has lots of kids/ doesn't have many kids. _____
Most admired writer, artist, actor/actress _____	Only child/ several broth-ers and sisters _____	Are oldest/ youngest in family _____	You live in an apartment/ condo/house _____	Favorite snack food _____

Age: 8–12

Activity Type: Storytelling

Activity Level: Quiet

Space: Any

Concentration
Level: High

Time: 30 minutes

Group Size: 4 or more

Prerequisite: None

WAKING UP TO CHANGE

In coed pairs, students share how their lives might be different if they were the opposite gender.

● ● ● ● ● ● ● ● ● ● ● ● ● ● ● ● ●

MATERIALS

❖ Pens and paper

SUGGESTED PROCEDURE

1. Start the activity by explaining that in our society, there are many differences in the ways that boys and girls are treated. Of course, not *everyone* treats *all* boys one way and *all* girls a different way, but our gender still affects our lives. As a way to think about how our gender might affect the way people treat us or the way we feel about ourselves, we will use our imaginations and talk with someone in the group who is of the opposite gender.

2. Divide the group, as best you can, into coed pairs. If you have an unequal number of boys and girls, then divide into groups of three or four, with at least one member of both genders in every group. The groups must be coed.

3. Ask the children to write silently for five minutes, completing the following thought, "If I woke up tomorrow morning and I were a girl/boy..." Encourage them to think about how their lives would be different in school, at home, in their afterschool program, on sports teams, and any other places they may go. Children will often focus on physical differences; help them think beyond these concrete, literal answers by imagining how every minute of a typical day might change. You may want to lead them through a guided imagery. To do this, have them close their eyes and listen as you describe their day in detail, "You wake up and walk to the bathroom, where you look in the mirror as you brush you teeth. Your brother or sister knocks on the door and tells you to hurry...."

4. After they have finished writing, have them exchange their ideas about how their lives would be different with their partner/group. Ask each student to listen carefully to their partner, checking to see if there are any additional changes they can think of, speaking from their own experience.

5. Come back together as a large group and discuss.

REFLECTION

❖ What did you discover might have been different about your life if you had been born the other gender? Did anyone's partner suggest something that you hadn't thought of on your own?

❖ Do people expect you to be a certain way because you are a boy/girl? What happens when their expectations are wrong? Do you expect other people to act a certain way because of their gender?

NOTES

● ● ● ● ● ● ● ● ● ● ● ●

Age: 8–12

Activity Type: Arts and crafts

Activity Level: Quiet

Space: Work tables

Concentration Level: Moderate

Time: 30 minutes

Group Size: Any

Prerequisite: None

SILHOUETTE PORTRAITS

Students attempt to identify portraits made by tracing their profiles onto paper and decorating them.

● ● ● ● ● ● ● ● ● ● ● ● ● ● ● ● ● ●

MATERIALS

❖ White paper

❖ Scissors

❖ Lamp

❖ Crayons, markers, paint, pastels

SUGGESTED PROCEDURE

1. Demonstrate how to trace someone's profile. Set a lamp close to the person's head, aimed at a piece of paper taped onto the wall. Ask the person to sit very still as you trace the child's profile with pencil. Once you have finished tracing, carefully cut the silhouette portrait along the line you have traced, so that you are left with a piece of paper the shape of the child's profile.

2. Have the students pair up and trace their partner's profile.

3. Children can now cut out their own silhouette portrait and decorate it to show something about themselves. Encourage students to be creative by drawing more than their own facial features. You may prompt them by asking them to draw the dreams they hold in their heads, or the best idea that they ever had, or what their imagination looks like. Be creative!

4. When they have finished their silhouette portraits, hang them on the wall and ask each child to guess which one belongs to which student. Give every child a list with everyone's name on it and number the silhouette portraits. Students then try to match the correct name with each number. After everyone has finished guessing, share the results!

REFLECTION

❖ Was it easy to tell which silhouette portrait belonged to whom? How did you guess? By the profiles? By the drawing inside the profiles?

❖ Do our silhouette portraits look more alike or different? What do they all have in common? What is different about each one of them? What do we all have in common? What makes each of us unique?

NOTES

● ● ● ● ● ● ● ● ● ● ● ●

Exploring Other Cultures

MULTICULTURAL SHOW AND TELL

Each student brings in something from home which shows her or his cultural background.

● ● ● ● ● ● ● ● ● ● ● ● ● ● ● ● ● ●

Age:	5–12
Activity Type:	Getting to know you
Activity Level:	Moderate
Space:	Any
Concentration Level:	High
Time:	45 minutes
Group Size:	Any
Prerequisite:	None

MATERIALS

❖ Five objects that represent American culture: such as a flag, a baseball, a photograph of the White House, a TV remote control, or a pair of blue jeans.

SUGGESTED PROCEDURE

1. Lay out the five objects and ask students to look at them, thinking about what they all have in common. Hopefully, the children will guess that these are all American objects.

2. Begin by explaining that although many of us are American, we consider our cultural background to be more than just "American." Discuss what the words "cultural background" mean, collecting ideas from the children and creating a list. Ask a few students to share what they know about their individual cultural backgrounds. Be certain that the students understand that cultural background includes things like language, beliefs, traditions, food, music, clothing, and art. Watch for students' feelings about their cultures, and be certain that everyone understands that our cultural background is something about which we should feel proud.

3. Ask the students to pair up and tell their partner what their individual cultural background is. Have students interview one another, asking the following questions:

   ❖ In which countries besides America do your relatives live?

   ❖ In which countries did your relatives who are no longer living live?

   ❖ What holidays do you celebrate at home?

   ❖ What language do you speak at home?

   ❖ Is there a special food that is from your culture that you eat at home? If so, what does it taste like?

4. If you have time and feel it is appropriate for your group, have the interviewers tell the whole group about the cultural background of their partners.

5. As an assignment for a second session, ask students to bring something to the next meeting that will help them tell the group something about their cultural backgrounds.

6. At the second session, have each child show her object and tell the group what it is and what it tells about her cultural background.

REFLECTION

❖ How many different cultural backgrounds does our group represent?

❖ Were you surprised by anyone's cultural background? Did you learn something new about anyone in the group? What was it?

❖ Did you learn anything new about a culture? What was it?

NOTES
● ● ● ● ● ● ● ● ● ● ● ●

MULTICULTURAL FEAST

Students collect and prepare recipes that represent the cultural backgrounds of group members and have a feast!

● ● ● ● ● ● ● ● ● ● ● ● ● ● ● ● ●

MATERIALS

❖ Cookbooks from the library that represent many different cultures

❖ Ingredients for whichever recipes your group chooses

❖ Kitchen equipment

SUGGESTED PROCEDURE

1. Review what the group learned about cultural backgrounds in the "Multicultural Show and Tell" activity (p. 221), including what multicultural means and what our individual backgrounds are.

2. Invite the children to search through the pile of cookbooks to find a recipe that the class can make that comes from each child's culture. Explain that some recipes are much more complicated than others and that we need to be able to make something that takes very little time to prepare. For younger children, you may need to do this work ahead of time. In that case, try to locate about ten simple recipes that represent as many cultures from your group as possible.

3. Once students have selected their recipes, go around the room and have each person describe theirs. They should include the name of the recipe, where it comes from, what's in it, and how difficult it seems to be to make. You may want to make a list of these questions on newsprint to help them remember what to say about their recipe.

4. As a group, decide which recipes you can make next time. You may be able to make a number of different dishes at once, depending upon your group and your facility. Set limits for the group that make the most sense for your situation (or, if your group works well together at making informed decisions, let them figure out what these limits are!). Help them consider all issues, including representation of different cultures, ease of preparation, taste, and the limits of your resources.

Age:	5–12
Activity Type:	Cooking
Activity Level:	Moderate
Space:	Kitchen
Concentration Level:	Medium
Time:	Two 45-minute sessions
Group Size:	Any
Prerequisite:	"Multicultural Show and Tell" (p. 221).

5. For the second session, make the recipes that the group has chosen and have your yummy multicultural feast! You may want to bring in decorations, clothes, posters, flowers, or music that come from cultures represented in the group that were not chosen for the recipes. Ask for help from the group in doing this.

REFLECTION

❖ Do the dishes from anyone else's culture taste like something from a different culture that you have tried before? Which ones? Are those two cultures related in some way?

❖ Did you try anything new from a culture different from your own? Did you like it?

❖ Did the food from a certain culture taste like you expected?

NOTES

● ● ● ● ● ● ● ● ● ● ●

WHAT IF SLEEPING BEAUTY WERE A BOY?

Children discuss gender-based stereotypes through variations on traditional fairy tales.

● ● ● ● ● ● ● ● ● ● ● ● ● ● ● ● ●

Age:	8–12
Activity Type:	Storytelling
Activity Level:	Quiet
Space:	Any
Concentration Level:	High
Time:	30 minutes
Group Size:	Any
Prerequisite:	None

MATERIALS

❖ Any traditional fairy tale (*Sleeping Beauty, Rapunzel, Little Red Riding Hood,* etc.)

SUGGESTED PROCEDURE

1. Choose a fairy tale ahead of time that contains very stereotypical gender roles. Rewrite it or make notes for yourself, so that the male characters become female and the female characters are male. Change the names and pronouns accordingly.

2. Read the story aloud to the children. Watch for Teachable Moments – like students laughing at a female wolf or calling male characters who cry "fags" or "wusses."

3. Discuss why the story was different, or funny, or strange.

REFLECTION

❖ How was this story different from ones we usually hear?

❖ What surprised you in the story?

❖ Was there anything that a character did that you thought was strange, considering that she/he was female/male? Why was that strange?

❖ How can stereotypes about what girls and boys can or cannot do hurt us? Has anyone ever told you that you can't do something because you are a boy/girl?

Understanding Stereotyping, Prejudice, and Discrimination

WHAT'S PREJUDICE?

In small groups, children share examples of discrimination, then role play for the rest of the group.

● ● ● ● ● ● ● ● ● ● ● ● ● ● ● ● ●

Age:	8–12
Activity Type:	Drama
Activity Level:	Moderate
Space:	Any
Concentration Level:	High
Time:	20 minutes
Group Size:	Large
Prerequisite:	None

MATERIALS

❖ Chart paper and markers

SUGGESTED PROCEDURE

1. Begin by writing the word "prejudice" on a sheet of chart paper and doing a web around it to help students define it. Make sure that some or most of the "isms" are written on the web (i.e., sexism, racism, ageism).

2. Break into small groups and have the children share stories of a time they felt discriminated against or saw someone else being prejudiced. Have each member of the small group complete the following sentence, "I felt or saw prejudice once when…"

3. Each group now chooses one story from their collective experience to role play for the large group. Give them enough time to assign parts and rehearse.

4. After each small group presents their role play, ask the large group to define what type of prejudice that scene shows.

5. Write the word "prejudice" on another piece of chart paper and ask the students what words they see in this word. Assist them in identifying the prefix "pre" as something that means before by suggesting other "pre" words, like preview, predict, preface, and premature. Point out that the word "judge" is in there, too, and that the dictionary definition of "prejudice" is "an adverse judgment or opinion formed beforehand or without knowledge or examination of the facts." You may want to write this definition down ahead of time.

6. Talk about how people judged the characters in the role plays "without knowledge," or before they had all "the facts."

REFLECTION

❖ Why is it bad to judge someone before you have all the facts? What might happen? What happens when people do this to you? How does it make you feel?

❖ Do you ever "pre-judge" people?

NOTES

● ● ● ● ● ● ● ● ● ● ●

BEAT THE WAVE

Children move from chair to chair in a wave-like fashion. The person in the center tries to find an empty chair.

Age:	8–12
Activity Type:	Circle game
Activity Level:	Very active
Space:	Any
Concentration Level:	High
Time:	30 minutes
Group Size:	15 or more
Prerequisite:	None

MATERIALS

❖ One sturdy chair per person

SET THE SCENE

Arrange the chairs in a tight circle so that there is no space between the chairs. To start the game, you will be "it."

Ask the children, "Who here knows what a wave at a sporting event is? Well, we are going to do a variation of this wave in our chairs."

At this point, you should get up off your chair, thus leaving an empty spot in the circle.

"The wave works by the person to the left of the empty chair moving into it. Then, as quickly as possible, the next person moves into the new empty chair. The object is to fill the empty chair as quickly as we can. Let's give it a try."

Have the group practice the chair wave.

"OK, now try it moving to the right! Good. Looks like we are ready to play."

SUGGESTED PROCEDURE

1. *Explain the rules to the group,* "I am 'it.' My goal is to get into the empty seat before one of you can fill it.

   "Your job is to keep the wave moving as quickly as possible so I can't get the seat."

2. The person who is "it" has one minute to get in. If the person who is "it" is not in a chair after the time is up, switch to a new person who is "it." You be the judge of how long to leave the person who is "it" in the center of the circle.

3. As a variation, have the person who is "it" control the direction of the wave. If that person calls out "right," the person to the right of the empty seat starts the wave. If they call out "left," everyone moves left.

229

REFLECTION

Introduce and discuss how it feels to be a person on the outside of a group trying to get in. There are many metaphors in this activity – the group is moving so fast there isn't any place for a new person, people trying to get in (those who are "it") feel like they will never fit in, etc. There is often someone who feels compassion for the person who is "it" and slows the wave down to let them in. For most people, the only way they will get in is if someone on the outside lets them in or if someone is not paying attention.

- ❖ How did it feel for the people who were "it" to be "it"?
- ❖ How did it feel to be on the inside keeping the person who was "it" out?

Use the reflection time to help the children explore these metaphors for group inclusion and exclusion. This activity can prompt discussion about various groups or cliques and how it feels to be in or out of a given group. It can also help sensitize children to how exclusion might feel to a child who is not a member of their group.

NOTES

● ● ● ● ● ● ● ● ● ● ● ●

SALAD BOWL OR MELTING POT

Discuss assimilation and integration
by making a salad and cheese fondue.

Age:	5–12
Activity Type:	Cooking
Activity Level:	Moderate
Space:	Kitchen
Concentration Level:	Medium
Time:	60 minutes
Group Size:	Any
Prerequisite:	None

MATERIALS

- ❖ Ingredients for green salad and cheese fondue, (see recipes on the next two pages)
- ❖ Kitchen equipment

SUGGESTED PROCEDURE

1. Split the group into two. One half of the group makes a green salad and the other makes cheese fondue, following the recipes on pages 232 and 233. The two recipes will take about the same amount of time.

2. Explain that the terms "salad bowl" and "melting pot" are sometimes used to describe the United States of America. Ask if anyone has ever heard these names before and if anyone knows what they mean. If not, explain the difference between the two concepts by having the children look at what happens to the ingredients in the salad (lettuce, tomato, carrots, cucumbers, etc.) versus the ingredients in the cheese fondue, which is like a melting pot (Swiss cheese, cheddar cheese, cornstarch). While the salad ingredients remain separate, the fondue ingredients all melt together to form one, unified thing.

REFLECTION

Over salad and fondue discuss:

- ❖ What might people mean when they say America is like a melting pot? How is it different when people call America a salad bowl?

- ❖ If your family came to the United States from a different culture, why might you not want to change or "melt" into American culture? What might be an advantage of "melting" into the melting pot?

- ❖ Do you think that in America we are more like each other or more different from each other? Do you think of America more as a melting pot or as a salad bowl?

Salad Bowl

- ❖ 1 head lettuce

- ❖ 1 cucumber

- ❖ 2 tomatoes

- ❖ 3 carrots

Wash the lettuce and rip it with your hands so that it is in pieces small enough to fit into your mouth. Wash and chop the vegetables. Take turns chopping, and make sure that an adult is supervising whoever has the knife. Mix it all together in a big bowl and add salad dressing – or put a few different kinds on the table and let everyone choose their own!

Melting Pot

- ❖ 2 Tbs. butter

- ❖ 1/2 lb. medium-sharp cheese

- ❖ 1 medium clove of garlic

- ❖ 1 tsp. dry mustard

- ❖ 1 Tbs. fresh lemon juice

- ❖ 2 loaves crusty French or Italian bread

Cut the cheese into half-inch cubes and the bread into one-inch cubes. Try to make all of the bread cubes so that at least one side is crust (this will keep the bread cubes from falling apart when they are dunked into the fondue). Crush the garlic clove.

In a heavy skillet or saucepan (cast iron works best), melt the butter over medium-low heat. Add the cheese and stir constantly as it melts and begins to bubble. Add the garlic, dry mustard, and lemon.

Serve immediately, with the bread cubes. Careful – it will be hot!

Conflict Resolution

Helping children acquire
the skills and understandings
they need to resolve conflict independently

Conflict is a natural part of any school-age childcare program. Conflict can be positive when it is handled well. It can be a signal that you need to improve a part of the program or solve a recurring problem. It can tell you what kind of conflict resolution skills the children in your program have or need to learn. It can lead to improved relationships. The activities in this chapter are designed to help children learn the skills they need to handle conflict productively, in what is called a Win-Win fashion.

You will find that many of the activities are more structured and instructional than is usual for many childcare programs. Suggestions for incorporating these into the program are included in chapter three. If these do not fit into your program, several of the activities have suggestions for adapting them.

There are four types of activities in this chapter:

1. Conflict Resolution Skill Building

2. Exploring Conflict and Conflict Resolution

3. Practicing Conflict Resolution

4. Peer Mediation Training

Using Teachable Moments

❖ Look for opportunities to label conflicts and reinforce the idea that a conflict can be more than a fight. You will be helping children become comfortable with the vocabulary of conflict when you model its use. Also, whenever possible, try to point out ways in which classroom conflicts can be constructive or valuable. For example, "Tanesha and Jerome had a conflict in the block corner and figured out a way to share."

❖ Group meetings provide an excellent forum for discussing conflict, solving problems, and teaching new skills. As children become familiar with the idea of conflict, have them share conflicts they've seen around the school. How did they start? Did they get better or worse? Did the participants solve the conflict? What were the consequences of the conflict?

❖ Encourage a problem-solving frame of mind in the group by using both the ABCD Problem-solving process (p. 256) and the "Thumbs Up/Thumbs Down" activity (p. 260) to solve a problem. Have the children brainstorm a list of group problems. Then, ask them to choose one and brainstorm ways to solve it. When the brainstorming is finished, discuss which idea or ideas might be a Thumbs Up solution and propose possible ways to implement the solution.

❖ Help children become more comfortable with the language of problem solving and Thumbs Up solutions by using it when you intervene in conflicts. You don't need to use the entire ABCD method. You can save time by simply helping children identify what the problem is and then asking, "Can you think of a Thumbs Up solution to this conflict?" The more children hear you use this language, the more likely they will use it themselves.

❖ The Conflict Escalator is a tremendously useful concept both for helping children to better understand conflict and encouraging them to take responsibility for their behavior. Make an effort to incorporate it into the daily life of the group room. When the children have conflicts, ask them, "How did you get onto the Conflict Escalator?" "What sent you up the Conflict Escalator?" "How could you come down the Conflict Escalator?" If you have a conflict with a child yourself, you might say, "Andrea, I think you and I are on the Conflict Escalator. How are we going to get off?"

❖ The Conflict Resolution Chart (p. 252) is also a very useful tool in the group room. Post it in a prominent place and refer to it often. If two children have a conflict, for example, you might intervene by asking them which of the conflict resolution methods on the chart they would like to use. Similarly, when you intervene in conflicts, point out which methods you are using.

❖ One of the goals of this chapter is to encourage children to expand the conflict resolution choices and options they have and go beyond the conflict resolution methods with which they are most familiar. Try some new approaches yourself. For example, if you find yourself constantly telling children to share, try giving them the responsibility for solving the problem by asking them to "talk it out" and come up with a solution. The solution they develop may be to share, but solving the problem themselves will help children develop and internalize conflict resolution skills.

❖ Here's a simple technique for encouraging children to use the techniques on the Conflict Resolution Chart. Keep a timer with you. When students come to you with a conflict or when you interrupt one in progress, ask them to choose a method from the chart and resolve their problem. Set the timer for three minutes. Assure them that after three minutes, if they haven't worked out a solution, you will help them, but they should try to work it out themselves. Often they will be able to work it out, and your role can change from arbitrator to time-keeper!

❖ Once children have tried a conflict resolution approach, help them evaluate how it worked. (This is discussed in more detail in chapter ten, *Peacing It All Together.*) For example, during a group meeting you might ask them to describe what they did and how it worked. This gives children an opportunity to reflect on their actions, acknowledges any success they had, and helps other children learn how to use the conflict resolution method in a real-life situation.

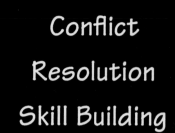

Conflict Resolution Skill Building

WHAT'S CONFLICT?

Children explore the many words that describe conflict and discuss different types of conflict.

● ● ● ● ● ● ● ● ● ● ● ● ● ● ● ● ● ●

Age:	5–12
Activity Type:	Chart
Activity Level:	Quiet
Space:	Any
Concentration Level:	High
Time:	20 minutes
Group Size:	Any
Prerequisite:	None

MATERIALS

❖ Chart paper and markers

❖ Pictures of common objects, such as a TV/VCR, sneakers, watch, etc., mounted on paper

SUGGESTED PROCEDURE

1. Write the word "conflict" on the paper and read it aloud. Ask if anyone knows what it means. After a few children have responded, build on their responses by explaining that a conflict is a disagreement between people.

2. Create a web chart. Write the word "conflict" on chart paper. Draw a circle around it. Have the children brainstorm all the words they can think of related to conflict. Record each suggestion on the board, drawing a line from the word to "conflict." Words that are related to previous contributions can be linked to each other. For example:

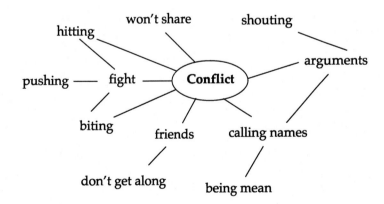

239

Mini-Reflection

- ◆ Can anyone give me an example of a conflict?
- ◆ What kinds of conflict have you been in?
- ◆ What kinds of things do you think of when you hear the word "conflict"?
- ◆ What kinds of conflicts do grown-ups have?

3. Show the magazine pictures of common objects and ask children to describe what the object could have to do with conflict. If they cannot think of a way that object could relate to conflict, move on to the next picture.

REFLECTION

- ❖ What could this picture have to do with conflict?
- ❖ Have you ever had a conflict like that?
- ❖ Have you ever seen a conflict related to this object?
- ❖ Did the conflict involve behaviors other than physical fighting? What were they?

NOTES

● ● ● ● ● ● ● ● ● ● ● ●

CONFLICT ESCALATES

Using storytelling, children discuss how conflicts get worse and what behaviors contribute to the escalation of conflicts.

● ● ● ● ● ● ● ● ● ● ● ● ● ● ● ● ●

Age:	8–12
Activity Type:	Storytelling
Activity Level:	Quiet
Space:	Any
Concentration Level:	High
Time:	20 minutes
Group Size:	Any
Prerequisite:	None

MATERIALS

❖ Conflict Case Study, "A Hatful of Trouble" (p. 244)

❖ Chart paper and markers

❖ Drawing paper and pencils

SUGGESTED PROCEDURE

1. Ask the children to describe an escalator. If they are unfamiliar with escalators, explain that an escalator is a set of stairs that moves either up or down. Draw the following escalator graphic on the chart paper:

Explain that when conflicts get worse we say that the people involved are on the Conflict Escalator.

2. Read the following story to the group (feel free to change the story):

Jermaine and Janet sat next to each other. Jermaine asked Janet if he could borrow a pencil. Janet was trying to hear the teacher so she said, "Will you shut up!"

This made Jermaine mad, so he pulled on Janet's braid.

Janet punched Jermaine in the arm. Jermaine pushed her books on the floor.

The teacher said, "What's going on over there?"
Jermaine and Janet both pointed to each other and said, "He/ She started it!"

3. Discuss the conflict with the children as suggested below. As you do, map the conflict onto the Conflict Escalator so that it looks like this:

"He/She
started it!"

The teacher said
"What's going on?"

Jermaine pushed
her books on the floor.

Janet punched
Jermaine's arm.

Jermaine pulled
her braid.

Janet said
"Shut Up!"

Jermaine asked to
borrow a pencil.

Mini-Reflection

◆ What happened to make this conflict escalate?

◆ How did Jermaine and Janet feel as the conflict started?

◆ How did they feel at the top of the escalator?

◆ What do you think their teacher said next?

◆ When you're in a conflict, what makes you go up the escalator?

4. Divide children into groups of two or three and distribute the Conflict Case Study to each child and a piece of drawing paper to each group. Have them read the story (you may also read it aloud).

Mini-Reflection

◆ What was the first step in this conflict?

◆ What was next?

◆ Do you think your group could put this whole conflict on a Conflict Escalator?

5. Have the groups draw an escalator on the drawing paper. Then have them write an incident from the conflict on each step. Be sure they write specific behavior, not generalizations. (For example, they should write: Shanda said, "You jerk!" *not* Shanda called names.)

6. Have groups share their escalators.

REFLECTION

❖ What behaviors made the conflict escalate or get worse?

❖ Have you ever had a conflict like this?

❖ How could Shanda and Tyrone come down the escalator?

❖ When you are in a conflict, what sends you up the Conflict Escalator?

NOTES
● ● ● ● ● ● ● ● ● ● ●

A Hatful of Trouble

Tyrone wanted a new ball cap, but his mother said, "No."

Shanda came to school wearing a new Red Sox cap and Tyrone told her it looked stupid.

Shanda said, "Not as stupid as that old one you wear."

Tyrone grabbed Shanda's cap and put it on his head.

Shanda tried to grab it back, and it fell to the floor. Tyrone stepped on it to keep Shanda from picking it up and left a big footprint on the cap.

Shanda was furious. "You jerk! You're going to buy me a new cap!" she yelled. Then she grabbed Tyrone's shirt. When he tried to get away from her, his shirt ripped.

"You're going to buy me a new shirt!" he yelled.

CONFLICT ESCALATES
Primary Grade Version

Using puppets and storytelling, children explore conflict-escalating behavior and how conflicts get worse.

● ● ● ● ● ● ● ● ● ● ● ● ● ● ● ● ●

Age:	5–7
Activity Type:	Drama
Activity Level:	Quiet
Space:	Any
Concentration Level:	High
Time:	20 minutes
Group Size:	Any
Prerequisite:	None

MATERIALS

- ❖ Peace Puppets (see p. 280)
- ❖ Five feathers
- ❖ Activity Sheet, "The Lunch Box Conflict"
- ❖ Chart paper and markers
- ❖ Paste, scissors, and crayons

SUGGESTED PROCEDURE

1. Ask the children to describe an escalator. If they are unfamiliar with escalators, explain that an escalator is a set of stairs that moves either up or down. Draw the following escalator graphic on chart paper:

   Explain that when conflicts get worse we say that the people involved are on the Conflict Escalator.

2. Say that you are about to introduce the children to some friends of yours. Take the Peace Puppets out of their bag or box and explain that the Peace Puppets are special puppets. They are called the Peace Puppets because although they have problems, with the children's help they can peacefully solve their problems.

3. Read the following story to the group, acting it out with the Peace Puppets as you do:

Marcus and Stephanie were working on an art project. They were making masks. Their teacher, Ms. Chen, had put on the table some markers, paste, colored feathers, and sequins for the children to use on their masks. Stephanie took three big yellow feathers and five small red feathers. "I'm going to put these on my mask," she said.

"Hey!" said Marcus. "I was going to use them." Stephanie said, "I got them first." "You should share," said Marcus. Stephanie said, "I need them all. You just want them because I got them. You can use the green feathers or the sequins."

"I want to use those feathers," said Marcus and he grabbed the yellow feathers away from Stephanie. "Give them to me," Stephanie yelled and she pulled at the feathers.

They broke into pieces. "Look what you did," said Marcus. "You wreck everything." "I'm telling," said Stephanie and she went to get Ms. Chen.

4. Discuss the conflict with the children as suggested below. As you do, map the conflict onto the Conflict Escalator so that it looks like this:

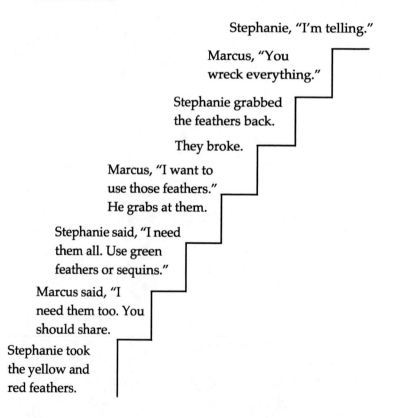

Stephanie, "I'm telling."

Marcus, "You wreck everything."

Stephanie grabbed the feathers back.

They broke.

Marcus, "I want to use those feathers." He grabs at them.

Stephanie said, "I need them all. Use green feathers or sequins."

Marcus said, "I need them too. You should share.

Stephanie took the yellow and red feathers.

Mini-Reflection

- ◆ What things did Marcus and Stephanie say that made them go up the escalator?

- ◆ How could they have come down the escalator and solved their problem?

- ◆ What do you think Ms. Chen said to them?

5. Review the key points of the lesson and explain that they will get a chance to practice using the Conflict Escalator themselves. Read the following story:

While Danielle was getting her snack out of the coat closet, her lunch box accidentally fell and clunked Giorgio on the head. "Ow!" said Giorgio, rubbing his head. "You should be careful, you big jerk."

Danielle felt bad about hitting Giorgio, but she didn't like being called a jerk. It was an accident! "Don't be such a baby. You shouldn't get in the way," said Danielle. Giorgio felt himself getting really angry. As Danielle bent over to pick up her lunch box, Giorgio kicked it into the group room.

Mr. Avazian, their teacher, came back to the coat closet. "What's all this shouting about?" he asked. Danielle and Giorgio pointed at each other. "He/She started it!" they both said.

6. Divide children into cooperative groups of two or three and give each group a copy of the Activity Sheet, "Lunch Box Conflict," a piece of chart paper, some paste, scissors, and crayons. Have the children draw an escalator with four steps on the paper. Reread the story to the group. As you read, have the children place the appropriate statements on the sheet, identifying how the conflict escalated.

REFLECTION

- ❖ What was the first thing that happened in this conflict?

- ❖ Which picture represents that? Where would (or did) you place this picture on the Conflict Escalator?

- ❖ What is the top of this Conflict Escalator?

- ❖ What things did the children do that made this conflict worse?

- ❖ How do you think they solved their problem?

- ❖ If you were helping them solve their problem, what would you tell them to do?

- ❖ Have you ever had a conflict like this? How did it escalate? How did it de-escalate?

The Lunch Box Conflict

- -

Danielle's lunch box fell and it hit Giorgio's head.

- -

Giorgio said, "Ow! You should be careful, you big jerk."

- -

Danielle said, "Don't be a baby."

- -

Giorgio kicked Danielle's lunch box.

- -

The teacher said, "What's all the shouting?"

- -

CONFLICT RESOLUTION CHART

Children explore various techniques for dealing with conflicts.

Age:	5–7
Activity Type:	Chart
Activity Level:	Quiet
Space:	Any
Concentration Level:	High
Time:	20 minutes
Group Size:	Any
Prerequisite:	None

MATERIALS

❖ Conflict Resolution Chart (Make a copy of the Conflict Resolution Chart on a sheet of chart paper, or enlarge the page on a copy machine)

❖ Role-play Cards

❖ For younger children: Peace Puppets

SUGGESTED PROCEDURE

Note: There's a lot for children to absorb in this activity. You may want to take a few days and introduce the chart a few items at a time.

1. Ask the children to brainstorm all the ways people can solve conflicts that don't hurt other people. Record these on the board or a sheet of newsprint. When the brainstorming is finished, discuss the list by asking for examples of each conflict resolution approach. (If, during the discussion, children suggest violent or destructive methods, ask if their suggestion would hurt anybody. Remind the children that you are looking for ways to resolve conflicts that don't hurt others.)

2. Show the Conflict Resolution Chart to the group. Discuss each item on the list, comparing the chart to the list the children developed. If there are any that are new or confusing terms, either ask the group for, or give them, an example.

   Talk It Out – Lots of conflicts can be solved by people just sitting down and talking about the problem.

   Listen to Each Other – The people in the conflict have to be willing to listen to each other. Good listening helps each person understand what the other is thinking and feeling. Listening helps them see where the misunderstanding is.

   Share – If people are having a conflict about who gets to use something, maybe there's a way they can both use it at the same time.

Posting the Chart

If the direct instruction in this activity does not fit with your program style, make a copy of the chart as suggested and simply post it in a prominent place. As the staff begin to refer to and use the chart, children will pick up on it.

For Younger Children

For younger children substitute the Peace Puppets for role playing.

Take Turns – One way to share is to decide that first one person uses it, then the other person has a turn. Taking turns makes sure it's fair.

Compromise – If both people give in a little, that's called a compromise.

Make a Peace Offering – One person gives the other a little gift or something that shows they want to solve the conflict.

Say "Sorry" – "Sorry" can mean different things. One reason to say "sorry" is when you were wrong. It can also be a way of saying, "I feel bad we're having this conflict."

Build Trust – Sometimes during a conflict the people don't believe what the other says. They need to trust each other.

Work Together – Sometimes a conflict can be solved by the people agreeing to work together on a project or idea.

Solve the Problem – Conflicts are problems. If the people solve the problem, the conflict will be solved.

Put It Off – Sometimes people are too angry to talk it out or solve the problem. They may need to take a break and work on it later.

Skip It – It is not worth bothering with some conflicts. Just forget about it.

Get Help – Sometimes you can't come to a solution by yourselves, and you need to ask either a grown-up or another child to help you.

Mini-Reflection

- ◆ Can you give an example of a time you used any of these?

- ◆ What happened when you did?

3. Explain that the group will be doing some role playing to practice conflict resolution. Ask for two volunteers to role play. Give the players copies of one of the Role-play Cards and ask them to act out the conflict. When the conflict has escalated, call "Freeze!"

Mini-Reflection

◆ What is the conflict about?

◆ How do they feel right now?

◆ What techniques from our chart do you think would be helpful in this conflict?

4. After some discussion, have the actors de-escalate the conflict using one or more of the techniques on the chart.

Mini-Reflection

◆ What techniques from the chart did you see the actors use?

◆ Do you think they worked well?

◆ Have you ever used this technique? What happened?

5. Continue with two new actors and a new situation. Repeat the process above.

NOTES

● ● ● ● ● ● ● ● ● ● ●

Conflict Resolution Chart

Talk It Out

Listen to Each Other

Share

Take Turns

Compromise

Make a Peace Offering

Say "Sorry"

Build Trust

Work Together

Solve the Problem

Put It Off

Skip It

Get Help

Conflict Resolution Chart
Role Plays

- -

Child 1 is drawing while sitting at a desk. Child 2 walks by and accidentally bumps him or her. Now the drawing is wrecked. Child 1 is furious.

- -

Children 1 and 2 were walking down the hall on the way to gym. Child 1 goes through the swinging doors first. Suddenly, Child 2 says, "Hey watch it! You squished me in the door!"

- -

Child 1 wants to be by herself and read. Child 2 keeps bugging her about playing together.

- -

Child 1 is visiting Child 2. Child 2 wants to rent a movie. Child 1 wants to play Monopoly.

- -

Child 1 says he will beat up Child 2 if Child 2 doesn't give Child 1 his lunch money.

Age: 8–12

Activity Type: Drama

Activity Level: Quiet

Space: Any

Concentration Level: High

Time: 20 minutes

Group Size: Any

Prerequisite: None

ABCD PROBLEM SOLVING

Children practice solving conflicts using role playing and a conflict-solving process.

MATERIALS

❖ ABCD Conflict-Solving Chart

❖ Role-play Cards

SUGGESTED PROCEDURE

1. Refer to the Conflict Resolution Chart (see p. 252). Explain that what many of the conflict resolution methods on the chart have in common is that they involve some kind of problem solving. Display the ABCD Conflict-Solving Chart and go over it with the group.

    Ask: What's the Problem?

    Brainstorm Some Solutions

    Choose the Best Solution

    Do It.

2. Walk the group through the ABCD method by having volunteers role play the following story as you read it aloud:

    The children in Mr. Aronstein's afterschool group had been waiting for weeks for the new set of books for their afterschool library. Finally the box arrived. The children gathered around watching as Mr. Aronstein opened the box and took out copies of seven new books. "I want the one on top," called Urvashi. "I want the other one," shouted Santel. All over the room children called out to be the first ones to read the books. "Quiet down everyone, " said Mr. Aronstein. "Boy, we've got a problem." said Jim.

Mini-Reflection

◆ What problem does Mr. Aronstein's group have?

◆ What are some ways they could solve this problem?

◆ Which solution do you think would be best?

◆ How could the group "do" the solution?

◆ Have you ever worked out a conflict by following steps like these?

Posting and Brainstorming

If the direct instruction in this activity does not fit with your program style, make a copy of the chart as suggested and simply post it in a prominent place. As the staff begin to refer to and use the chart, children will pick up on it. If your children are unfamiliar with brainstorming, do the activity "Brainstorming" (p. 269) before you introduce the ABCD conflict-solving process.

3. Have two volunteers role play a conflict from the role-play cards. After the conflict escalates, call "Freeze!" Have the group use the ABCD method to solve the conflict. After they have identified what they think is the best solution, have the actors show how it might look.

4. If there is time, repeat the above procedure with two new actors and a new situation.

5. Review the key points and explain that in the next lesson the group will learn more about evaluating solutions.

NOTES

● ● ● ● ● ● ● ● ● ● ●

A B C D
Problem Solving

A ASK
What's the problem?

B BRAINSTORM
possible solutions

C CHOOSE
the best solution

D DO it

A B C D Problem-Solving Role Plays

Child 1 and Child 2 were playing a game and Child 1 lost. She feels mad. Now it's time to clean up and Child 2 won't help.

Child 1 has a bag of candy. He is passing it out only to certain group mates. Child 2 is being left out.

Child 1 and Child 2 are good friends. Child 1 calls Child 2 a name in a friendly, teasing kind of way. But Child 2 is insulted and the conflict starts to escalate.

Child 1 invites Child 2 to be in a club. One of the rules of the club is that no one can talk with Child 3. Child 2 has always liked Child 3 and doesn't want to hurt her.

As Child 1 sits down, Child 2 pulls the chair out from under him. Child 1's pants rip as a result.

Safety Note
Be careful when you do this role play. Don't let Child 1 get hurt when he or she falls!

Age:	5–7
Activity Type:	Drama
Activity Level:	Quiet
Space:	Any
Concentration Level:	High
Time:	20 minutes
Group Size:	Any
Prerequisite:	"Making Peace Puppets" (p. 279)

ABCD PROBLEM SOLVING
Primary Grade Version

Children practice solving conflicts using role playing and a conflict-solving process.

● ● ● ● ● ● ● ● ● ● ● ● ● ● ● ● ● ● ●

MATERIALS

❖ ABCD Conflict-solving Chart (p. 256)

❖ Peace Puppets created in "Making Peace Puppets" (p. 279)

SUGGESTED PROCEDURE

1. Refer to the Conflict Resolution Chart (see p. 252). Explain that what many of the conflict resolution methods on the chart have in common is that they involve some kind of problem solving. Display the ABCD Conflict-Solving Chart, and go over it with the group.

   Ask: What's the Problem?

   Brainstorm Some Solutions

   Choose the Best Solution

   Do It.

2. Walk the group through the ABCD method using the Peace Puppets. Have the Peace Puppets run a race that ends in a tie. The first puppet says he won; the second puppet says she won. They bicker back and forth. Then stop and discuss, using the ABCD method as a guideline for the discussion.

3. Repeat the ABCD method with the following story:

   Ernest and Miriam are doing a science project together. They have eight containers of dirt and are going to plant different seeds in the containers. Ernest is planting the seeds, Miriam is watering them. "You're planting them too deep," says Miriam. "You better let me plant them."

   Ernest looks at a container that Miriam has watered. "You're giving them too much water," he says. "Give me the watering can. You can't do anything right."

▼ TIP!

Posting and Brainstorming

If the direct instruction in this activity does not fit with your program style, make a copy of the chart as suggested and simply post it in a prominent place. As the staff begin to refer to and use the chart, children will pick up on it. If your children are unfamiliar with brainstorming, do the activity "Brainstorming" (p. 269) before you introduce the ABCD conflict-solving process.

REFLECTION

❖ How did this conflict escalate?

❖ What's the conflict now?

❖ How do Ernest and Miriam feel?

❖ What could they do to solve this conflict?

NOTES

● ● ● ● ● ● ● ● ● ● ● ●

Age: 5–7

Activity Type: Storytelling

Activity Level: Quiet

Space: Any

Concentration Level: High

Time: 20 minutes

Group Size: Any

Prerequisite: None

THUMBS UP, THUMBS DOWN

Through storytelling and group problem solving, children develop Win-Win solutions.

● ● ● ● ● ● ● ● ● ● ● ● ● ● ● ● ● ●

MATERIALS

- ❖ Chart paper and markers
- ❖ Activity Sheet: The Win-Win Grid (included with this activity)
- ❖ Conflict Case Study: Guessing Game (included with this activity)
- ❖ Rubber Thumb

SUGGESTED PROCEDURE

1. Explain that when we are trying to resolve conflicts, some solutions are better than others. Ask the children what makes a good solution to a conflict. Write children's suggestions on the chart paper. If it doesn't come up during the discussion, emphasize that the best conflict solutions are those in which no one is hurt and everybody in the conflict can say, "That's okay with me."

2. Draw the Win-Win Grid. *Explain*:

   Winning in a conflict is being able to say, Thumbs Up (demonstrate using the rubber thumb), "That's okay with me." Losing is Thumbs Down, "That's not okay with me." If both people say Thumbs Up, "That's okay with me," we call that a Win-Win resolution. If both people say Thumbs Down, "That's not okay with me," we call that Lose-lose. If one person says Thumbs Up and the other says Thumbs Down, we call that Win-Lose or Lose-Win.

3. Present the following situation:

   In Ms. Lopez's group room the children love to put jigsaw puzzles together. There are ten boxes of puzzles. Lately, when the children have gone to get puzzles, they've found that pieces from different puzzles have been mixed together. Ms. Lopez gathered the group and said, "We've got a problem. The puzzle pieces are getting mixed together."

   ### Mini-Reflection
   - ◆ Why would this be a problem for the group?

    ◆ How do you think the children felt when they tried to put puzzles together and found pieces that didn't belong?

    ◆ How could they solve the problem?

4. Continue the story. Ask the children to listen to all the solutions Ms. Lopez's group thought of without evaluating them. (In the next step, you will ask them to evaluate the solutions as Thumbs Up or Thumbs Down.)

    ❖ Ms. Lopez takes all the puzzles away and no one gets to use them.

    ❖ Ms. Lopez buys all new puzzles.

    ❖ Some children volunteer to sort the puzzle pieces.

    ❖ The group sets up a procedure for putting puzzles away so pieces don't get mixed.

    ❖ Once the puzzle pieces are sorted, the back of the pieces are marked with a color so it's easy to tell where they belong.

    ❖ Everyone promises never ever to mix puzzle pieces again as long as they live.

5. Go through the list again, asking children to evaluate the solutions as either Win-Win, Win-Lose, or Lose-Lose. Write them in the appropriate box on the Win-Win Grid you drew on the chart paper. For each solution, ask the children what they think would be the consequences or outcome of the solution. Would it be Win-Win for everyone? Win-Lose for everyone? A winner for some and loser for others? Finish the activity by having children identify which solution(s) are the most workable.

6. With older children, continue the activity by distributing the Conflict Case Study to children and reading it aloud as they follow along:

Maria has finished her report on her favorite hobby. She decides that she wants to play a new board game that the after-school teacher just brought into the game area. She's not sure of the rules, so she wants to play with someone who won't make fun of her.

Jeanie says that she gets the board game now, because she's doing her hobby report on games and she especially wants to use this one. Last week Jeanie made fun of Maria when they played checkers.

7. Have the children work in cooperative groups and use the Win-Win Grid to come up with four different solutions to the conflict.

REFLECTION

❖ What solutions did you develop?

❖ Which box on the grid was easiest to fill?

❖ Which solution do you think is best?

NOTES

● ● ● ● ● ● ● ● ● ● ●

The Win-Win Grid

WIN-WIN

Both people get what they want.

WIN-LOSE

Person 1 gets what he or she wants but person 2 doesn't.

LOSE-WIN

Person 1 doesn't get what he or she wants but person 2 does.

LOSE-LOSE

Neither person gets what he or she wants.

Guessing Game

Maria has finished her report on her favorite hobby. She decides that she wants to play a new board game that the afterschool teacher just brought into the game area. She's not sure of the rules, so she wants to play with someone who won't make fun of her.

Jeanie says that she gets the board game now, because she's doing her hobby report on games and she especially wants to use this one. Last week Jeanie made fun of Maria when they played checkers.

Exploring Conflict and Conflict Resolution

Age:	5–12
Activity Type:	Chart
Activity Level:	Quiet
Space:	Any
Concentration Level:	High
Time:	20 minutes
Group Size:	Any
Prerequisite:	None

CONFLICT VOCABULARY

The group creates a chart of conflict vocabulary to post in the program space.

MATERIALS

❖ Chart paper and markers

SUGGESTED PROCEDURE

1. Create a "Conflict Words" chart to post in a prominent place. Begin with the words generated during "What's Conflict?" (p. 239). Add more words to the chart as they come up during other activities in this book. As you add words, discuss their meaning. Try to use the words from the chart during discussions of conflict and refer to the chart when you do.

CHARTING YOUR CAUSE

Children look for and discuss examples of the various conflict resolution techniques.

Age:	5–12
Activity Type:	Drama
Activity Level:	Quiet
Space:	Any
Concentration Level:	High
Time:	10 minutes
Group Size:	Any
Prerequisite:	"Conflict Resolution Chart" (p. 252)

MATERIALS

❖ Conflict Resolution Chart (p. 252)

SUGGESTED PROCEDURE

1. Have children bring in examples of various conflict resolution techniques they observe during the day. These can be observed during recess, on the playground, during lunch, after school, etc.

2. Ask for volunteers to demonstrate the techniques by role playing the incidents.

REFLECTION

❖ Where did the conflict take place?

❖ What conflict resolution techniques did the people involved use?

❖ Do you think the techniques were successful?

❖ What might have made them more successful?

Age: 5–12

Activity Type: Getting to know you

Activity Level: Quiet

Space: Any

Concentration Level: Medium

Time: 15 minutes

Group Size: Any

Prerequisite: None

WHAT COLOR IS CONFLICT?

Children pick a color that reminds them of conflict and describe why they chose it.

● ● ● ● ● ● ● ● ● ● ● ● ● ● ● ● ● ●

MATERIALS

❖ Lots of colored paper (have different colors, but especially lots of red).

SUGGESTED PROCEDURE

1. Place the pieces of colored paper in a pile at the front of the room. Ask children to think about what color comes to mind when they hear the word "conflict."

2. In groups of two or three, have them come and pick a piece of paper from the pile and return to their seats.

3. When everyone has a piece of paper, go around the room. Have each child hold up his or her paper and say, "I think of _____ when I think of conflict because _____." It helps if you model this first.

REFLECTION

❖ What did you notice about the different colors people chose?

❖ If you were going to choose another color what would it be?

❖ What color represents peace to you?

BRAINSTORMING

Children practice brainstorming by thinking of as many uses for a common object as possible.

● ● ● ● ● ● ● ● ● ● ● ● ● ● ● ● ●

Age:	5–12
Activity Type:	Brainstorming
Activity Level:	Quiet
Space:	Any
Concentration Level:	High
Time:	20 minutes
Group Size:	Any
Prerequisite:	None

MATERIALS

❖ An ordinary object such as a box, a wooden spoon, or a cardboard tube

❖ Chart paper and markers

SUGGESTED PROCEDURE

1. Brainstorming is a skill that can and should be practiced often in all types of problem solving, not just conflict resolution. Explain that the purpose of brainstorming is to come up with as many ideas as possible in a short period of time. During the brainstorm no one says whether the ideas are good or bad, sensible or silly, workable or not workable. The point is simply to get out as many ideas as you can. After the brainstorm is finished, the ideas are evaluated.

2. Set the object in front of the group. Ask them to suggest all the things they can think of that they could do with that object. Write their suggestions on the board. After a few minutes, or after their energy runs down, end the brainstorm and begin evaluating the ideas.

REFLECTION

❖ What does the group think it would like to do with the object? If at all possible, do what the group decides.

Age:	5–12
Activity Type:	Team challenge
Activity Level:	Moderate
Space:	Large open space
Concentration Level:	Medium
Time:	20 minutes
Group Size:	6 or more
Prerequisite:	"Conflict Escalates" (p. 241)

THE CONFLICT FIELD

Blindfolded children explore concepts of de-escalating conflict as they try to make their way through a field of obstacles.

● ● ● ● ● ● ● ● ● ● ● ● ● ● ● ● ● ●

MATERIALS

❖ Assorted props to create the obstacle field – these can include stuffed animals, ropes, boxes, anything. (Be creative here to add to the fun.)

❖ Blindfolds (half the number of the group)

❖ Paper and pencil for each person

❖ Chart paper and markers

SET THE SCENE

You will need to set up an obstacle field before the group arrives. Clear a 10' wide by 18' long space and clearly mark the boundaries. Fill the inside of the space with a variety of "obstacles." Set it up so there is no clear walking path through the area. Do not put so many obstacles, however, that there is nowhere to walk.

Tell the children, "We have learned that there are many ways that conflict can escalate. We have also learned that we can help to de-escalate a conflict. I'd like you to think of one way you know of to de-escalate a conflict. Once you have thought of it, I'd like you to write it down on this paper."

Ask the children to read their de-escalation skills to the rest of the group and place their paper on the ground at the end (one end of the marked area) of the field.

Explain, "This is our conflict field. Inside here are lots of things that get in the way of de-escalating conflict. What are some of those things?

"Our job is to make our way through this field, without touching any of the escalators. We want to make it to the other side to get our de-escalation skills."

▼ TIP!

For Younger Children

To complete this activity with a younger group, allow only one person to navigate through the field at a time. As the partner pair is working, the rest of the group is quietly observing. To more actively involve a group, have the observers act as the obstacles inside the field. Once they are in place, they cannot move or speak.

SUGGESTED PROCEDURE

1. Ask each person to find a partner.

2. One partner will be blindfolded. The other partner will help to guide the blindfolded partner through the field. The guide may not step inside the field or touch the blindfolded partner. Verbal instruction only is allowed.

3. Start the blindfolded people at one end of the field (the long way).

4. Have partners switch roles.

REFLECTION

Help children think about what they need to do to de-escalate conflict and to avoid hitting escalators. Ask the pairs to find a quiet space within the room. Their job is to create a newspaper headline describing one strategy they used that helped them from hitting any of the obstacles in the field. For example, "Josh tells Louise to take baby steps!"

Once the headlines are created, share them. Use the headlines to talk about what the group has learned from the activity.

NOTES

Age: 8–12

Activity Type: Team Challenge

Activity Level: Active

Space: Large open space

Concentration Level: Medium

Time: 20 minutes

Group Size: 10–16

Prerequisite: None

TIP TOE TENSION

Children try to keep steady while trying to tip their partner off balance.

MATERIALS

❖ One rope 20' long

❖ Two carpet squares about 1' in diameter

SET THE SCENE

Explain to the group, "When conflict happens, at least two people are involved. Sometimes, one person is trying to incite another; other times they are both looking to get their own way. Conflict isn't always the best way to get what you want. When you are in a conflict, try to think of what you want *and* what you really need. In order to get through conflict, you may have to let go of what you want to reach an agreement between the two of you."

SUGGESTED PROCEDURE

1. Place the two carpet squares about 15 feet from each other on a surface where they won't slip.

2. Tell the group about the ancient test of wisdom and balance called "Tip Toe Tension." In this challenge two young people are tested to see who can keep their balance while holding a rope between them. Have one child stand on each rug and squat down, while staying on their tip toes.

3. The object of this game is to remain balanced on your rug while trying to move the other person off balance. Keep score by counting the number of times each person touches the ground. Stop at a low number or after a few minutes and let another pair try. If a player never touches the ground, they receive a bonus of five points.

4. Another variation is to play without keeping score. Tell the children only that they must keep their balance on the rugs and keep hold of the rope. They will likely interpret this to mean that they should try to knock the other person off their rug as well. See if any pairs choose to cooperate. Discuss this as part of getting lured into a conflict.

REFLECTION

After everyone has had a chance to try Tip Toe Tension, gather the group into a circle with the rope in the center. Ask them about how it felt to play the game.

❖ What were strategies they found for not losing their balance? How about for getting the other player off balance?

❖ Did they enjoy playing the game or did they feel pressure to win?

Next, try to create parallels between this game and being in a conflict. Ask them to think of the rope as a conflict they have had.

❖ What are some ways they could have dealt with the conflict and still played the game? (Remind the group about their strategies for not getting thrown off balance.)

❖ Did they feel distanced from each other while playing? How about afterward?

❖ Did having goals that were the opposite of the other player affect how they felt about each other?

Draw the discussion to a close by asking the group to think about what it might mean to have a *positive* conflict.

Age:	8–12
Activity Type:	Team challenge
Activity Level:	Very active
Space:	Large open space
Concentration Level:	Medium
Time:	45 minutes
Group Size:	10 or more
Prerequisite:	None

DON'T TOUCH ME!

Children try to pass through a hoop, two at a time, without touching each other, as a way to explore personal space.

● ● ● ● ● ● ● ● ● ● ● ● ● ● ● ●

MATERIALS

❖ One hula hoop

❖ Stopwatch

SET THE SCENE

Ask the children, "Have you ever been in a small place with another person? How about riding in a car? Have you ever wished your sister or brother would stop touching you? Well, here is your chance to practice not touching."

SUGGESTED PROCEDURE

1. Divide the group into two even teams (use four teams if you have more than 12 children). Place the hoop on the ground in the middle of an open space.

2. Line one team up on one side of the hoop and the other team directly across the hoop from the first.

3. *Tell the children,* "Our goal is to get as quickly from one side of the hoop to the other. So, team A is trying to get to team B's side and vice versa.

   "This is a very sensitive, technologically advanced hoop. In order to pass through it, there must be at least four feet in the hoop at a time – two feet from one team, and two feet from the other team. If there are less than four feet in the hoop, then the group must start over (i.e., one person cannot pass through the hoop alone).

   "The hoop likes to hear loud noises. As you are passing through the hoop, you must yell to the person who is passing through with you, 'Don't touch me!' (An enthusiastic demonstration of this from you can help to set the tone!)

   "You may not touch the other person while passing through the hoop. If a touch takes place, three seconds are added to your time.

"If the hoop is touched, three seconds are also added to the time."

4. Ask the group to take a few minutes to figure out how they want to solve the problem.

5. Do a test run to set the base time. Ask the group to set a time goal. Give them 15 to 20 minutes to reach the goal.

REFLECTION

Give the group a chance to reflect on what they have just done.

❖ How did they go about solving the problem? Were they successful at reaching their goal?

Once they've had a chance to talk about the problem, use the activity to begin discussing the relationship between conflict resolution and space.

❖ Have you ever felt like you did not have enough space? Where were you? What were you doing?

❖ Have you ever heard the expression "In your face"? What do you think this means?

❖ How can imposing on someone's space escalate an argument? What about touching someone during an argument? Why do you think this escalates the argument?

Age: 8–12

Activity Type: Team Challenge

Activity Level: Quiet

Space: Any

Concentration Level: Medium

Time: 20 minutes

Group Size: 6 or more

Prerequisite: Some conflict vocabulary

IT'S A CONFLICT WORD

Small teams compete to create words from the letter cards.

● ● ● ● ● ● ● ● ● ● ● ● ● ● ● ● ●

MATERIALS

❖ 4" x 6" index cards

❖ Colored markers

SET THE SCENE

You will need to create sets of word cards. Using the conflict words below, write one letter per card to form the words. Color code the cards so that all the letters of one word are in one color. Use the following words (or others you have introduced): mediate, communicate, arbitrate, negotiate, legislate, litigate.

Note: You will need one set of cards per small team of three to five children.

SUGGESTED PROCEDURE

1. Shuffle each set of cards so the words are not distinguishable. Give one set to each small team.

2. Each team's goal is to create the longest words they can from the cards provided. They can use only one color in a word (i.e., don't mix the yellow letters with the red).

3. Allow 15 to 20 minutes for problem solving.

REFLECTION

Have the teams share their solutions.

❖ Did anyone find words to use up all the cards of one color?

INSTIGATOR

A detective tries to find the instigator in a group.

● ● ● ● ● ● ● ● ● ● ● ● ● ● ● ● ● ●

Age:	5–12
Activity Type:	Team Challenge
Activity Level:	Moderate
Space:	Any
Concentration Level:	Medium
Time:	20 minutes
Group Size:	10 or more
Prerequisite:	None

MATERIALS

❖ Detective hat (optional)

SET THE SCENE

Ask the children, "How does a conflict get started? When someone sets out to start a fight what are they called? Instigator! Today we'll look for instigators."

SUGGESTED PROCEDURE

1. Select one child to start as the detective and have them leave the room for a few moments. Once they are gone, pick the first instigator.

2. The instigator will make different movements (e.g., rub their tummy, hop up and down, clap hands, etc.) and the rest of the group will try to follow as accurately as possible. Have them practice a few moves.

3. Ask the detective to return. They now have three guesses to find the instigator while the group makes different movements, following the lead of the instigator.

4. When the detective guesses or uses up their three questions, select a new detective and instigator and continue play.

5. Bring this game to a close by asking the group to start performing actions together. Then, have them take turns randomly as the instigator, changing the movement when they feel like it. Encourage them to enjoy each movement and to share the role of leader.

REFLECTION

❖ Who is the instigator in a conflict? Was it difficult to spot them in this exercise? Why? What did you look for?

❖ When you were part of the group, what did you do to keep from giving the instigator away?

❖ How was the final activity, where you shared the leader role, different from being an instigator?

Practicing Conflict Resolution

MAKING PEACE PUPPETS

Children make Peace Puppets to use to act out conflicts.

Age:	5–10
Activity Type:	Arts and crafts
Activity Level:	Moderate
Space:	Work tables
Concentration Level:	Medium
Time:	30 minutes
Group Size:	Any
Prerequisite:	None

MATERIALS

❖ Socks

❖ Yarn, felt, material scraps

❖ Scissors

❖ Glue

SUGGESTED PROCEDURE

1. Explain that the children will be making puppets to use in the group for the remainder of the program year. These Peace Puppets will help the group to look at conflicts that might come up, so that they can consider lots of different ways to deal with problems between people. Because they are *Peace* Puppets, the one thing they will not be able to do is fight; these puppets have to figure out other ways to deal with whatever disagreements they may have.

2. Make one puppet ahead of time, so that children can see what a finished product might look like.

3. Use a sock for the main body of the puppet, yarn for hair, and felt or material scraps for eyes, mouth, and clothes.

4. Help children make their own puppets. They may work in groups if they wish, but each child should have her or his own puppet in the end, as these puppets will be used to represent specific individuals in the future.

5. Once the puppets are finished, store them in your room in a specially marked place.

REFLECTION

❖ Can you think of a time when you could have used a Peace Puppet to help you think about creative ways to solve a problem?

For the Future

The Peace Puppets can be used to help children consider their options anytime a conflict arises in the future.

Age:	5–10
Activity Type:	Drama
Activity Level:	Moderate
Space:	Any
Concentration Level:	Medium
Time:	60 minutes
Group Size:	Any
Prerequisite:	"Making Peace Puppets" (p. 279)

PEACE PUPPET SHOW

Use the Peace Puppets to think in a nonthreatening way about alternative resolutions to conflict in your group.

MATERIALS
❖ Peace Puppets, created in "Making Peace Puppets" (p. 279)
❖ Desk or table with a skirt, to use as a puppet stage

SUGGESTED PROCEDURE
1. When you notice a conflict in the group, take time out from what you are doing or remember the event for a later time. Act out the conflict situation, using the Peace Puppets created by the children who were involved in this specific conflict. Try to be as accurate as you can be, repeating the children's words as closely as possible.

2. Stop the play at the moment that the conflict has escalated to its highest point and ask both the children who were involved and the other children in the group to identify the problem. Focus on what each child involved in the conflict wants or needs. Check with the children involved in the conflict to be certain that the group has accurately assessed each individual's needs and desires.

3. Have the whole group brainstorm possible resolutions to this conflict. Then vote on the best resolution among those choices.

4. Check with the children involved in the original conflict to see if this was the resolution they came up with. If it wasn't, have them share their actual resolution.

5. Finish the puppet show according to the resolution the whole group chose.

REFLECTION
❖ Did the resolution that the group came up with satisfy everyone's wants and needs? Did the resolution chosen by the actual participants in the conflict do this?

❖ How did you decide which solution to this problem was best? What factors did we take into consideration?

❖ Next time you have a conflict with someone, what can you remember from this play that might keep you from fighting?

BRAINSTORMING CONFLICT SCENARIOS

The group collects ideas for potential conflict situations which can be used in other activities.

●●●●●●●●●●●●●●●●●●●

Age:	5–12
Activity Type:	Brainstorming
Activity Level:	Moderate
Space:	Any
Concentration Level:	Medium
Time:	15–30 minutes
Group Size:	Any
Prerequisite:	None

MATERIALS

❖ Chart paper and markers

SUGGESTED PROCEDURE

1. This activity will give children another opportunity to practice the skill of brainstorming. Explain that in some cases, getting lots of ideas out quickly is more important than making sure that the ideas we generate are reasonable, good, or wise. Brainstorming is the process by which a group can generate many ideas quickly. The rules for brainstorming are as follows:

   ❖ For the time period that the group is generating a list of ideas, nobody responds to anyone else's ideas (i.e., no one can say, "That's dumb!" or even, "Yeah, and then we could...").

   ❖ Everyone must raise his hand to be called on so that we speak one at a time.

   ❖ Any idea is acceptable, no matter how outrageous it may seem.

2. Explain that today we will brainstorm "conflict scenarios." A scenario is like a scene from a play or like a very short story. Give a couple of examples, such as, "Two five-year-old children are fighting over who gets to play with the blocks in the group room." or "A husband and wife disagree about what to eat for dinner." Explain that conflict scenarios need to include two pieces of information: *who* is fighting and *why* they are fighting.

3. Draw a big storm cloud border on the paper, to represent a brainstorm. Tell the children that you will brainstorm for ten minutes as a group. When they understand the rules, begin brainstorming.

4. After you have generated a list of conflict scenarios, choose one and brainstorm a list of things that might make that conflict escalate. Explain that things that escalate a conflict are things that make it get worse, instead of better. Give a couple of examples,

TIP!

For Younger or Older Children

This activity can be adapted based on your ultimate goal. For example, if you are working with younger children and using puppets, frame the discussion around developing Peace Puppet scenarios. If you are working with older children in drama, talk about the conflicts in those terms.

such as, "One person says, 'You *always* say that!'" or "One person turns her back on the other person." Put this list into some sort of chronological order once it is finished, so that you have created, as a group, a very detailed account of a conflict scenario.

5. You can use brainstorming in many ways. If you have time, you might try brainstorming de-escalating strategies or possible resolutions to a particular scenario.

6. Keep the lists of conflict scenarios and escalating causes posted in the room for later reference.

REFLECTION

❖ Was it difficult to keep yourself from commenting on other people's ideas during the brainstorm? Why?

❖ Is this an effective way to generate a lot of ideas quickly? Were some of the ideas good ones? How do you decide which ones to keep?

❖ Do any of these conflict scenarios or escalating causes sound familiar to you? Do you have any similar stories?

CONFLICT SPINNER

Children practice conflict resolution techniques using role playing and a spinner.

● ● ● ● ● ● ● ● ● ● ● ● ● ● ● ● ● ● ●

Age:	(5–7) 8–12
Activity Type:	Drama
Activity Level:	Quiet
Space:	Any
Concentration Level:	High
Time:	20 minutes
Group Size:	Any
Prerequisite:	None

MATERIALS

- ❖ Conflict Resolution Chart p. 252
- ❖ Spinner from a game
- ❖ Sticky labels
- ❖ Role-play Cards (see "The Lunch Box Conflict," p. 248; "Conflict Resolution Chart Role Plays," p. 253; or "A B C D Problem-solving Role Plays," p.257)

SUGGESTED PROCEDURE

1. Write conflict resolution techniques on the sticky labels and make a spinner by sticking the labels on the game spinner.

2. Read role-play cards to the group. Have volunteers act out the conflicts showing how they escalate. Then have the role players spin the spinner.

REFLECTION

- ❖ How well did the conflict resolution technique work?
- ❖ Can you think of another way to handle this conflict?
- ❖ Have you ever been in a conflict like this?

For Younger Children

Be sure the conflict resolution techniques are appropriate for younger children. Encourage them to use the spinner with their Peace Puppets

Age:	5–12
Activity Type:	Drama
Activity Level:	Moderate
Space:	Any
Concentration Level:	High
Time:	30 minutes
Group Size:	Any
Prerequisite:	None

CRAZIEST CONFLICT RESOLUTIONS

Children try to come up with creative, crazy solutions to a conflict.

MATERIALS

❖ Zany props and disguises (optional)

SUGGESTED PROCEDURE

1. You may use the conflicts that your group concocted in "Brainstorming Conflict Scenarios" (p. 281) for this activity. Otherwise, invent a conflict of your own or use one that has happened in your group.

2. The goal of this activity is for children to be as creative as they possibly can when generating solutions to a conflict. There are no solutions which are too unrealistic, too silly, or too outrageous. Be clear about this when introducing the activity to the children.

3. Divide the group into smaller groups and explain that you will describe a situation where two people are having a seemingly difficult conflict. The group must try to come up with the most creative solution to this problem. The most creative solution will be determined by a vote once each group has shared their solution with the others.

4. One person in each group is the "Creative Genius." Try to find a few zany hats, wigs, or some other silly props for these children to wear (a rubber chicken, a kazoo, or a clown nose will work, too!). This person's job is to keep encouraging the group to be as outlandish as possible.

5. Give the groups about ten minutes to work out their resolutions.

6. Gather together as a large group and have the Creative Genius of each group present their solution. Encourage silliness!

7. Have a group vote to determine which group designed the most creative conflict resolution. (Of course, the group can choose to have everyone win.)

REFLECTION

❖ Could this conflict resolution ever work? What about some of the others? Why or why not?

❖ Did the other groups think of solutions that were very different from your group's?

❖ How did it feel to have the Creative Genius asking you to be more and more creative? Did he help you make your solution crazier and crazier? Did he keep you laughing?

❖ If you were the Creative Genius, was it hard to keep pushing the group to be creative? Did people get tired of you trying to get them to think harder and further?

❖ Were there any parts of anyone's conflict resolutions that really might work? Which parts?

NOTES

Age: 8–10

Activity Type: Video

Activity Level: Moderate

Space: Any

Concentration Level: Medium

Time: 45 minutes

Group Size: Any

Prerequisite: "Brainstorming" (p. 269)

MORPHIN' THE POWER RANGERS

Children watch this popular TV show to brainstorm alternative conflict resolution strategies to the Rangers' violent ones.

MATERIALS

- ❖ TV and VCR
- ❖ Recorded episode of the *Mighty Morphin' Power Rangers* program

SUGGESTED PROCEDURE

1. Tape an episode of the TV show and watch it first yourself, thinking about the places where you might stop the tape when watching with the children to address conflict situations.

2. Explain that the group will be watching the *Power Rangers* today, but that they will watch it in an unusual way, as conflict resolution experts, who may be able to help the Power Rangers expand their use of nonviolent conflict resolution strategies. Ask the children to help you decide when to stop the tape during the show. You will be looking for any point in the program when any one of the Power Rangers finds herself or himself in a conflict situation with someone else. At that point the group will think of strategies, *besides fighting,* that the Power Rangers could use to resolve their conflict.

3. Roll the tape!

REFLECTION

- ❖ Did the Power Rangers ever use any conflict resolution techniques other than fighting? When?
- ❖ Do you think that the Power Rangers fight too much? Why or why not?
- ❖ What do you think about TV programs for kids that have a lot of violence in them? Do you think they are fun to watch? Do they ever bother you?
- ❖ What lessons do you think kids learn from watching shows like the *Power Rangers* or *Roadrunner*?

THE VERY BEST PART IS THE BRIDGE

After reading the story *The Tree House*, by Lois Lowry, children discuss building bridges that resolve conflict.

● ● ● ● ● ● ● ● ● ● ● ● ● ● ● ● ● ●

Age:	5–10
Activity Type:	Storytelling
Activity Level:	Quiet
Space:	Work tables
Concentration Level:	Medium
Time:	30 minutes
Group Size:	Any
Prerequisite:	"Conflict Escalates" (p. 241)

MATERIALS

❖ *"The Tree House"* by Lois Lowry, in *The Big Book for Peace*, Ann Durrel and Marilyn Sachs (ed.). Dutton Children's Books; New York, 1990.

❖ Chart paper and markers

SUGGESTED PROCEDURE

1. Settle the children for story time. Read Lois Lowry's story *The Tree House* to them.

2. After finishing, draw an escalator on the chart paper and have the group identify the actions in the story which escalated the conflict between Leah and Chrissy. See the "Conflict Escalates" activity (p. 241) for more details.

3. In the end of the story, Leah and Chrissy resolve their conflict by building a bridge between their tree houses. Draw a bridge on another piece of paper and ask the children where they might like to build bridges in their own lives. Help them think about the metaphorical bridges as well as literal bridges that they might want to build by suggesting a few examples, such as, "I would like to build a bridge between my neighborhood and the East side of town, because people don't usually travel between these two places." Or, "I'd like to build a bridge between the older kids and the younger kids in this afterschool program, because we don't spend very much time with them, and we could share a lot more."

4. Follow up with the "Building Bridges" (p. 289) or "Human Bridges" (p. 74) activities.

REFLECTION

❖ Why do you think Chrissy hung up a sign on her tree house that said "Keep Out!"? Have you ever hung up a sign like that? When and why? Have you ever hung a welcome sign, like the ones the girls hung up at the end of the story?

❖ Whose tree house was better, Chrissy's or Leah's? Why? How do you know? Does more money always make something better?

❖ Have you ever been in a fight with one of your best friends? Why did you fight? Did you build a bridge to resolve your conflict? What kind of bridge was it?

❖ Why did Chrissy say that her favorite part about a tree house is "the bridge"?

NOTES

● ● ● ● ● ● ● ● ● ● ● ●

BUILDING BRIDGES

Children build models of bridges that they would like to see, as inspired by the story *The Tree House,* by Lois Lowry.

Age:	5–10
Activity Type:	Arts and crafts
Activity Level:	Moderate
Space:	Any
Concentration Level:	Medium
Time:	30 minutes
Group Size:	Any
Prerequisite:	"The Very Best Part is the Bridge" (p. 287)

MATERIALS

❖ Cardboard, small boxes, paper towel rolls

❖ Popsicle sticks

❖ Markers, paint, crayons

❖ Construction paper

❖ Glue, tape

❖ Glitter, yarn, felt, material scraps

SUGGESTED PROCEDURE

1. Using the list that the group generated at the end of "The Very Best Part is the Bridge" activity (p. 287), have each child choose a bridge that they would like to build.

2. Build models of bridges using cardboard, paper, and whatever else the children find inspiring.

3. Give each person a chance to share their bridge with the group, describing why a bridge would be a good idea in that particular place or situation.

REFLECTION

❖ Why isn't there a bridge built where your bridge would go? Could a bridge be built there? How?

Age: 8–12

Activity Type: Arts and crafts

Activity Level: Quiet

Space: Work tables

Concentration Level: Medium

Time: 30 minutes

Group Size: Any

Prerequisite: None

CONFLICT RESOLUTION COMICS

After reading comic strips that have to do with conflict resolution, the group creates its own funny pages.

●●●●●●●●●●●●●●●●●●

MATERIALS

❖ Pens and paper

❖ Markers, crayons, colored pencils

❖ Comic strips from the newspaper

SUGGESTED PROCEDURE

1. Show the comic strips you have collected and ask what they have in common. Discuss the common elements in comic strips. Explain that they will be making their own comic strips about conflict and conflict resolution.

2. Children may choose to work in groups or alone. Have them create a comic strip using characters they develop. The theme of the comic should be dealing with conflict, either successfully or not. The comic strip doesn't have to be funny.

3. When they have finished, have the children share their comics with the others in the group by posting them on a wall. Give everyone enough time to circulate around the room and read other people's creations.

4. For next time, photocopy everyone's comic strip and distribute the group's Conflict Resolution Comics to everyone.

REFLECTION

❖ Why are the comic strips we saw first funny?

❖ Is a comic strip an effective way to get a message across? Does it make you think as you laugh?

❖ To whom could we give our group's Conflict Resolution Funnies?

TAKE A WALK IN MY SHOES

Children work together to walk in "shared shoes"
(shoe boxes).

Age:	5–10
Activity Type:	Arts and crafts
Activity Level:	Very active
Space:	Work tables; then large open space
Concentration Level:	Medium
Time:	40 minutes
Group Size:	6 or more
Prerequisite:	None

MATERIALS

- ❖ One shoe box per person
- ❖ Markers, construction paper, glue, etc.
- ❖ Boundary markers
- ❖ Cassette player and age-appropriate music cassettes (optional)

SET THE SCENE

Ask each person to find a partner. If needed, allow for a three-some. Give each pair one box (two boxes to a threesome).

Tell the children: "Do you know what the expression 'take a walk in my shoes' means? Could taking a walk in another person's shoes help to resolve a conflict? Well, we're going to see.

"We will begin by creating our shoes. Our shoes need to tell people something about us. Use these art supplies to decorate your shoes (boxes). The decoration should tell all of us something about what you are like when you are angry or mad. For example, are you quiet? Do you like to be alone? Do you yell? Do you try to work it out? Think of how you usually act when you are angry."

SUGGESTED PROCEDURE

1. Allow ample time for the children to create their shoes. Move around the room coaching and helping the children to think about how they are when they are angry.

2. Once the children are finished, have each pair share their box with the larger group. Encourage each partner to explain to the rest of the group what their partner is like.

3. *Say,* "Now, it's time to see if we really can walk in each other's shoes."

4. Ask everyone to line up across an open area (staying with their original partners).

5. Begin by asking the partners to try walking shoulder to shoulder with their middle feet in the box. See how far they can walk in a given time limit. If you would like, use music to mark the

time. When the music starts, the children start moving. When the music stops, the children stop.

6. Now see if they can get as far by partnering up with another pair. Add an extra box (eight feet need three boxes!). Give the same amount of time. How far could they move?

7. Continue adding groups together (have plenty of extra boxes available) until the whole group is moving together. How far could they travel? Allow several tries. Encourage creative problem solving.

REFLECTION

Your group will find that they are much more efficient when the numbers are small. It's easier to share one shoe than it is to share ten!

❖ Why is this? What happened as the groups became larger? What did they need to do differently to travel the same distance?

Once you have discussed the activity, ask the children to think about how this activity is like conflict.

❖ What do they need to do to resolve a conflict between two people?

❖ How is this different when there are four, or eight, or more people? How do things get more complicated when more people become involved? Encourage children to begin a discussion about point of view.

Peer Mediation Training

Age: 8–12

Activity Type: Drama

Activity Level: Quiet

Space: Any

Concentration Level: High

Time: 30 minutes

Group Size: Any

Prerequisite: "Conflict Escalates" (p. 241), "ABCD Problem Solving" (p. 254)

PRACTICING MEDIATION

Children are introduced to mediation and practice using it to resolve conflicts.

● ● ● ● ● ● ● ● ● ● ● ● ● ● ● ● ●

MATERIALS

❖ ABCs of Mediation Chart (make a copy on a sheet of chart paper, or enlarge the page on a copy machine) (p. 295)

❖ ABCs of Mediation Chart copied for each child

❖ Role-play Cards

SUGGESTED PROCEDURE

1. Ask children to describe a time someone helped them solve a conflict. What did the person do? What did they say? What were some of the helpful things they did? Record the key qualities you hear on a chart, such as, "Good listener," "Fair," "Didn't let us call names," and so on.

2. Write the term "mediator" on the board or on paper. Explain that a mediator is someone who helps other people solve their conflicts. The mediator does this not by telling them what to do, but by helping the people talk to each other and focus on solving the problem.

3. Distribute a copy of the ABCs of Mediation Chart to each child. Discuss the steps and how they think those steps will be helpful in solving conflicts.

4. Using the role-play cards that follow, have the children practice using the ABC process to mediate a conflict. After the role play is complete, reflect with the children.

REFLECTION

❖ Were you able to solve your problem with the help of a mediator?

❖ What was easy or hard about being a mediator?

❖ What conflict resolution skills did you use as a mediator?

❖ What skills do you think you need to be a good mediator?

The ABCs of Mediation

Introduce yourself. Ask if they want help solving the problem.

Review the ground rules:

- ❖ One person talks at a time.

- ❖ No name calling or put downs.

- ❖ Be honest.

- ❖ Ask them: Are you willing to work and try to solve the problem?
  Do you agree to follow these ground rules?

Ask questions

- ❖ Decide who will speak first.

- ❖ Ask each person: What happened? How did it make you feel?

- ❖ After each person talks, summarize what was said.

- ❖ Say what you think the problem is.

Brainstorm possible solutions

- ❖ Get ideas from each person about how to solve each part of the problem.

- ❖ Don't let them criticize the ideas right now. That happens next.

- ❖ If there are a lot of ideas, write them down.

Choose solutions

- ❖ Good solutions make everyone feel like a winner.

- ❖ Be specific. The solution should say Who, What, When, Where, How, How Much.

- ❖ Check to see if the solution is realistic and fair.

- ❖ Write it down and read it back to them.

Mediation Role Plays

- -

Pam:

We're trying to put on a play and Sam keeps coming around and bothering us. He wants to be in the play but there's no room. He keeps bumping into people and saying, "Sorry." I don't think it's an accident. I think he does it on purpose so that it will wreck our play.

- -

Sam:

Whenever there's a play Pam always gets to be the director and she never lets anyone into the plays. She has to boss everything. I know there's room in this play because some people have two parts. I could play a part. I only bumped two people. One was an accident and the other was Andy because he said, "Ha, ha, you can't be in the play."

- -

Slip Sliding Away

The Conflict (Read to the group)

Felicia and her friends are playing on the slide at recess. There is a large muddy puddle at the bottom of the slide. No one wants to slide into the puddle, so as each person takes their turn, others stand at the bottom and catch the person sliding. Malcolm was supposed to catch Felicia, but he didn't. Now she's covered with mud. Malcolm and the other kids laugh. Felicia says, "It's not funny. You did this on purpose. You always do mean things."

Slip Sliding Away – Felicia

Felicia's Point of View:

You think Malcolm purposely let you fall into the mud. Look at how he laughed! Ever since he moved here a month ago he's been doing mean things to other kids. Usually he doesn't get caught, but you know he does them.

Felicia Background:

You hate to be embarassed or have other kids laugh at you. You say what's on your mind when you're angry, even if it hurts other people. You jump to conclusions and make global kinds of statements. ("You always...You never...")

Slip Sliding Away – Malcolm

Malcolm's Point of View:

You didn't mean to let her fall in the mud and you didn't mean to laugh. But she did look funny all covered with mud and squaking like a chicken! She thinks she's so big and always makes accusations about you, even though you've never done any of the things she says. Before she came down the slide it sounded like she said, "I bet he screws this up." That was embarassing.

Malcolm's Background:

You just moved to this school a month ago. You still don't feel you fit in. Kids like Felicia seem to have it in for you. It feels to you like they keep you out of things.

Girl Groups

The Conflict (Read to the group)

Carol approached a group of girls on the playground and asked if she could play with them. The leader of the group, Stephanie, said that the group didn't want to be friends with Carol today. Carol responded by calling Stephanie a pig. Soon there was a back and fourth shouting match between the two girls, with the rest of the girls encouraging Stephanie.

Girl Groups – Carol

Carol's Point of View:

You and Stephanie have been friends off and on since the first grade. In third grade you were best friends most of the year, but now she seems to have changed. She's become good friends with a new girl, Angelina. You feel hurt and left out. Today was not the only day you were excluded.

Carol's Background:

In third grade you and Stephanie once went horseback riding together. You also liked to go to get ice cream together and rent videos together. In the second grade, Stephanie ruined one of your Barbie dolls by cutting her hair, but you forgave her.

Girl Groups – Stephanie

▪ ▪

Stephanie's Point of View:

You and Carol have been friends, off and on, since you were in the first grade. This year you've become friendly with a new girl, Angelina. You and Angelina have a lot in common – you both like to read the same books and you are both interested in science. You're going to be working on a science project together. Carol only likes to rent videos and seems kind of babyish to you now. Look at how she calls you nasty names just because you didn't want to play.

Stephanie's Background:

You've always felt as though you have had to do the giving in in your relationship with Carol. Whatever she wants to do is what you usually end up doing, like the getting videos she wants to watch.

▪ ▪

Bicycle Bickering

The Conflict (Read to the group)

Chris lent Pat his bicycle. While Pat was using the bike, the chain broke. Pat crashed the bike, and now it has a bent front wheel. Chris and Pat disagree about who should pay to have the bike fixed.

Bicycle Bickering – Chris

Chris' Point of View:

You feel that Pat should pay to have the bike fixed. She says the chain was rusty, but it wasn't that bad. You think Pat was just careless about riding it. Your family can't afford to buy a new bike or to get this one fixed.

Chris' Background:

You and Pat have been friends for years, but is not the first time she wrecked something of yours. Pat always treats your stuff carelessly. You sometimes feel that if Pat really liked you, she would treat your things with more respect.

Bicycle Bickering — Pat

Pat's Point of View:

You feel that you shouldn't have to pay to have the bike fixed. The chain was really rusty. Chris hasn't taken proper care of the bike, now he is more worried about repairing the bike than the fact that you might have been really hurt.

Pat's Background:

You and Chris have been friends for years, and you feel bad about the bike. But come on, it's not the end of the world. Chris always acts like his stuff is really precious. It's not that big a deal to get the bike fixed, but it's not your responsibility. You sometimes feel that Chris cares more about his things than your friendship.

Peacing It All Together

Giving children a chance to practice peacemaking skills through creative projects

Once children have some conflict resolution skills under their belts, they can become proficient with these skills by practicing them in a variety of forms. The activities in this chapter are all creative, fun projects that give children a chance to use what they have learned from the activities in previous chapters. Some of the projects are one-session activities, some will take several sessions. All encourage children to have fun as they practice the skills of peacemaking.

Peacing It All Together

MAKING PEACE PUNCH

Children create a recipe for a special fruit or vegetable juice which will help people resolve conflicts creatively.

● ● ● ● ● ● ● ● ● ● ● ● ● ● ● ● ● ●

Age:	5–10
Activity Type:	Cooking
Activity Level:	Moderate
Space:	Kitchen or work tables
Concentration Level:	Medium
Time:	20 minutes
Group Size:	10 or more
Prerequisite:	None

MATERIALS

- ❖ Fruits and vegetables
- ❖ Juicer
- ❖ Paper and pencils

SUGGESTED PROCEDURE

1. Explain to the children that you need their help in concocting recipes for Peace Punch, a drink which will help people who are having conflicts to be really creative in thinking of ways to deal with them peaceably.

2. Have children work in small groups. Ask each group to create and agree upon their recipe, using the fruits and vegetables available. Have them give their concoction an outrageous, original name. Make sure that the children remember what they put in their recipe, and ask them to write down the ingredients.

3. Make the juices! Let children experiment with ratios of different ingredients until they have a Peace Punch that they think is delicious, healthy, and good at helping people resolve conflicts.

REFLECTION

- ❖ How did your group decide what to put in the juice? How did you create a name? Were everyone's ideas heard? Did one person make all the decisions?

- ❖ What's funny about the name Peace Punch?

- ❖ Can you remember a time when you could have used a cup of Peace Punch? What was the conflict? How did you react? What do you wish you had done?

Age:	5–10
Activity Type:	Drama
Activity Level:	Very active
Space:	Any
Concentration Level:	Medium
Time:	30–45 minutes
Group Size:	3 or more
Prerequisite:	"Making Peace Punch" (p. 309)

PEACE PUNCH ROLE PLAYS

Children role play conflict situations, using their Peace Punch to help them creatively de-escalate the conflict.

● ● ● ● ● ● ● ● ● ● ● ● ● ● ● ● ●

MATERIALS

❖ Peace Punch from "Making Peace Punch" (p. 309)

❖ Conflict scenarios from "Brainstorming Conflict Scenarios" (p. 281) or conflict scenarios developed by the children

SUGGESTED PROCEDURE

1. Ask children to break into groups of three. Give each group one of the Conflict Scenarios they developed in "Brainstorming Conflict Scenarios" (p. 281) or have them develop their own scenarios.

2. Give them time to read over their scenario, decide who will act out which part, and rehearse their scene a couple of times, so that they will be prepared to perform it for the others.

3. Have each group take a turn acting out their scenario. The audience's job is to stop the action by saying, "Peace Punch!" when they think that the conflict has escalated to a point when things are really out of hand. When the audience stops the action, have the actors involved in the conflict drink their Peace Punch. This will help them think of alternatives to fighting over their differences. Ask the audience to help the actors devise as many creative solutions to the conflict as they can. Choose the best alternative to fighting and ask the actors to act out that resolution.

REFLECTION

❖ How did you know that the conflict was getting worse as you watched? What did the actors do with their faces? With their bodies? What did they say?

❖ When you were deciding which way to end the play and the conflict, how did you decide which one of the endings was the best? What are some of the things we think about when we decide how to deal with conflicts?

❖ Have you ever been in a situation like the one this group presented? What did you do? Could you have used a cup of Peace Punch at the time?

NOTES

● ● ● ● ● ● ● ● ● ● ● ●

Age:	5–10
Activity Type:	Arts and crafts
Activity Level:	Moderate
Space:	Work tables
Concentration Level:	Medium
Time:	30–45 minutes
Group Size:	Any
Prerequisite:	"Making Peace Punch" (p. 309)

PEACEMAKER'S COOKBOOK

The group collects all of their Peace Punch recipes and others they have created and writes a cookbook to share with the community.

● ● ● ● ● ● ● ● ● ● ● ● ● ● ●

MATERIALS

❖ Construction paper

❖ Markers, glitter, glue, tape

❖ Staples or string to hold the book together

SUGGESTED PROCEDURE

1. Let each team decide together how they want to decorate the page in the cookbook that will describe their recipe. Make sure that each group lists the ingredients, including the amount of each, the name of their juice, the directions for making it, and the number of servings their recipe makes. Have them look at other cookbooks for help with measurements and format.

2. Once each group has decorated their page, compile the recipes into one bound volume, along with any other recipes the class may have developed.

3. Have the group decide collectively upon a name for their cookbook. Brainstorm a list of ideas. Let students talk about which name they like best and why. Take a vote or decide by consensus.

4. As a group, write an introduction for the cookbook, explaining how Peace Punch can help people think about creative solutions to conflict situations.

5. If possible, make copies of the cookbook and share it with the community. Sell it to raise money for your center or group!

REFLECTION

❖ How did your group's page turn out? Do you like the way it looks? Could someone easily follow your directions?

❖ Do you know any peacemakers to whom you would like to give this cookbook? What makes that person a peacemaker?

AND NOW, A WORD FROM OUR SPONSORS...

Students watch and discuss public service announcements, then write their own.

● ● ● ● ● ● ● ● ● ● ● ● ● ● ● ● ●

Age:	8–12
Activity Type:	Writing
Activity Level:	Moderate
Space:	Any
Concentration Level:	High
Time:	60 minutes
Group Size:	Any
Prerequisite:	None

MATERIALS

❖ TV and VCR

❖ Videotaped public service announcements

❖ Paper and pencils

SUGGESTED PROCEDURE

1. Explain to the children that they have just been hired to write television advertisements for a high profile campaign. The goal of the campaign is to get other kids in their communities to stop using violence as a way of dealing with conflict.

2. Watch the videotape of other public service announcements to give the children some ideas (for example, "The More You Know" series). Talk as a group about which advertisements they liked and didn't like. Did they have music or celebrities in them? Were they funny? Make a list of things that describe the best ads.

3. Have students work in small groups to create their own ads. Ads should be about one minute long.

4. Make sure everyone has a role within the group (for example, fact checker, creative consultant, celebrity contact, or time-keeper).

REFLECTION

❖ What was the best part about working in your group? The hardest part?

❖ How did you agree upon how your video would look and what it would say? Did you all come to consensus? Did you compromise? Did one person make all the decisions? Were your ideas heard? Did your group need to come up with any Win-Win solutions?

❖ What would be your reaction to your own advertisement if you actually saw it on TV? How would it make you feel?

Would it make you think or act differently? Would you change the channel?

❖ What are some alternatives to violence available to young people when they find themselves in conflict situations? Brainstorm a list, and keep it hanging on the wall to refer to in future sessions.

NOTES
● ● ● ● ● ● ● ● ● ● ● ●

FILMING PEACE ADS

Students film the public service announcements they have written to raise community awareness around nonviolent conflict resolution.

●●●●●●●●●●●●●●●●●●

Age:	8–12
Activity Type:	Drama
Activity Level:	Very active
Space:	Large open space
Concentration Level:	Medium
Time:	60 minutes
Group Size:	Any
Prerequisite:	"And Now, A Word from Our Sponsors..." (p. 313)

MATERIALS

❖ Video camera and video cassettes

❖ Props as necessary

SUGGESTED PROCEDURE

1. Have students form the same groups they were in for the "And Now, A Word from Our Sponsors..." activity (p. 313), so that they can review their written scripts for public service announcements.

2. Give the children time to rehearse their advertisements, making certain that everyone participates, even if they are not acting in the ad. Non-actors can take the role of director, timekeeper, prop person, or even act out inanimate objects. Try to get everyone involved!

3. Let the students film their advertisements, making sure that they are as close to one minute long as they can get.

REFLECTION

❖ How well did your group work together in filming your advertisement? Did everyone participate equally? Were everyone's opinions taken into consideration?

❖ What resources might you use to make your advertisement more effective than it is now? What were the limitations within which you needed to work?

❖ How does your advertisement compare with the ones you watched before writing your script?

❖ Who is your audience? Who do you wish could see your advertisement? Who do you think your ad could help?

Age:	8–12
Activity Type:	Video
Activity Level:	Moderate
Space:	Large open space
Concentration Level:	High
Time:	Varies
Group Size:	Any
Prerequisite:	"And Now, A Word from Our Sponsors..." (p. 313); "Filming Peace Ads" (p. 315)

A PREMIER SCREENING

The student filmmakers show their public service announcements to the community via this celebratory screening party and critique.

● ● ● ● ● ● ● ● ● ● ● ● ● ● ● ● ●

MATERIALS

❖ Completed videos of advertisements

❖ VCR

SUGGESTED PROCEDURE

1. Invite friends and family to join your group for a screening and critique. Have the students describe the project to the audience once everyone has gathered.

2. Show the advertisements!

3. Have a feedback session, where students describe what they think makes an advertisement like this effective, using the list they generated in the "And Now, A Word from Our Sponsors..." activity (p. 313). Be sure that students and guests give both positive feedback and constructive criticism to the filmmakers. Suggest that the critics complete the following sentences:

   ❖ "Something I really liked about your advertisement was..."

   ❖ "One thing that might make your advertisement even more effective is..."

   Make sure every filmmaking team receives feedback.

4. Discuss the alternatives to violence that the students envisioned in their advertisements. Invite guests to contribute their ideas for other alternatives that were not mentioned and to share stories about times when they resolved a conflict peacefully.

REFLECTION

❖ What made the advertisements effective? What could have made them even more effective? What would you do differently next time?

❖ How did it feel to receive feedback from others about your work? Was it helpful? Hard to hear? Annoying? How can we learn to listen to criticism without getting defensive?

❖ What are the alternatives to violence that were pictured in the advertisements? Have you ever used any of these alternatives? When? What was the situation?

NOTES
● ● ● ● ● ● ● ● ● ● ● ●

Age:	5–12
Activity Type:	Drama
Activity Level:	Moderate
Space:	Large open space
Concentration Level:	Medium
Time:	120 minutes
Group Size:	Any
Prerequisite:	"Making Peace Punch" (p. 309); "Peacemaker's Cookbook" (p. 312); "Peace Punch Role Plays" (p. 310)

COMMUNITY PEACEMAKERS PARTY

The group throws a party to celebrate members of the community who have creatively resolved conflicts.

● ● ● ● ● ● ● ● ● ● ● ● ● ● ● ● ●

MATERIALS

❖ Peace Punch (p. 309)

❖ Peacemaker's Cookbook (p. 312)

❖ Arts and craft supplies for decorations

SUGGESTED PROCEDURE

1. Collect any art projects your group has done to this point and ask the students to help you display them so that guests can see what your group has done.

2. Make decorations for the party.

3. Give the children time to rehearse their Peace Punch role plays again, using the conflict resolution idea that the group created to end the play. Have the entire group decide how they will explain what Peace Punch does to their audience at the party. Write scripts and divide up the speaking responsibilities equally.

4. Make invitations and send them to parents and friends.

5. Make a few batches of Peace Punch and any other recipes from your version of *A Peacemaker's Cookbook*.

REFLECTION

❖ Are there peacemakers at this party? Who are they? Why are they peacemakers?

SNAP, CRACKLE, PEACE

Children create box designs for a breakfast cereal with a peacemaker theme.

● ● ● ● ● ● ● ● ● ● ● ● ● ● ● ● ● ● ●

Age:	8–12
Activity Type:	Arts and crafts
Activity Level:	Moderate
Space:	Work tables
Concentration Level:	Medium
Time:	60 minutes
Group Size:	Any
Prerequisite:	None

MATERIALS

❖ Construction paper (white and colored)

❖ Cereal boxes (or other similarly shaped boxes)

❖ Markers, crayons, colored pencils

❖ Scissors

SUGGESTED PROCEDURE

1. Playing the role of a business executive, explain to the group that your company would like to design and market a breakfast cereal for adults and/or children that celebrates peacemakers and makes people want to resolve conflicts nonviolently. The cereal can have anything in it, sugary or more healthy, hot or cold. The most important thing is that it have a peacemaker theme.

2. Divide the large group into smaller working groups, each of which will design their own version of a peacemaker cereal box. Make a list of things that each group will need to decide, including: the cereal name, what the box will look like, what kind of cereal it will be, if it will have a prize in it.

3. Give the groups plenty of time to work on their boxes.

4. When they are finished, display the cereal boxes and have each group present their pitch to the rest of the class.

REFLECTION

❖ How did you decide what your cereal box would look like? Did your group work together effectively?

❖ How does your cereal portray a peacemaker's theme? Would your box be something interesting to read at the breakfast table? Would it make people think about conflict resolution?

❖ What do your cereal boxes look like at home? Do the prizes in them promote peace?

Age: 8–12

Activity Type: Arts and crafts

Activity Level: Moderate

Space: Work tables

Concentration Level: Medium

Time: 30 minutes

Group Size: Any

Prerequisite: None

BALANCING PEACE

The group makes mobiles symbols that represent peace.

MATERIALS

- ❖ Construction paper
- ❖ Markers, crayons, colored pencils
- ❖ Scissors, hole puncher
- ❖ Wire hangers
- ❖ String or yarn
- ❖ Paper clips

SUGGESTED PROCEDURE

1. As a large group, brainstorm any symbols that you can think of that represent the concept of peace. You may include things like doves, the hand peace sign, olive branches, the peace symbol, and other personalized symbols from your group or community.

2. Break into working groups of about five students. Create the symbols by drawing them and then cutting them out of construction paper. Create mobiles using these symbols. Each student should make one or two symbols.

3. The group must collectively figure out how to turn these symbols into a mobile, or "balance peace," using the available resources. You may want to provide examples, or make this more challenging by letting them figure out on their own how to successfully balance their peace symbols.

4. When they have successfully created mobiles that "balance peace," hang them in your group's room.

REFLECTION

- ❖ Did your group peacefully figure out how to make your mobile work? Did any group have conflicts around deciding the best way to keep the balance?
- ❖ Sometimes it's difficult to balance everyone's opinions, ideas, and needs in a group. Did your group "balance" well?

❖ Who were the peacemakers in your group? Were you all responsible for keeping the peace and for peaceably resolving any conflicts that might have occurred?

NOTES
● ● ● ● ● ● ● ● ● ● ● ●

Age: 8–12

Activity Type: Music

Activity Level: Moderate

Concentration
Level: Medium

Space: Any

Time: 30 minutes

Group Size: Any

Prerequisite: None

TOP FORTY TROUBLE

Children listen to the lyrics of popular songs and discuss whether they suggest peaceable or violent ways to resolve conflicts.

● ● ● ● ● ● ● ● ● ● ● ● ● ● ● ● ●

MATERIALS

❖ Radio/cassette tape player

❖ Blank cassette tapes (one per child)

SUGGESTED PROCEDURE

1. Ask children to listen to songs they hear on the radio or have at home, recording several that have to do with solving problems between people or resolving conflicts. Record a few yourself. Allow children time during the session to listen to the radio and record songs as well.

2. Listen to a few of the songs. Make a list of the different ways of dealing with conflicts that appear in the songs. Examples may include approaches like listening carefully, talking it out, or fighting.

3. Keep a tally of how many times each conflict resolution approach is mentioned.

REFLECTION

❖ Do songs on the radio generally promote peaceable conflict resolution strategies?

❖ How might a peaceable song sound? Could you write a peaceable conflict resolution song or rewrite the lyrics to an existing song we talked about to make it more peaceable?

❖ Do music videos encourage kids to be peacemakers? Should they? Why or why not?

TIP!

Follow-up Idea

Record a few music videos that portray interpersonal conflicts. Have the children watch and discuss the various conflict resolution techniques presented.

PEACEMAKER MUSIC VIDEOS

Children create music videos of songs which promote peaceable conflict resolution.

● ● ● ● ● ● ● ● ● ● ● ● ● ● ● ● ●

Age:	8–12
Activity Type:	Drama
Activity Level:	Moderate
Space:	Large open space
Concentration Level:	Medium
Time:	60 minutes or more
Group Size:	Any
Prerequisite:	"Top Forty Trouble" (p. 322)

MATERIALS

❖ Video camera and blank tapes

❖ VCR

SUGGESTED PROCEDURE

1. Divide into small groups to write songs that are about resolving conflicts peaceably.

2. Give the students enough time to write a song, plan a video for it, and rehearse.

3. Film the music videos!

4. Share the finished product.

REFLECTION

❖ How is your video different from most of the ones you see on MTV? Are your lyrics different? Do you ever see kids on MTV? What are most of the songs on MTV about?

❖ Would a music video be an effective way to spread the message that conflict can be resolved without fighting? Why or why not?

❖ Can a music video star be a peacemaker? Are any of the stars that you see on MTV peacemakers?

Age:	8–12
Activity Type:	Arts and crafts
Activity Level:	Moderate
Space:	Work tables
Concentration Level:	Medium
Time:	60 minutes
Group Size:	Any
Prerequisite:	None

PEACEMAKER T-SHIRTS

Working individually, students make T-shirts that celebrate the fact that they are peacemakers.

MATERIALS

- ❖ T-shirts
- ❖ Clothing paints
- ❖ Clothing dyes
- ❖ Rubber bands and string
- ❖ Vinegar (to set the dye)
- ❖ Plastic basins and kettles

SUGGESTED PROCEDURE

1. Prepare for tie dyeing by heating the dye, assembling piles of rubber bands and string, and preparing basins of different colors.

2. Let the children design and make their own T-shirts, using both tie dye and paints. If they want to dye and paint their shirts, you will need to plan two sessions for this activity so that the dye can dry before using the clothing paint.

3. If they need help figuring out what to put on their T-shirts, remind the group about other conversations they have had and activities they have done, such as "Balancing Peace" (p. 320), or "Snap, Crackle, Peace" (p. 319).

REFLECTION

- ❖ What will you say when someone asks you to describe what your peacemaker T-shirt is all about?

- ❖ For whom would you like to make a peacemaker T-shirt?

PEACEMAKER POEMS

Children write acrostic poems celebrating a peacemaker they know.

● ● ● ● ● ● ● ● ● ● ● ● ● ● ● ● ●

Age:	8–12
Activity Type:	Writing
Activity Level:	Quiet
Space:	Any
Concentration Level:	High
Time:	45 minutes
Group Size:	Any
Prerequisite:	None

MATERIALS

❖ Paper and pencils

❖ Chart paper and markers

SUGGESTED PROCEDURE

1. Describe acrostic poems to the group. Acrostic poems are special poems which spell a key word when you read the first letter in each line. You may want to bring in an example to illustrate what this kind of poem looks like.

2. Ask students to think of someone they know who is a peacemaker. This person can be someone they know personally, someone who is famous, or even someone from history.

3. Using the name of the person whom they have identified and the word "peacemaker" as the first letters (as in Mary Raphael, peacemaker), the children now work on their poems individually. Students should attempt to describe the peacemaker they have chosen through the words of their poem.

4. If they finish early, have students write their acrostic poems on chart paper with markers, highlighting the acrostic letters. Decorate the posters and hang them up.

REFLECTION

❖ What are some words that a lot of you used to describe the peacemaker you chose to write about?

Age:	5–12
Activity Type:	Arts and crafts
Activity Level:	Quiet
Space:	Any space with windows
Concentration Level:	Medium
Group Size:	Any
Time:	45 minutes
Prerequisite:	None

HELPING HANDS MURAL

The group paints a mural on a facility window, including every person's handprints.

● ● ● ● ● ● ● ● ● ● ● ● ● ● ● ●

MATERIALS

❖ Water-based paints

❖ Paintbrushes

❖ Paper towels

SUGGESTED PROCEDURE

1. Choose a picture window in your building on which you can create a mural.

2. As a whole group, write the words "Peacemakers lend helping hands!" on the mural.

3. Have every student (and you, too!) add his or her handprint to the mural.

4. Decorate with other peace signs and symbols.

REFLECTION

❖ Can you think of a time that you lent someone a "helping hand"? What did you do? Did you help someone make or keep peace?

BIG BOOK OF PEACE

The group creates a book containing ideas about keeping the peace.

● ● ● ● ● ● ● ● ● ● ● ● ● ● ● ● ● ● ●

Age:	(5–7) 8–12
Activity Type:	Arts and crafts
Activity Level:	Quiet
Space:	Work tables
Concentration Level:	Medium
Time:	30 minutes (can continue for several sessions)
Group Size:	Any
Prerequisite:	None

MATERIALS

❖ One sheet of heavy paper or card stock for each child (9" x 12" is enough, but bigger is better)

❖ 1 yard heavy string, twine, or yarn

❖ Art supplies such as markers, glue, scissors, crayons, colored paper, magazines for clipping, paint, etc.

❖ Photograph of each child (optional)

SET THE SCENE

Tell the children, "We have so many different kinds of people in this group that I thought we should make a book about being together. That way, when people come to visit they can look through the book and learn about us and our ideas of peace."

SUGGESTED PROCEDURE

1. Begin this project by talking with the children about their ideas for the meaning of peace. Write down these ideas and post them where the children can refer to them.

2. Tell the group that you'd like to make a book about peace, giving one page to each person. If you have photographs of everyone, begin by having them glue their picture and write their name on the page.

3. Have them personalize their page of the book with artwork about peace on one side and something about themselves on the other.

4. This activity is designed to be a project that continues over a few sessions. Spend time on the discussion about peace. Encourage the children to take as much time as they need with their page and to bring things from home if they would like. Support them as much as you can with any materials they would like to put on their page.

5. Some children may need more guidelines and ideas for what to put on their page. Try to define most of this through discussion about peace and the way they want to be together as a group.

For Younger Children

Younger children enjoy this activity but will need more guidance than older children.

Versatile Uses

This book has the potential to be many things for the group. You may have the children develop specific rules for being together and create a page for each, or you may have it be a memory book for each student's most peaceful memory. Through the completion of this book, the children will develop a better sense of the meaning of peace and of the other people in the group.

As much as possible, develop the book through their ideas ("What should we include on the page about ourselves?"), but supply more help if they need it.

6. Some students may finish early. If so, have them do a second page or work on the front or back cover.

7. To bind the book, use a hole punch to create three or four holes down the side of each page and tie a loop of string through the stack. Leave enough slack to turn the pages. If the book seems impossibly bulky, create two volumes.

REFLECTION

Once the book is put together, gather as a group to look through the book and have each child share the contents of their page.

NOTES

● ● ● ● ● ● ● ● ● ● ●

MANY HATS

The group creates different hats representing various ideas of peace and then acts out a scene with them.

● ● ● ● ● ● ● ● ● ● ● ● ● ● ● ● ● ●

Age:	(5–7) 8–10
Activity Type:	Arts and crafts
Activity Level:	Moderate
Space:	Work tables
Concentration Level:	Medium
Time:	30 minutes
Group Size:	Any
Prerequisite:	None

MATERIALS

❖ Art supplies such as markers, glue, scissors, crayons, colored paper, magazines for clipping, paint, etc.

❖ Paper to create hats (chart paper, newspaper, drawing paper, etc.) With younger children, make the hats from paper bags.

SET THE SCENE

Tell the children, "We are all asked to wear different hats at different times. This means that we are asked to play different roles in different situations. For example, when I am here I am the group leader and I do certain things, but at other times I wear different hats. Sometimes I'm a daughter, sometimes I'm a store customer, sometimes I'm a friend, sometimes I'm a cook. We all have many hats that we wear in different situations."

SUGGESTED PROCEDURE

1. First, spend time brainstorming a list of as many different kinds of hats as possible. (They should be able to think of 30 or 40 easily. For example: top hat, baseball cap, chef's hat, beret, sombrero, crown, etc.)

2. Have each student think about a kind of hat that they could wear that would help them to keep the peace (e.g., listener, policeman, teacher, friend, helper, etc.). Encourage them to make up a new kind of hat or use an old one and decorate it for its peaceful purpose.

3. Make a hat yourself and wear it as a good way to break the ice. Each child should make a hat or two, time permitting.

4. When everyone has made their hat, gather together wearing your hats and go around the group sharing the kind of hats they made and the story behind the hats.

5. If the energy is high, divide the group into smaller groups of three or four and have them develop a skit about a brief conflict and its resolution, portraying the roles indicated by their hats.

TIP!

For Younger Children

Have younger children decorate paper bags to make their hats.

6. Afterward, the children may take their hats home, or display them around the room.

REFLECTION

Tell the children, "Congratulations on all of the different hats you made. You are all very creative."

❖ What are some of the many hats that you wear everyday?

❖ Which ones can help you when you are in a conflict?

❖ Which ones would you try not to wear when you see a conflict coming?

NOTES

● ● ● ● ● ● ● ● ● ● ●

TOWER OF POWER

Children make and decorate a tower out of cardboard boxes that promotes peaceful conflict resolution.

● ● ● ● ● ● ● ● ● ● ● ● ● ● ● ● ● ● ●

Age:	(5–7) 8–12
Activity Type:	Arts and crafts
Activity Level:	Quiet
Space:	Work tables
Concentration Level:	Medium
Time:	30–45 minutes
Group Size:	4 or more
Prerequisite:	None

MATERIALS

❖ Cardboard boxes that can be closed, one per child

❖ Paint and markers

❖ Collage materials such as feathers, buttons, cardboard, Styrofoam® pieces, magazines, etc.

SUGGESTED PROCEDURE

1. Each child will need a box. The top and the bottom of the box should be closed. Children will be decorating the four sides of the box.

2. *Ask,* "If you were going to give advice to someone about resolving a conflict, what kinds of things would you say?" List their suggestions and expand on the promising ones by asking, "How would it look if someone did that?"

3. Have each child paint, decorate, or draw on each side of his or her box a picture, symbol, or design that indicates a way to resolve conflict. There are four sides so they will need to think of four things, unless they want to work with a partner. Along with the graphic they can put a message about resolving conflict.

4. When the boxes are complete and dry, stack them into a tower. The tower can stay in place for a while to decorate the program area. When this purpose is finished, each child can take his or her box home.

REFLECTION

❖ Why do you think this activity is called "Tower of Power"?

❖ How would you explain to other people what your pictures mean?

TIP!

For Younger Children

Younger children enjoy this project, but may not be able to think of four things to include on their boxes. Let them draw a symbol of conflict resolution on one side of the box, then have them simply decorate the other sides.

Age: (5–7) 8–12

Activity Type: Arts and crafts

Activity Level: Quiet

Space: Work tables

Concentration Level: Medium

Time: 20 minutes

Group Size: 3 or more

Prerequisite: None

PEACEMAKER POSTERS

Children make posters about imaginary peacemakers who have specific powers and skills in conflict resolution.

● ● ● ● ● ● ● ● ● ● ● ● ● ● ● ● ●

MATERIALS

❖ Chart paper and markers

SUGGESTED PROCEDURE

1. *Ask,* "What are the things you need to be able to do if you are a peacemaker?" "If you could have superpowers as a peacemaker, what would they be?"

2. Have children work either independently or in groups to invent peacemakers who have some of these powers. When they have an idea of what peacemaking powers they want to use, have them make a poster of their peacemaker that illustrates their various powers.

3. Display the Peacemaker Posters prominently in the program space.

REFLECTION

❖ How might your peacemaker use each of his or her skills and powers?

❖ How could an ordinary person have similar powers?

For Younger Children

Younger children need help with this activity. It works best if they work on one poster in small groups.

WHAT PEACE MEANS TO ME

Children draw a picture or write a story about a time they experienced peace.

● ● ● ● ● ● ● ● ● ● ● ● ● ● ● ● ● ●

Age:	5–7 (8–12)
Activity Type:	Arts and Crafts
Activity Level:	Quiet
Space:	Work tables
Concentration Level:	High
Time:	15–20 minutes
Group Size:	4 or more
Prerequisite:	None

MATERIALS

❖ Drawing paper

❖ Lined paper

❖ Crayons and colored pencils

❖ Chart paper and markers

❖ Pencils/pens

SUGGESTED PROCEDURE

1. Write the words "Peace is" on chart paper and explain that you are going to write or draw about a time that made them feel peaceful. Give the group an example of a time when you felt peaceful, "I feel peaceful when it's summer and I'm playing in the sand."

2. Have the group offer times that they felt peaceful and record them on the chart.

3. Distribute art and writing supplies and ask the group to draw or write about a time that they felt peace. They may entitle their creations, "Peace Is..." or create their own titles.

REFLECTION

When the group finishes, have them share their creations.

Age Level: 8–12

Activity Type : Arts and Crafts

Activity Level: Moderate

Space: Art area

Concentration Level: Medium

Time: 30 minutes plus

Group Size: Any

Prerequisite: Some experience with conflict resolution skills

THE PEACEMAKER TOOL KIT

Children make a kit composed of objects that represent peacemaking skills.

● ● ● ● ● ● ● ● ● ● ● ● ● ● ● ● ● ●

MATERIALS

An empty cardboard box big enough to hold objects; other materials will vary (If you can, have a variety of miscellaneous objects children can use for this project. These can include cardboard tubes, empty cans, pieces of foam, etc.)

SUGGESTED PROCEDURE

1. Peacemakers use many skills or tools when they resolve conflicts. With your group, identify at least ten skills you think peacemakers need to have.

2. Have the children divide into small groups, then find objects that represent those skills. For example, if "good listener" is one of the skills, they should find something that represents listening. It might be a toy telephone, or it might be a cardboard tube – anything that might be used for listening. The group should do this for each of the skills they identified.

3. When the group has finished collecting tools, they will need a box in which to put the tools. As a group, decorate the box and label it. Be sure to have group members write their names on the kit.

4. The group can share its tool kit with other groups in a variety of ways. One is the Tool Kit Advertisement that is described next. Another, simpler way is to have the group show each of the "tools" to the larger group and have them guess what conflict resolution skill that object might represent.

REFLECTION

❖ Which skills do you use most often?

❖ What are some skills that you couldn't find objects for?

❖ If you were going to make a kit for a specific group of people, such as a Peacemakers Tool Kit for Parents or a Peacemakers Kit for Kids, how would it be different from yours? How would it be the same?

TOOL KIT COMMERCIALS

After making Peacemaker Tool Kits, childen create TV commercials to advertise the kit.

● ● ● ● ● ● ● ● ● ● ● ● ● ● ● ● ● ●

Age Level:	8–12
Activity Type:	Drama and Art
Space :	Work tables
Concentration Level:	Medium
Time:	45 minutes
Group Size :	Any size, but don't let groups get bigger than five
Prerequisite :	Peacemaker Toolkits

MATERIALS

Paper and crayons or markers

SUGGESTED PROCEDURE

1. Once the group has completed its "Peacemakers Tool Kit," have them create a TV commercial to sell the Kit. Encourage them to make the commercial both visual and dramatic.

2. First, the group should discuss ideas, then write a script. Finally, give them an opportunity to cast and rehearse the commercial. Ideally there should be a role for everyone in the group who wants to be part of it. When everything's ready, present the commercial to the larger group.

3. There are several variations on this activity. A simpler version is to have the children make poster advertisements to promote the kit. A more complex version that older children enjoy is to make the advertisement an informercial, with an audience that responds to the wonderful innovations of this kit. If you have access to video equipment, any of the dramatic versions of the the activity can be videotaped.

REFLECTION

❖ What do you think would make people want to buy a Peace-makers Tool Kit?

❖ If you wanted a specific group of people to buy your kit (such as parents, teachers, grandparents, or kids), what kind of commercial would you create?

Age Level: (5-7) 8-12

Activity Level: Quiet

Space: Work tables

Concentration Level: Medium

Activity Type: Art and Writing

Group Size: Groups of four

Prerequisite: Some experience with conflict resolution skills

SUPERHEROS FOR PEACE

Children invent superheros who do not use violence to solve problems.

● ● ● ● ● ● ● ● ● ● ● ● ● ● ● ● ● ● ●

MATERIALS

Large sheets of poster paper; drawing paper; writing paper; crayons or markers

SUGGESTED PROCEDURE

1. The goal of this activity is for children to create superheros who do not use violence to solve conflicts. It's helpful to begin this activity with a discussion that will start children thinking about some of the alternatives to violence that these heros/sheros might use.

Mini Reflection

♦ What do you think of when you think of a superhero? What kinds of powers do superheros usually have?

♦ Have you ever seen or read of a superhero who didn't use violence to handle conflicts?

♦ What are some of the strategies that a nonviolent superhero might use?

2. After the discussion, have the children meet in groups of no more than four. Their task is to invent at least one superhero – they may invent a team of heros/sheros if they wish. The group should decide what powers the superhero has, how he or she uses the powers, what he or she looks like, etc.

3. Once they make these decisions, have them draw their superheros and mount them onto the poster paper. Underneath the picture, they should paste a written description of what powers the superhero has, how the superhero uses his or her powers, and so on.

4. When the groups finish their posters, display them for the larger group to see. Children can follow-up this activity by making comic strips of the adventures their superheros have. Another follow-up activity is to design and make a costume for the hero/shero.

REFLECTION

- ❖ How would your hero/shero rescue you if you were in trouble?

- ❖ With what kinds of villains do you think your superhero would have conflicts?

- ❖ How would your hero/shero handle those conflicts?

NOTES

● ● ● ● ● ● ● ● ● ● ● ●

Age Level: 5-12

Activity Type: Art

Activity Level: Moderate

Concentration
Level: Medium

Time: 30 minutes

Space: Work tables

Group Size: Any size

Prerequisite: None

THE PEACEMAKER ROBOT

Using cardboard boxes, children make robots that have specific peacemaking skills.

● ● ● ● ● ● ● ● ● ● ● ● ● ● ● ● ●

MATERIALS

Large cardboard boxes, preferably ones with that can be closed – try to have about five boxes for each group of four; paints and/or markers; assorted art materials, such as foil papers, cardboard tubes, sponge pieces, etc.

SUGGESTED PROCEDURE

1. Explain the task to the children: they will be making peacemaker robots out of cardboard boxes. The boxes will be stacked on top of each other, with the top box serving as the head, the next two boxes as the torso, and the bottom two as the legs or base of the robot. But this is no ordinary robot, this is a peacemaking robot, so it needs to be constructed with peacemaking skills in mind. For example, if the robot is able to see other points of view, perhaps its head should be able to turn completely around. If it is good at asking clarifying questions, it might have a "question control panel" built in. Giving a few of these examples should help children get the idea.

2. Discuss with the group possible skills or attributes they think the robot should have. Ask for ideas on how these attributes might be represented. Display the materials you've collected and, if necessary, divide children into groups. (There is a lot to do to make one of these robots, so groups can be fairly large. It's most successful if each child or pair of children has a box and decides in advance what skill they will be giving the robot.)

3. This makes a good painting project, but if that's too messy or complicated in your program, paper cutouts and drawings can be attached to the sides of the boxes.

4. Once the robot is assembled, put it on display. A fun follow-up is to have one or two children act as voices for the robot who then gives conflict resolution advice to people. Another follow-up if you have a very ambitious group is to write a play based on the robot.

REFLECTION

❖ What advice do you think the robot would give you about a conflict you're having?

❖ Give the children some hypothetical conflict situations and ask what they think the robot would say to them (or have a child act as the robot's voice).

NOTES

● ● ● ● ● ● ● ● ● ● ●

Age Level: 5-12

Activity Type: Arts and Crafts

Activity Level: Moderate

Space: Work tables

Concentration Level: Medium

Time: 30 minutes

Group Size: Any size

Prerequisite: None

PEACEMAKER POSTERS II

Children make posters promoting the use of a particular conflict resolution skill.

● ● ● ● ● ● ● ● ● ● ● ● ● ● ● ● ● ●

MATERIALS

Poster paper; crayons or markers

SUGGESTED PROCEDURE

1. Have each child in the group identify a conflict resolution skill at which he or she is particularly good. There may be more than one person in the group who is good at any one skill. Ask how they might encourage others to use and develop that skill.

2. Give each child poster paper and drawing materials to make a poster that illustrates and promotes that particular skill.

3. When the posters are finished, display them around the program space as part of your campaign to create a "Peaceable Program." After a week or so, take these posters down and have another group create new posters.

REFLECTION

❖ What skills do you see other kids using?

❖ What skills do you think kids need to practice?

❖ How did you learn the peacemaking skills you have?

❖ If it was your job to teach the skills to other kids, how would you do it?

Activity Index

Activities categorized by chapter, age and type

About Project Adventure

Since 1971 Project Adventure has been creating learning programs that challenge people to go beyond their perceived boundaries, to work with others to solve problems and to experience success. The Project Adventure concept is characterized by an atmosphere that is fun, supportive and challenging. Noncompetitive games, group problem solving Initiatives and ropes course events are the proincipal activities we use to help individuals improve self-esteem and self-confidence.

About Educators for Social Responsibility

ESR's primary mission is to help young people develop the convictions and skills to shape a safe, sustainable, and just world. We support educators and parents with professional development, networks, and instructional materials. ESR is nationally recognized for promoting children's ethical and social development through its leadership in conflict resolution, violence prevention, intergroup relations, and character education.

We distribute a full line of conflict resolution resources from early childhood through high school levels. In addition, we carry resources in classroom management, diversity, violence and the media, teaching conflict resolution through children's literature, and many others. In addition, we offer a wide range of training, resources, and consultation for preschool through adult settings. Our programs are designed for teachers, counselors, administrators, parents, and community members. We tailor the length, format, and content of our work to the unique constraints of each school, district, institution, or community.

For more information about ESR's resources and professional services, please call 1-800-370-2515.

For more information on conflict resolution resources and adventure programming, contact:
Educators for Social Responsibility, 23 Garden St., Cambridge, MA 02138 (617)492-1764, (800)370-2515 and Project Adventure, Box 100, Hamilton, MA 01936 (508)468-7981.

Bibliography

Carlsson-Paige, Nancy and Diane E. Levin. *Who's Calling the Shots? How to Respond Effectively to Children's Fascination with War Play and War Toys.* Philadelphia: New Society Publishers, 1990.

"Decisions, Decisions Series." Cambridge, MA: Tom Snyder Productions, 1986-1993. Computer software.

Kamiya, Art. *Elementary Teacher's Handbook of Indoor and Outdoor Games.* West Nyack, NY: Parker Publishing, 1985.

Kreidler, William J. *Creative Conflict Resolution: Over 200 Activities for Keeping Peace in the Classroom K-6.* Glenview, IL: Scott, Foresman and Co., 1984.

Kreidler, William J. *Elementary Perspectives: Teaching Concepts of Peace and Conflict.* Cambridge, MA: ESR, 1990.

Kreidler, William J. *Teaching Conflict Resolution Through Children's Literature.* New York: Scholastic Professional Books, 1995.

Levin, Diane E. *Teaching Young Children in Violent Times: Building a Peaceable Classroom.* Cambridge, MA: ESR, 1994.

Pirtle, Sarah. *Discovery Sessions: How Teachers Creative Opportunities to Build Cooperation and Conflict-Resolution Skills in Their K-8 Classrooms.* Greenfield, MA: Franklin Mediation Service, 1989.

Rohnke, Karl. *Silver Bullets: A Guide to Initiative Problems, Adventure Games and Trust Activities.* Project Adventure, 1984.

Schmidt, Fran. *Creative Conflict Solving for Kids.* Miami Beach, FL: Grace Contrino Abrams Peace Education Foundation, 1982.

Schniedewind, Nancy and Ellen Davidson. *Cooperative Learning, Cooperative Lives.* Dubuque, IA: Wm. C. Brown, 1987.

Schniedewind, Nancy and Ellen Davidson. *Open Minds to Equality.* Englewood Cliffs, NJ: Prentice-Hall, 1983.

"Solving Conflicts." Los Angeles: Churchhill Films, 1989. Videotape.

Youth Leadership: A Guide to Cooperative Games and Group Activities. Project Adventure, 1995.